The Way of KARMA

The Way of
KARMA

CHARLES BREAUX

SAMUEL WEISER, INC.

York Beach, Maine

First published in 1993 by
Samuel Weiser, Inc.
Box 612
York Beach, ME 03910

Library of Congress Cataloging-in-Publication Data

Breaux, Charles.
    The way of karma / by Charles Breaux.
        p.   cm.
    Includes bibliographical references.
    1. Karma—Case studies.   2. Reincarnation—Case studies.
  3. Reincarnation therapy—Case studies.   I. Title.
    BF1045.K45B74   1993
    133.9′01′3—dc 20   92-45543
                                                                  CIP

ISBN 0-87728-773-2
BJ

Cover art copyright © 1993 Richard Stodart
Used by kind permission.

Typeset in 11 point Palatino

Printed in the United States of America

The paper used in this publication meets the minimum requirements of
the American National Standard for Permanence of Paper for Printed
Library materials Z39.48-1984.

TABLE OF CONTENTS

FOREWORD

It would be difficult to trace the antiquity of the belief in reincarnation and karma. Regardless of their antiquity, they are
still key pieces in the puzzle of the human psyche.

Reincarnation and karma have provided a foundation for
the world views of Hinduism, Buddhism, Jainism, Sikhism,
and Zoroastrianism. Similar beliefs were held in such diverse
groups as the American Indians, Pre-Columbian cultures,
the Polynesian Kahunas, the Gauls, the Druids, and various
African tribes. Even in the Western European world, reincarnation was an important part of life.

In ancient Greece, the Pythagoreans, the Orphics, and
the Platonists incorporated reincarnation into their doctrines.
The same was true for the Essenes, the Pharisees, the Ka-
raites, and the Kabbalists, in the Jewish tradition. The Gnos-
tics and early mystical traditions of Christianity also
embraced the doctrine of reincarnation, until such ideas were
deemed heretical by the Second Council of Constantinople in
A.D. 553. With the verdict, "If anyone assert . . . the fabulous
pre-existence of souls and shall submit to the monstrous doctrine that follows from it, let him be anathema," the belief in
reincarnation was officially eradicated from the Western
mind.

Though Christian dogma and traditional orthodox science denounce reincarnation, research in transpersonal
psychology has, in the last twenty years, provided overwhelming evidence for past lives and karmic forces at play in
our present lives.

In the last three decades, science has peeled away the
flesh of physical reality. We no longer exist in a solid atom-

based, three-dimensional universe. World and being are losing their boundaries and a new, holographic, image of the world/psyche is emerging. The cutting edge of modern science is finally discovering the heart of wisdom pulsing through ancient mystical traditions.

This book was inspired by my German publisher, who asked me to compile a series of clairvoyant past-life readings to show how people develop karmic patterns and carry them over from one life to the next. After completing this task, I felt compelled to include transcripts of past-life therapy sessions. I wanted to address ways of working with karma based on my own experiences and the pioneering work of such innovative therapists as Roger J. Woolger, Ph.D. and Stanislav Grof, M.D.

Often oversimplified and overmoralized in metaphysical traditions here in the West, karma is as complex and multifaceted as the human psyche itself. As individuals we have each woven our own characteristic web of psycho/physical energies. Impressions of events, emotional responses, and belief systems weave an ever denser pattern of experience. It may at first seem paradoxical that this web is also a guide, a map. It shows the way we have come in, as well as the way out of the tunnel of the constricting boundaries of the ego matrix.

ACKNOWLEDGMENTS

This book has been a labor of love. The being who came through to talk to me about the ongoing process of life, Giaff, gave me a great deal of insight, for which I am eternally grateful. I also want to thank all the people who allowed themselves to be featured in this book. The names have been changed to protect the karmic innocent. Thank you for letting us delve into your karmic pasts to help us enlighten the present.

PART ONE

How
Karma Works

What is Karma?

Karma is a Sanskrit word meaning "action." The connotation in Hinduism and Buddhism refers to a process of cause and effect associated with our thoughts, emotions, and behaviors. As Jesus put it, "as you sow, so shall you reap." This is karma.

Thoughts and emotions, as well as physical actions, generate certain forces in the world at large. They also produce characteristic patterns of energy in the body-mind. These patterns of energy act as a vibratory grid for the creation of future experiences and govern our reactions to these events. This is all very much akin to self-fulfilled prophecy.

Western psychology assumes an infant's psychological makeup to be a tabula rasa. It has therefore believed that our individual characters are formed from birth in this present life. Terms like *complexes, patterning, personal myths, scripts,* and *family of origin* have all been used to denote the shaping affects of our childhood, i.e., parental and social conditioning. Western psychology has had to turn its back on the problems of special gifts and character traits that have no basis in the family history or gene pool. It has also remained relatively unsuccessful in treating the majority of psychological disorders.

What's missing in the Western model of the psyche is reincarnation, the continuity of the self from one life to another. The continuity model explains how our character and present life conditions have been predetermined from previous incarnations. Habitual psychological and physical activities, as well as those events which were charged with emotion, such as traumatic experiences, have structured our

4 ◊ *Charles Breaux*

psychological postures. Our present selves are gross charac-
terizations of the subtle mental and emotional elements that
have coalesced into attitudes and dispositions and carried
over from one life to the next.

Karma can be viewed as an extension of the Western concept of complexes to include the pathos of the soul stretching
back to its origin. In this expanded view, current family genetics and psychological environments are not primary causative factors in our psychological makeup. They are vehicles
through which a soul dramatizes its karmic patterns. Souls
gravitate to parents and social conditions that match their
karmic predilections. Genetics, family, and environmental
conditions offer the soul an opportunity to play out specific
karmic necessities.

Karmic patterns are integral with the dynamics of identification. Whatever we identify with we become, be it a belief
system, a social role (victim, oppressor, outcast, etc.), or an
emotional state. We believe, and therefore act as if it were so,
and so it is. The survival instinct controls our identification
with these karmic patterns. One of the greatest hurdles in
psychotherapy, for example, is to let go of our sense of identity associated with dysfunctional patterns. Like a dog fighting to protect its territory, we struggle to defend our sense of
identity as if our life depends on it. Thus, our wounds and
afflictions survive from one life to the next in emotionally
charged identities, with their associated attitudes. These unconscious subpersonalities dominate our existence with pro-
pensities to attract or create certain kinds of events, and then
react in prescribed manners. The sense of an individual identity is therefore germane to creation of karmic patterns.
Actions, and their karmic effects, are meaningless without a
self who performs them, and then experiences their results.

There are three distinct dimensions of the self: the ego,
the soul, and the Self. The ego is the most exterior and temporal self. It is our present conscious sense of identity.

The soul is the self that survives death and goes forth to project another ego-self. The term *psyche* once meant "soul." Hence, I will use the term *soul* here to include all levels of the personal psyche that are not integrated into ego consciousness. The term *soul* has some commonly associated attributes that are misleading. I'll address these later, but for now I'll use the term *soul* instead of coining a novel word.

The third, and most sublime, self is of a transpersonal nature. It is commonly projected into the image of God. It is the self that Jung refers to with his term *the Self*. In the microcosm of our psyche, the Self is a reflection of the central organizing force of All That Is. It is a transcendent and whole-making factor. The Self provides a blueprint for the soul to follow in its task of building a kingdom of consciousness.

The ultimate goal of the Eastern teachings on karma is to outgrow our belief in and attachment to an individual sense of identity. This makes it much easier to let go of old identities, or karmic patterns. It also allows us to function from a transpersonal level where we no longer create karma. When the soul becomes transparent, then only the light of the Self shines through. We no longer live for our personal needs and desires controlled by the pain and defenses of our personal histories. We become a vehicle for Life at large. In the world view of Eastern religions, the fires of desire cease and we become liberated from our involuntary treading on the wheel of birth and death.

The dynamics of karma do not seek to punish us. Punishment is always self-inflicted from the karmic point of view. Identification with patterns of guilt leads to a need to punish oneself, and is therefore self-inflicted punishment. Nor is karma fate. We have the freedom to let go of our attachments to the patterns we identify with. This is no easy task, I assure you. Nonetheless, it is possible—indeed, mandatory—for our psychological and spiritual maturation.

Only a small number of our soul's karmic patterns display themselves in any one lifetime. The entire body of our karma is too complex and large to manifest all at once. There's also the consideration of group karma and special types of conditions needed in the world at large for certain karmas to ripen.

In common usage, the word *karma* often carries a negative connotation. It is healthier to have a positive attitude toward karma. It is our most diligent teacher. The dynamics of karma are not only the basis for defining our individual characters, but the healing and development of the psyche, in truth the soul, as well.

THE SOUL: A MESSAGE
FROM GIAFF TO THE READER

Before I started work on this book, I did some research to see what else had been written on the subject of karma. While thumbing through one of Ruth Montgomery's books, *World Beyond,* I came across a passage in which the deceased Arthur Ford mentions how the disincarnate Irish-American psychic, Eileen Garrett, is looking for a person to write through. Reportedly she wants to carry on the psychic research she was doing while in the body. I thought, "Wouldn't that be an easy way to write a book," and attempted to contact Eileen on the inner planes to work out a deal.

Once seated in meditation, I became aware of a being approaching me. Instead of contacting Eileen, I realized I was meeting the being responsible for inspiring the publisher to have this book written, and responsible for choosing me to write it, as well. Giaff, the being who signed this essay on the soul, which it wrote through me for this book, was here to assist in the critical period of transformation occurring in our world. This is what he said.

For now, let us focus on the unit of life you call the soul. The soul is variably the seed of Life, the spark of the fire of creation. Just as there are many varieties of plants, there are many types of souls, each suited to specific environments or functions in the organism of the greater cosmos. However, regardless of the type of soul, all souls go through a similar process of birth, unfoldment, and death/rebirth. In this way souls are created equal. Souls all have the same opportunities to unfold through the stages of development, but different groups of souls, in different cosmic environments, will have specific tasks and duties to perform.

You've always thought the soul was immortal, was created at the beginning of time, and was the perfect part of yourself. But there was never a beginning to life. Life, as so often symbolized in ancient times, is circular. A circle has no beginning or end. You can see how fruitless it is to assign an arbitrary time in some ancient eon as the moment when all souls were created. Life is an ongoing process. Souls are continually being born, *and* returning to the Great Spirit.

You believe the soul is perfect, and logically deduce that all you must do is conquer the evils of your corporeal self and escape to heaven to be saved, as some of your religions propose. The soul is perfect in the same sense that a seed is perfect. Then again, all seeds are not perfect, a point I will only hint at now. A seed contains the blueprint, if you will, for the perfected plant, but only the appropriate conditions will ensure the growth of the plant toward its ultimate potential.

While there is assistance from spirit guides, each soul is largely responsible for absorbing the necessary nutriments, adopting attitudes and working hypotheses that will lead to positive actions toward its potential perfection. I want you to understand that neither the body nor the physical world are inherently evil. The body is the ground in which the soul is planted. Through it the soul will experience the events that will nurture its growth or lead to folly. Trial and error, learning from mistakes, practicing what's been learned, and teaching by example are the methods employed here in the garden of Earth.

Now, the soul is born and dies, or more correctly, is transfigured. As the soul blossoms and experiences a conscious reunion with All That Is, it goes on to perform duties that are on an entirely new level of the cosmic organism—a level in which the soul's whole focus is to be a vehicle for Universal Law and Harmony. Living for personal or self-related endeavors is no longer a concern for a perfected soul. A soul that has fulfilled its destiny (i.e., unfolded its innate potential) becomes a holographic projection of the Whole. The soul is immortal, in this sense, when it completes its life cycle and becomes a lens through which the Light of Creation shines without distortion. As the soul dies in its sense of individualness, it is reborn as a god, if you will, and returns in total awareness to embrace and express its original nature.

Your soul is the ground of your individuality. However, at the very core of your individual form is Life. It is your task to fathom the depth of your soul with the light of consciousness to activate this vital seed.

When you give yourself over to Life, you will be swept from the shores of your known world into the oceanic majesty of creation. You need only to let go and trust the movement of the cosmos through you, a simple but oh so trying task. For each step of the way you cling to your surroundings. You hold on to those things with which you identify to such a degree, that when change comes you feel it will be the end of you. If you could only learn how to alter your perspective to see yourself as part of the larger picture—an expression of Life, a part of all that is in transformation—how much easier your task, how much more enjoyable your incredible journey.

Unfortunately, you cannot learn from a book how you can perform this maneuver of letting go and trusting. However, you can perceive the tragedy of your folly and recognize the undue suffering and erroneous belief systems—indeed, entire civilizations—you construct to defend yourself from necessary growing pains. Is your pain not proportional to the amount of resistance you maintain against Life?

Please ponder carefully the stories you read here. I am sure you will realize that you have been living similar stories, over and over again. These dreams of life (in many cases nightmares) will continue until you and you alone have the desire and fortitude to awaken to Life—Life in its essential and universal nature. Perhaps, remembering through the stories in this volume of past-life readings how long you have wandered lost through the darkness of your dreams, you will finally harken the call of Life.

Life Readings

Most of us have lived numerable lives here on planet Earth, and therefore we have a huge backlog of karma. Often I have heard idealistic New Agers proclaim that they are going to work off all their karma this time so they won't have to come back. It makes me chuckle to myself. What a Herculean task.

One of the subjects of the life readings to follow complained that, though his reading elicited some core patterns, it did not present a complete picture. He was correct. His reading—as well as the rest of the readings included here—only traces the history of some of the more prominent karmic patterns the soul is dealing with in this present life, even at the present time.

There are many factors involved in how a soul incarnates, and I don't pretend to understand them all. I have some ideas, such as, the more conscious and cooperative a soul is determines how much freedom of choice it has in choosing the conditions of its next life. Other souls, who are less conscious or driven by extreme emotions and addictions, are at the mercy of the psychological states at their death in the most recent incarnation. For example, if a person dies in terror, the emotional state at death can trap the soul for a long period of Earth time. The soul will live in a nightmare on the astral plane, often oblivious to help and guidance from benevolent souls and spirit guides. An obsession with alcohol, or strong emotions like anger, or even sexual desire, can prove to be so irresistible that the soul is drawn back to the planet without any preparation or guidance.

In other situations, a soul may feel its life ended too soon and is anxious to return to the planet to complete the desires and purpose of the earlier life. In such instances we lose the opportunity to reflect or to receive wise counsel, and we are driven merely by habits and ulterior motives. For example, in one of my own past lives I was killed by a robber as I rode through the night to deliver an important message to a prominent colonial leader. I was so overwrought with frustration and concern for the outcome of the War of Independence that I reincarnated immediately. The conditions of my next life were unsuited for me, and I spent a whole life spinning my wheels.

Sometimes a soul will resist coming back into the body. In such cases the forces of karma will eventually pull the soul back to the planet. The soul may then have little control, or even awareness, of the upcoming conditions. In other circumstances, the soul may spend an extended period of time in an institution of higher learning on the inner planes and may return to the body fully aware of an intended purpose. Regardless of how the soul enters a new life, it is confronted with specific karmic themes. We either learn from our past mistakes, or we further complicate matters.

When I'm doing a past-life reading by just allowing the various lifetimes to come to me unsolicited, they may or may not appear in a linear fashion. (This is most probably related to the paratemporal nature of transphysical reality, an interesting topic, but one I will avoid in this work.) However, when I endeavor to do so, I can selectively view past lives from our normal perspective of historical time. Though some of the following readings are nonlinear, there are obvious networks of karma connecting the lifetimes.

Over the twenty-five years I have been doing readings and past-life regressions, I have pieced together a rather unconventional sketch of history. There are two periods that show up in the readings in this book that are potentially controversial: the ancient civilization of Lemuria and a particular phase of the matriarchal epoch.

My personal karma with Lemuria is very limited. To my knowledge I've had no incarnations there and I have worked with only a relatively small number of souls from Lemuria. In Appendix A, I have included some information and personal experiences that have led me to adopt my opinions about those times. On the other hand, I am aware of an extensive involvement in the Amazon era. My traumatic experiences in this period have left me with a hypersensitivity to the repercussions in people I have worked with. This is evident throughout the readings presented in this book. In Appendix B, I elaborate on my personal experiences and hypothesize on the affects of this period on the development of modern civilization.

In addition to my novel view of the founders of Lemuria and the Amazon era, I am under the impression that I, and many of the people with whom I have close karmic ties, came to this planet during the middle period of Atlantis. My own awareness of existence prior to coming to this planet has given me much insight into who I am and my reactions to being here on Earth. I have found such information helpful to many clients. A number of readings, therefore, include pre-terrestrial experiences and reactions of souls sent to Earth from other dimensions. The traumatic affect of a soul's birth and separation from its Twin Soul are also included in a few of the accounts given here.

Before we begin the readings, I want to encourage you to look for the karmic themes woven through the various lifetimes presented for each subject. These are actual transcripts of sessions and I have not analyzed them; the themes and patterns are clear enough. Each soul has its story to tell. I suggest reading one chapter at a time. Spend a while thinking about each soul's story before going onto the next.

HIROKO

Hiroko was a slender Oriental woman in her mid-20s. A cool, calculating person who possessed an alarming aura of self-assurance. She had just graduated from acupuncture school and was working for an importer of Oriental herbs while she prepared to begin her practice. After discussing a few details pertaining to her imminent profession as an acupuncturist, we began her life reading.

C: When I tune in to your soul, I sense something a little unusual. There is a lot of interference and the energy keeps changing. I'm going to just go on and look at your past lives.

The first life I see is in the southern part of China. You are a woman with a child. I see you doing laundry by hand. You're angry with your husband, who is a fisherman. I get the impression that you and he argue a lot. You are both strong-willed, and you can't always get your way with him. This seems to be the main characteristic of this life, the antagonism that you have for each other.

The next life I see is down in the Philippines. Once again you are a woman, a healer of some kind, practicing a primitive healing tradition in which you sacrifice chickens. This is like some sort of divination. When you cut up the chickens there are different omens inside that tell you what gods to pray to, etc. In your tribe you are the woman healer, and you are well respected. In this life, as well as the last one, your energy is very strong. You have a strong will, and are very self-assured. The significance of this life is centered around your role as the tribe's healer. It's a prominent and authoritative position. You don't have many personal relationships or a mate in this life; neither are very important to you.

When you leave the body in this life, you keep that same strength and sense of importance. You want to come back to the planet and do the same role over again. You come back into the same culture in the Philippines. Though a healer again, in this life you have a mate and children, and in that context I see the same anger I saw in your life in China. As the healer you can be in charge, but in your personal life you can not. That makes you angry. When you don't have control over the people in your personal life you get very upset. As a result, you end up alienating your family. Later in that life you feel alone. When you are dying you feel remorse about the way your anger has pushed those people who were close to you away.

When you leave the body this time, instead of feeling so self important, you are more humble. With this attitude you are open to your guides. They show you a place where they want you to go next on the Earth and talk to you about being kinder if you really want to be of service. They speak to you about compassion.

The next life I see is in Australia. You are a man in an aboriginal tribe. There is something about the placing of stones and prophecy. It is a hunting and gathering social structure dependent on moving in harmony with nature. The stones have something to do with going into Dream Time and contacting the Ancestors for guidance about the movement of the herds. Your religious and prophetic practices are integral with survival skills. You are like a shaman or a priest who acts as a mediator for the rest of the tribe.

Your disposition is gentler in this life. When you meet with opposition from others it is still difficult for you, but you get quiet and go inside rather than act out your anger on them.

There is a traumatic event in this life when you lose a son. You try to intervene and heal him, but he dies anyway. This makes you very sad and undermines your identity as the shaman, causing you to begin doubting your abilities. You continue in your role, but you're more removed. You don't believe in it as much, and you don't put your heart into it.

You are despondent when you leave the body. You had a lot of energy invested in your role as healer. With the loss of this identity, you feel confused and disoriented. When your guides come they try to comfort you and tell you that you made a lot of progress in terms of becoming more gentle and compassionate. Having your son die in that life was a way they were trying to open your heart. They feel it was a successful life, but you resent having lost your confidence in your capacity as a healer. You're very disillusioned despite their support. You are reluctant to come back to the Earth. You refuse to incarnate for a long period. Finally your guides convince you to come back again.

This life seems to be in a place like Thailand. I see a house built up on stilts in a tropical jungle setting. You're a woman again. You collect herbs and plants to make medicines. Your grandmother is your teacher in this life. She passes on the tradition to you and you become the medicine woman for your village. In this life you don't want to marry. You shy away from the men who try to court you. You don't want to open your heart again; you're protecting it. The more men try to win your heart, the more you push them away and close down. This reminds me of your strong will. Closing your heart becomes associated with displaying your will.

As you grow older in this life, you regain your confidence in your role as a healer. This feels good to you. In order to regain this sense of power and control, however, you once again alienate yourself. When you leave the body, you are feeling good and strong, but your guides are trying to encourage you to open your heart. They want you to have more interpersonal relationships in your next life. They want you to be with the soul who was your son in the aboriginal life to reconnect with the emotions you closed off then.

In this next life, you are a woman and this being is your son again. So this draws out your nurturing side. This life is somewhere in Asia—Japan. You also have a daughter, but you are closer to your son. Your husband is a fisherman. There is more respect and love between he and you than I've sensed in your previous relationships. Your home life seems a lot happier and healthier. You are very proud of your son as he grows up. He becomes a fisherman like his father. He has a very intuitive connection with the sea and knows where the fish are going to be, so he becomes the hero fisherman of the village. As his mother you take pride in this and feel respected yourself.

When he gets married you still want to control his life,* so you become the dominating mother-in-law. This puts a strain on your relationship. It is hard for your son because in this culture people are supposed to respect their parents, so he has to repress his own desires to do what will please you, but it's not a good energy for him. You're getting what you want, so you feel good about it.

I see you living in a small house near your son. At some point your husband is killed at sea. You are by yourself now, but you're still part of your son's family. You take care of his children, and you are still the one who runs the whole show, so toward the end of this life you feel satisfied. When you leave the body your guides encourage you to expand your horizons. Till now you've been following similar patterns in each life.

The next life I see is in Germany. You're a man. You feel out of place in this culture. As a boy growing up, everything feels foreign to you. You don't feel as if you belong there. You're the youngest of three children. Your father is a printer and you end up working with him on the printing press. This is almost a cloistered life. It feels safe to just work in the shop. You feel protected from the world outside. This is reminiscent of the lives in which you were a healer and didn't get involved with personal relationships. You feel so awkward in this culture that you withdraw and avoid relationships.

Moving ahead to when you're older, you still run the print shop. You have an employee who has a son. This boy comes to the shop often and you relate to him as if he were your own son. You teach him all about the printing business, and leave it to him when you die.

Your guides try to encourage you to return to the Western world again, but you don't want to. So once again you resist coming back to Earth. When you finally do, you choose to go back to the Orient—Mongolia or Tibet—and lead a nomadic life as a man. I see you loading tents and supplies onto yaks. Your wife is gentle and you have two kids. It's a big deal to always pack and unpack everything as you move from place to place. There doesn't seem to be a leader in the tribe. The men get together and have heated discussions, and eventually a plan is decided upon.

I'm seeing an avalanche in which you lose some of the people in your tribe. You have to turn back from the route you are on. You are upset because you had tried to persuade the tribe to go by another route. You're angry because they didn't listen to you. This life seems to be full of experiences like this in which you have difficulty in power struggles with the other males in your tribe. You feel frustrated in trying to get your way or force your will on them. After a while you develop the proverbial chip on your shoulder. In addition to your struggles on a psychological level, this life has many hardships because of the rough terrain and severe climate. To survive in this environment is a never-ending struggle. When you leave this life you bring with you that sense of hardship and struggle. You're frustrated and don't want to listen to your guides.

You come back in the western part of China as a woman. I'm seeing you working with herbs again. In different seasons you roam the countryside and mountains gathering herbs. In this life you are trying to return to what is most familiar and comfortable to you. You live in a small rural village and focus on the life of being an herbalist. You don't marry or have many personal relationships. You keep to yourself, keep things simple, avoiding interpersonal struggles or entanglements. This is like a passive-aggressive withdrawal, a way of acting out your resentment for the frustrations you experienced in your last life.

Toward the end of this life you begin to soften a bit. As an old woman you spend time with some of the young children in the village. This opens your heart, and you have some regret for how you isolated yourself emotionally. You die in this vulnerable condition. When your guides capitalize on this vulnerability, you become defensive and harden again, avoiding their intervention.

You come back as a Chinese man. I'm seeing you as a doctor in the palace of a feudal lord. You're practicing acupuncture and herbal medicine. As the doctor you have a prestigious position, one that gives you much recognition and respect. There is a poetic quality to this life. Oriental medicine is so filled with metaphors from the world of nature. You are really in tune with these qualities in people, with the fire energy, the water element, the wood, etc. You are very intuitive, and your healing work is a way of life, almost like a religion. In fact, the people believe in the medicine as if it were a religion. It's as if the gods were working through it, as if it were a way to stay in balance with the cosmos. I see that because of this, even when your treatments are not successful, people ignore the failures. They don't want to acknowledge that their "religious" beliefs are fallible. And of course your whole identity and social position are based on your ability to heal people, so you also have a desire to overlook the failures.

Once again you avoid an intimate relationship in this life. However, palace concubines or geishas are at your disposal. You are a real male chauvinist in the way you treat your servants and concubines. Indeed, in this life you develop a rather arrogant and calloused personality based on your position and medical abilities.

In your next life, I see you once again in China, on the coast near Japan. This time you are a woman and the period seems more modern. Your husband is a businessman and you are his oppressed housewife. You appear obedient, but remain rebellious on the inside. You have a lot of resentment for how controlled your life is. You want to study medicine again, but your role as wife doesn't allow you to, and you have a lot of frustration about that. Your husband in this life is very much like you were in your last life.

When you leave that life you are very angry and determined to come back as a woman and get your own way. You want to be a doctor in a woman's body. Consequently you have come into this life, and it seems that you are well on your way to fulfilling that desire. Do you have any questions?

H: Would you say that you got every life?

C: No, definitely not. When I do a reading like this there are certain patterns that come up. Usually these are patterns directly influencing your present life.

H: So possibly if I came back at another time, I would get other lifetimes?

C: Yes, that could be. There might be other issues that would be appropriate for you to look at. It seems most of the information today was related to the topics we discussed at the beginning of the session. We saw your background as a shaman and herbalist/doctor. We also saw patterns of frustration and anger, and a need to develop more compassion, which could apply to your role as a healer, as well as your personal life. I didn't consciously control or edit the lives that I saw today.

H: Do you see auras?

C: Yes.

H: What do you see in mine?

C: The first thing I notice is that you hold your aura in close to yourself. This reminds me of the lifetimes we saw today in which you kept to yourself and didn't want to get tangled up with other people. You hold your aura in tight because you're not very interested in reaching out to people. You have your own interests and you're rather self-contained in them.

I'm also seeing a metaphoric image of a computer screen over here in your aura. It's telling me that you have stored a lot of information in your mind, information on Oriental medicine, and it's all very organized. You can access this information easily.

In general, there is not much passion or emotion. It's very calm, almost too dry and logical. There's a lack of joy and zest for life. The energy seems cut and dried, almost mechanical.

H: I'm afraid I'll have to agree.

C: On the whole, it seems very organized and down to business, and I don't mean monkey business. (laughter) I see the energy coming down through your crown chakra, which is quite open, but there is a lid over it on top of your aura. This reminds me of the difficulty I had in reading your soul in the beginning of the session. I feel your soul is somewhat closed regarding the spiritual dimension. It has its focus and control in what it's doing on the Earth now and fears that if it opens to spiritual realms it will lose its power.

H: Do you think that is something I should work on?

C: Well, sooner or later. I get a sense from the reading we did today that in the past you have not really opened to these realms. When you are ready, you will do it. And that probably won't happen until you either get bored or feel trapped in the karmic patterns you have been operating within. It's not something you work on from the outside, or in an intellectual way. When the seed of the Spirit germinates within you, you will feel an inner compulsion to unfold like a flower stretching up to face the warmth of the sun.

H: Do you think that this could be blocking my intuitive abilities?

C: Yes, it could very well be having that affect. You seem to be a person who is primarily focused in a mental and rational mode. That's a highly developed function for you, so you feel comfortable with it. What you may not realize is that often your intuition operates through your mental processes. Perhaps you could become more aware of that instead of needing to make a distinction between the intellect and intuition. They can and do work together.

H: Well I guess I don't have any more questions. Thank you.

GARY

Gary is the editor for the German publisher who asked me to write this book. He is married and has three children. I did this absentee reading for him at his request. I have never met him, but in my correspondence with him I have been impressed with his integrity and dedication.

C: A knight in shining armor, a knight in search of the Grail; that's the description that best expresses the quality I see in your soul. My first impression is that the things keeping you from growing spiritually are ironically your purity and goodness as a soul. You have fought hard and long to uphold all that is good and true here on the planet. But this principle of using might for right, of defending and fighting for the truth, has polarized you and set you apart from others and not without a certain air of self-righteousness. Let's face it, it's difficult to relax and just have a good time dressed up in a shiny suit of armor. It would tend to make one a little stiff and rigid, and most people would feel a little intimidated having a casual conversation with a knight in shining armor.

Let's look at some of your past lives and see what you have been doing. Ancient Egypt is the first life I see. The time period is around 2000 B.C., after the prehistorical esoteric theocracy has been secularized. The Pharaoh is now worshiped as a god and the religious life of the culture is no longer guided by the higher-dimensional beings who originally established it. Many of the religious ideas and symbols still remain, but their true meaning has been lost, altered, or confused with new mythologies. You work in the palace or headquarters of the Pharaoh. You are the captain of the guards, or something like that. You take your job very seriously. It's an important and prestigious position, and you take pride in your service to the Pharaoh. It is a time in Egyptian history when there is much dissension, political conflict, and subversive factions trying to gain control. The Pharaoh's life is often in danger. You are a firm believer in his divinity and are totally committed to protecting him and his reign of power.

As a result of your dedication, your personal life suffers. You are so gung-ho in your service to the Pharaoh that you are not able to relax and spend quality time with your wife and family. Your whole world revolves around your job, and when conflicts occur at home because of this, you become defensive and feel as if you are being forced to make a choice between your service to the Pharaoh and your family responsibilities. When put in this position, you feel you must honor your commitment to the Pharaoh since it has religious overtones. Your sense of self-esteem and worth as a being have become associated with your position as captain of the guards. This conflict becomes quite a bone of contention between you and your wife, and the essence of the love you feel for one another is eclipsed by the struggle between the two of you over your loyalties and priorities. The pressure you feel from your wife hurts emotionally. You don't feel supported or understood by her. In fact you feel as if she is attacking something very sacred and important to you. I'm beginning to sense that this creates a schism in your heart, a belief that your religious convictions are opposed to the more personal needs of your heart for intimate relations with a partner. We'll see how that plays out as we go on.

As I scan this life for significant events, I see an episode where a rebellious faction has infiltrated the palace. It failed to harm the Pharaoh, but you feel responsible nonetheless. You don't lose your position, but you do lose a great deal of confidence and precious self-esteem as a result of the ordeal. You become more anxious, almost paranoid, and the tension in your home life escalates, causing this pattern to become more deeply ingrained in you.

At your death in that life, your wife begins to feel some compassion and understanding for you. She begins to see things from your side and empathize with you in your struggles. It helps a great deal to feel this emotional resolution with her as you leave the body. Ironically, to feel such love for one another only makes the schism in your heart that much more poignant. You carry this dilemma with you over to the other side.

As you struggle with your problem on the inner planes, guides come to you and try to help. But once ideas are set in your mind it's as if they are etched in steel. It is very difficult for you to see things from a different perspective, let alone change your ideas. Your guides are unable at that time to change your mind about the way you are perceiving the dilemma. One reason your ideas are so staunchly held is because you have a desperate need to feel you are right. It's a matter of pride, self-esteem, worth as a being.

Allow me to digress for a moment to seek the source of this. Back in Atlantis you found yourself in a place where

your loyalties to the theocracy of the higher-dimensional beings were challenged. There are several layers to this. First of
all, as a member of the human evolution on this planet, you
were in awe of the inner-dimensional beings. You compared
yourself to them, and at the same time wanted to win their
favor. Your internal logic went something like this: "If I can
win their favor and approval then I can feel equal to them."
Hence, your sense of self-esteem became associated with
gaining the approval of these higher-dimensional beings
who were like gods come to Earth in many ways, especially
in your eyes.

Things became complicated when you found yourself in
the middle of some power-hungry inner-dimensional beings
working toward overthrowing the theocracy. Because of your
eagerness to please, you were a good choice for them to attempt to enlist for their purposes. You knew what they were
doing was wrong, and wanted to warn the others in charge,
but you also had a need to be accepted, and feared what they
might do if you revealed their plot.

In the end you did nothing, neither assisting the bad
guys, nor alerting the good guys. When things went crazy
and Atlantis was eventually destroyed, you felt guilty about
not having done something to stop it. You felt as if you had
done something very wrong, and this left you with a need to
compensate. Your internal logic went like this: "If the good
guys knew what I did, they would never accept me, hence
I'm a worthless being. Therefore I must prove myself, I must
do things right, I must *be* right. I must fight for what is right
and make up for the wrong I've done."

Unfortunately, this self-serving need to redeem yourself
taints all the good you struggle to do and has come into conflict with your ability to avail yourself to goodness for goodness's sake. Your acts are serving this—by now—neurotic
need to redeem yourself. This seems like such a generic pattern in your makeup that from your perspective I imagine it

would be very difficult to separate your true identity from its affects on you. So my friend, I pose a riddle: Who are you? The Pearl of Great Price, which is your essential goodness and divinity, has been stolen by a powerful subpersonality of your ego. What heroic character of your True Being can you enlist to retrieve this treasure? How would this aspect of yourself be and act in the world? How would it regain the treasure?

Perhaps it's too soon for me to make such drastic conclusions. Let's continue, and see. The first image I see is a life where you were a commodore of a Phoenician fleet of ships. The patterns I have already spoken about have now crystallized into a very stern and rigid person. You have great responsibilities and your stature is well braced to carry their weight. In this life you have foregone family life and have devoted yourself fully to your career. You spend great amounts of time at sea. Your exploits include protecting your homeland from enemy ships, as well as exploration and imperialistic adventures. You are a very fair sovereign, but rule your men with an iron fist. You laws are just but exacting. None escapes due punishment for transgressions.

In this life you are projecting your own self-condemnation and need to be right outside of yourself onto those under your command. You are no more stern and rigid with your men than you are with yourself. This life is barren emotionally. Beneath the facade of law and order there is a vast emotional wasteland, a private world you share with no one. Many nights are spent alone in your cabin on the ship, often in the numb netherland of inebriation. Here we see that schism in your heart; outwardly you are an important and competent commodore in the navy, inwardly there is an emotional vacuum. In this life you have swung to the extreme outward polarity in the service of your king. Though you are courageous, victorious, and excel in your duties, you die with a confusing sense of discontent. You have fulfilled all your outer ideals and responsibilities but have no way of understanding your inner emptiness.

On the other side you sink into a torpor, not unlike your states of inebriation while in the body, except that you are painfully aware of your state. There is no escape from your sense of alienation and forlornness. Your depression surrounds you like a thick cloud, a cloud that veils your guides from you. Because you denied your emotions so avidly while in the body, they overwhelm you now. The polarity has swung to the inner, immersing you in the feelings on the other side of the schism in your heart. Your next birth is looked forward to as an escape from this emotional hell.

As a young boy in the Minoan culture, you are reserved and aloof. You feel apart from your brothers and sisters and spend a lot of time by yourself. You are fascinated by your imaginings of great warriors, and play by yourself acting out these fantasies of being a great hero/warrior. You join the army when you come of age. I'm seeing you marching with a helmet, shield, and spear. You are a diligent soldier and quickly advance through the ranks to achieve a leadership role. Exuding pride and confidence, you soon fall in love with a young woman who lives at home with her parents. They disapprove because you are a soldier, and therefore a poor candidate for a husband. You are confused and hurt by their disapproval because you are proud of your position.

You manage to persuade the woman to marry you in spite of her parents' protests. At the outset you are infatuated with her, and all the love that has been repressed for so long in your being gushes forth. Unfortunately your adoration of her is not based on a mature caring and empathy. When the glamour wears thin, both of you find you are unable to communicate or nurture your mutual emotional needs. In frustration, you turn your attention and energies once again to your life as a soldier. In its dynamics, this life is similar to your Egyptian life. The main difference here is that your spouse in this Minoan life is a weaker, less articulate woman, and hence puts less pressure on you. Though you remain together, there is a severe lack of emotional and verbal communication between you. Even though you have a family, once again you experience an inner emotional wasteland. Because you are in a relationship, this is not fully apparent to you. Eventually the schism becomes more insidious, camouflaged beneath a carpet of orthodoxy and mediocrity. The polarities existing on either side of the schism in your heart appear to be in a process of reconciliation only because they have been swept under the same carpet.

In this life, while there seems to be a movement toward balancing the inner and outer, not much ground is actually gained on either side. However, at least an attempt is being made to balance the two. The end result for you, when you leave the body, is that you feel stymied and frustrated, experiencing a lack of satisfaction both inwardly and outwardly. But this time the dilemma is more poignant. You stand near the center of the schism, and your awareness is more precise. In this condition you are more available for assistance from your guides. In fact you spend time in a retreat on the inner planes. Here you are schooled in the basics of spiritual love. In the presence of angelic beings, you are shown how Universal Love welds the cosmos into one whole organism. For the time being you leave behind the mundane and petty problems of your little world. You lose yourself in the grandeur and inspiration of Universal Love. In your innocence and naiveté, you discover numerous religious connotations in your introduction to the Bliss of Love, and you become a champion of this new level of understanding with the same zeal that you pursued your military endeavors in the past.

In the life that follows, you partake in an esoteric community that is laying the groundwork for the advent of the Christian Era. Born in Jerusalem to parents of the gentile segment of the Jewish culture, you rebel against the materialistic orientation of your parents and eventually join a group of desert ascetics, the Essenes, and become a zealous adherent to their austere beliefs.

In this life you are returning to the original intent of your efforts to fight for what's good and true. And this is happening in a context where you have an opportunity to live out the lessons on Universal Love you received while out of the body in the physical world. You are making strides in healing the two polarities within you, but your efforts are tainted by a holier-than-thou attitude.

Only dimly aware of the significance of the project you are involved in, you work to help lay the foundation for the religious edifice that Jesus, The Christ, would later build. Your service here is still motivated to a large degree by your need to feel important, rather than from a self-effacing attitude. I don't mean to belabor this point. Admittedly there's a fine line here but an important one—the *bottom* line, so to speak. It's the boundary that is keeping you trapped in the realm of personal karma.

Also in this life, due to nearly fanatical emphasis on purity and righteousness, you refrain from entering into an intimate love relationship with a woman. In fact, this issue becomes further confused by your religious beliefs regarding celibacy and the evil desires of the flesh. Nonetheless, at the end of this life you feel a great deal of satisfaction for what you have accomplished. There is more peace in your heart, and the stirrings of religious fervor, as well as a sense that you have found The Path and a goal that is really worth moving toward.

In the past, whether it was for the theocracy in Atlantis, the Pharaoh, or king, you have labored to uphold and further the cause of what was good and true. But now you feel you are in the service of God, the ultimate sovereign. In reality it's only your concept of the ultimate power that has changed, not your motivation or will to act.

After living this saintly life, you assume you are going to heaven to join the entourage of the Most High. You are a little confused when the trumpets are not blaring and the banners are not waving for you when you cross over to the other side. Your guides are supportive and positive about the growth in your recent life, but they don't seem to be quite as pleased as you think they should be. This is disconcerting to you. Regardless, you are ready to go on to the next big project. Meanwhile they are thinking it's time to trim your hubris a little. You are confused by their suggestions for your next life, but without understanding the implications you are eager to please and go along with their plan.

Once again you are born in the Holy Land. This time your parents are of the poorer class. As you grow into adulthood, there is very little opportunity for you to escape the harsh realities of life. You do not receive much education and are required to help your father in his trade as a carpenter/handyman. As the eldest son, you also have responsibilities to stay with the family and help support and raise the younger children. This life is focused on family and emotional issues. Your mother is sickly and you often have to care for her, consequently your predilection for involving yourself in a grandiose way in the matters of the external world is being curtailed. You are forced by your surroundings to pay attention to basic human needs. Early in that life you do not feel the strain of this constraint as much as you do later.

You are an older man with wife and family of your own when Jesus begins his mission. You long to leave your family and follow him, to be one of his champions, but you can't leave your family. They would perish without you. The tension of the opposing forces within you causes much anguish.

Your wife in this life is so nurturing and gentle that you cannot resent her for preventing you from going out to save the world. She does a lot to soften your hard edges. Though it is difficult to overcome the patterns within you that inhibit your expression of personal love, she is such a wonderful person that it is also damn hard not to love her.

The tide of religious sentiment is running high and the forces of oppression in your culture become more and more unbearable after the death/disappearance of Jesus. Still tied to the needs of your family, you suffer extreme dismay over not being able to throw yourself wholeheartedly into the Christian revolution. Hence, in this life you experience the result—the karma, if you will—of your attachment to being a champion. Your ability to enjoy life and to be nourished emotionally in your relationships of personal love is tainted by your desire to perform great acts in the eyes of the outer world. It's a difficult life for you, and a lesson you refuse to learn at that time.

When you cross over this time, you are angry with your guides. Not understanding the intent of their actions, you feel somewhat betrayed by them. This further undermines your confidence and sense of security. You don't feel so sure of your direction now; you do not know who to trust. They were the main emissaries between you and your idea of what or who God is. Now you feel unsure of that connection, of your relationship to that ultimate power, and this is one—if not the prime—basis for your sense of individual identity. This is very traumatic for you, threatening the roots of your identity.

In your confusion, you go through a period of rebellion in which you resist incarnating. Your state of anxiety is such that you are not available for the assistance of your guides, and you spend a considerably long time in this limbo.

Finally, still without a definite sense of direction, you come into the body once again. You find yourself in the Dark Ages at a time when Christianity is fighting to eradicate paganism. It's a brutal and barbaric time in which you act out your desire (from your previous life) to champion Christian dogma. In this life you are literally a knight in armor enmeshed in the bloody wars of the chaotic European continent. Instead of glamour and glory, you are confronted with the atrocities of war. Though struggling to uphold the values from your previous lives, it is difficult to feel noble and proud about your pursuits as a warrior for God. You keep fighting nonetheless, expending as much energy combating inner feelings of hopelessness about your efforts as you do in your outward involvement in the muddle of hostility and aggression that surrounds you.

Dying on the battlefield, you leave the body consumed with disgust for what seems a futile life. On the other side, you sit pensively on a metaphorical battlefield strewn with the gory byproducts of human aggressions. Deep in your being you struggle to comprehend the horror and absurdity of it all. You compare these activities to the glimpses of Universal Love and Law you experienced in the inner-plane lessons several lifetimes ago. It doesn't make sense to you. The human "battlefield" on the planet seems totally insane compared to the way it's supposed to be according to your lessons and growing inner awareness. Your old identity as champion, warrior, etc., is becoming tainted with negative associations. This is an identity crisis par excellence!

So deep is your depression that the guides are again unable to communicate with you. Again you resist returning to the physical world because you lack any positive motivation or sense of meaningful direction.

Upon returning, you continue to work out your dilemma. Your desire to bring the Law and Love of God to the planet is acted out in the Crusades. You throw yourself wholeheartedly—or more correctly, desperately and neurotically—into the quest to reestablish the allegorical Holy Land. This is a last-ditch effort on your part to validate your identity as champion of the Almighty and Most High, and to vanquish what by now appears to you to be great evil in the world.

The aftermath of this tour de force is bittersweet. There is an almost righteous sense of satisfaction from having spent the energy of your frustration in the heat of battle. But the realization that not much really changed in the world due to your efforts is sobering at first, and then gradually demeaning. You return from the holy wars to your family and a life of mediocrity, a life of increasingly quiet desperation in a Bavarian village. A life in which the trouble and confusion deep in your soul insulates you from the love and warmth of your family. You live out the rest of your days in this emotional winter, numb even to your sense of alienation.

Upon leaving the body you remain in this state of emotional paralysis. The pain of your failure to once and for all validate your identity as champion, and your failure (yours because you identified with the desire to make it so) to drastically change the world by bringing God's Kingdom to the Earth is devastating to you. This is an auspicious time, ripe for the sowing of wisdom in your soul, but you shroud your vulnerability in emotional armor, wall yourself in, keeping the forces of transformation at bay. Your guides are shut out as you curl up in a fetal position, nursing your hurt pride and fatally wounded values. Meanwhile, centuries pass beneath you on the planet.

This fetal slumber is much like a gestation period. Though unconscious of your guides, they are surrounding you in an embryonic environment of love and nurturance. Slowly there is a breaking down of old defense systems, and a gentle spirit from deep within you begins to grow. All the alchemical magic of Life is working inside you, and when you are born again into the world an entirely new aspect of being comes forth.

A female child in your familiar Germanic homeland, you live in a rural area of rolling pastures. You enjoy an almost fairy-tale existence communing with the forces of nature that surround you. Growing up you retain the innocence of your childhood. So innocent and shy are you that the young men of the nearby village have a hard time winning your favors. There is one, an especially gentle and sensitive young man, who finds his way into your heart. After a long, and very formal courtship, you settle into the family life.

Everything that was lacking in your previous lives in regard to family and personal love is experienced fully in this life as a woman. Your experience of motherhood is akin to rapture. Your spouse turns out to be someone who has emotional patterns similar to those you have exhibited in the past as a male. From your feminine incarnation, you develop compassion for that part of yourself. Your love for your husband is unconditional, though at times he is unavailable for your love due to his aloofness.

In this life you have entered the Kingdom of Love. So complete is your immersion in it, when you die you ascend buoyant with bliss. Your guides are there to embrace you, and you are overwhelmed with a sense of gratitude at your reconciliation with them. You experience great peace in your soul after this life. There's a sense of having arrived at the place you have fought so hard to attain, and you revel in it.

You understand completely when your guides suggest that you need to come back as a man again with this level of awareness to dispel the old patterns associated with your male identity. You suffer a tinge of remorse about having to leave your rapture and return to the old patterns in the male body. You know it won't be easy to change those patterns quickly. Putting on the male body is somewhat like putting on clothes that are filthy just after you've taken a bath. But you understand that you need to go back and dissolve those old patterns; you need to finish the dirty work.

After a brief sojourn in a rarified realm on the inner planes where you once again go to school, you get a behind-the-scenes look at how spiritual work is carried out on the planet before coming back to Earth in your present body.

Today, in your work as editor of metaphysical books, you are learning how to take part in the gradual uplifting and transformation of consciousness here on Earth. Your old pattern of being a champion is being integrated into a more effective and humble outlet. And you are coming in contact and working with many spiritual beings, both incarnate and disincarnate. In fact, before coming into the body this time you agreed to act as a conduit for the dissemination of new spiritual ideas. There are guides and spirits working through and with you, much more than you realize in your Earth-side consciousness.

In addition, you are making great strides in this life to heal the old schism in your heart. Your present spouse is none other than the soul who was your wife in ancient Egypt. With her, you are integrating your spiritual work with your personal relationships. Your family unit this time is strong and rooted deeply in love.

What lies ahead for you is more inner work. Going within and basking in the Light, grinding away at the hard edges, and pushing aside the layers of armor and personal identity so the Light is free to shine forth unobstructed. Further softening and letting down your guard will come as you uproot that old need to prove yourself, which will happen as you continue to allow yourself to be absorbed into the Light. This is the Light of your True or Essential nature. Always remember that it's not your life you're living, but Life that is living you.

BARBARA

I met Barbara in Key West, Florida, where I was taking a holiday from lecturing and teaching. She was there with her first daughter visiting friends. Later that spring I briefly stayed with her and her husband in their country home in Tennessee. They sponsored some workshops of mine on their property, and I returned to visit them frequently over the next couple of years. I haven't seen Barbara for nearly four years. She has two more children now and has gone on to study and practice Iridology and natural healing methods. Her husband, Don, has completed his education and is now a professor of literature. In a letter, I mentioned that I was working on this book and asked Barbara if she would like a past-life reading.

C: Mother hen; that's how I would describe the quality I see in your soul. This preoccupation with mothering and fostering seems a little imbalanced to me. At any rate, you are anxious in the way you perform your mothering. Let's see how this image might relate to your history of lifetimes on the planet.

The first life I see is in primitive times. You are holding a baby in your arms as you huddle inside a cave. You are alone and some natural disaster is occurring, like an earthquake. When the walls of the cave begin to give way, you run outside. The ground is moving and breaking up all around you. You're terrified and don't know what is happening. You don't know whether you should run or stand still. Finally you begin to run, but as the ground moves, you stumble and fall. The child flies from your arms just as the cliff collapses. You manage to scurry to safety, but the child is crushed beneath the falling rocks and earth.

After the calamity is over, you remain in shock for many days. Your home was destroyed, and your child was killed by the mysterious shaking of the earth. The intensity, horror, and mystery of the event left a deep impression in your psyche. You're also plagued with a sense of guilt because you survived and your child has died. In this primitive life you are unable to reason and deal with your guilt. The logic of the guilt it created in your unconscious mind remains unaltered. The irrational logic went something like this: "A mother should protect and care for her offspring. My child died and I survived without protecting her, therefore I've done something wrong."

As I've already said the event was highly charged. In addition, you responded to the irrational logic with all the fear and superstition a primitive mind is prone to. Hence this guilt and the resulting need to appease it have become generic factors in your psychological makeup. You wandered in a daze over the countryside punishing yourself unconsciously by refusing to eat or take care of your own survival needs because you were so distraught, and of course you soon died in this state.

The first thing I see in your next life is an image of you holding a baby. I'm not sure where this life is yet. I get the sense you are in a large tent and are a member of a nomadic tribe. The main focus in this life is your child, to the extent that you neglect all the other aspects of your life. Your social responsibilities and your relationship with your spouse suffer. The sun rises and sets on your role as nurturer to your son. Soon you give birth to another child, and many more are to follow. You abandon everything else in order to care for your children. In this culture it is a sign of prosperity to have a large family, and though your emotional relationship with your spouse is curtailed, he is actually proud of his lot. As proud as you are satisfied with your ability to appease your guilt.

I get a sense this pattern has carried through up to your present life. Instead of tracing it through the many lives between now and then, I feel it would be more constructive to look at other themes. Let me just say before changing the subject, that you have made some progress with this theme in that you have managed to expand your field of endeavors beyond your role of mother/fosterer, though it still demands a large portion of your focus.

I'm seeing a life in a tropical, somewhat primitive existence. It's a tribal life and in this initial image I see you cooking mashed tubers over an open fire. You are childless in this life and jealous of the other women who have children. Your desire to nurture is sublimated by being a medicine woman. I see you hunting in the jungle, collecting plants and other substances used in healing. Though you dedicate your life to healing others, you harbor a free-floating resentment for your lack of children. You refuse the love of your spouse, and later other men, as a way to express your resentment. You also resist being part of the tribal family on an emotional level.

I can really understand your resentment in that life, since I have a similar resentment toward life in general for denying me the fulfillment of my desire—perhaps addiction—for romance. Seeing you in that life helps me see how futile my own stubborn passive-aggressive stance toward life is. Your lifelong self-imposed alienation had no affect on the Universal Forces moving you relentlessly along the path of evolution and perfection as a soul. However, after you leave the body in that life, your guides decide to allow you to persist in your pattern rather than trying to set up more situations whereby you would be given the opportunity to move on to other realms of development. Their attempt in your last life only escalated the issue with you, and their plan to help you move on backfired. You are more resolved than ever to hold on to your role as mother/fosterer.

In your next life I see you with a child at your breast. Your husband is a fisherman. You live in a seaside village in the South Pacific; a Polynesian culture. In this life you seem to be enjoying a sense of victory in that you have returned to your favorite role. As you go on to have other children, you become more demanding of your spouse. You assume, and even demand, that your spouse support you in your role. He is merely a pawn in your game, so to speak. He is not someone you love and respect for who he is as a person, but someone you are using simply to satisfy your need to have children.

Well it doesn't look as if I'm going to be too successful in moving on to another theme. It seems this guilt-powered instinct has become like a demon in you. Psychologists might say you have become possessed by the archetype of the Great Mother. In the lifetimes we've looked at so far, this archetype has controlled you and curtailed your own individualness. Because of your original sense of guilt and fear, you have become trapped in the service of this instinct.

Your sense of victory is carried over to the inner planes after you die. In regard to your guides, you are quite competent in your ability to resist them and continue on your one-track course of rearing children. They try to explain to you the need to go on and have other kinds of experiences for the purpose of developing the various parts of your being. But you are smug, and tenaciously pursue your own path.

The next life that comes to me seems to be in the Roman Empire. As a young woman growing up you peruse your social environment, keen on seeking the most auspicious mate to serve your purpose. You eventually choose an ambitious young soldier. To be a soldier in the Roman army was one of the most prestigious positions a man could attain. This particular fellow was well on his way to a leadership role in the army, thus ensuring you, and your offspring, security.

Once you decide, you set out to lure this robust young officer. This turns out to be no easy task, for the young man had been your spouse in the Polynesian life. He is attracted to you, indeed he had truly loved you in your previous life together, but he's also weary of your ulterior motives. Nonetheless, you persist and he eventually submits to his desire for you.

You were no less demanding in this Roman life. It's not that you didn't have genuine feelings of affection for him, but unconsciously you had a built-in safeguard that did not allow you to forego your prime objective as mother/fosterer. To allow yourself to become vulnerable to love would have been a psychic event that might prove to be more powerful than your prime objective. This unconscious governor made sure that other types of experiences did not gain precedence. Everything but the prime objective must be repressed or subverted; this was the task of the survival mechanism and the built-in safeguard. For example, when your affection for your spouse threatened to become too important, it was immediately and assuredly repressed by a staunch and rather demanding attitude.

After the children were grown and left your household, you had a difficult time knowing what to do with yourself. You became increasingly nervous and anxious, and had a compulsive need to keep yourself busy. In that life, you became real finicky about your house and were very critical of the servants working for you. You drove everybody nuts, including yourself. So distraught were you that you became ill and passed away. Not only were those in your household relieved at your passing, but you yourself breathed a sigh of relief as you passed over to the other side. You did not understand that your anxiety was caused from your addiction to being a mother, but you were glad to be free of the emotional tension your withdrawal caused (after the children moved out of your house).

Your guides capitalize on this opportunity to try to help you see the dynamics of your plight. But by now this area of your being has become sacred, and any threat to it is met with powerful defenses. Once you get the gist of their communication, you close yourself in, and them out. You spend some time in this self-imposed retreat until the old instinct takes hold of you again, and you obey without questions. At this point you are not consciously choosing your next life or its conditions. The blind drive to reproduce and mother is on automatic pilot. The only personal interest you have is reconnecting with souls who were your offspring in previous incarnations, and perhaps joining with a spouse who you have used before, which is the case I see coming up in the next life.

On the eastern side of the Mediterranean in a Byzantine culture, you come into a family of prestigious lineage, one that will ensure a secure upbringing and marriage. Your early life seems to be heading in one direction only, toward your marriage and role as a mother. Your husband, the Roman soldier from your previous life, is a statesman. When you meet in this life there is no question as to what you will do together. By now it's like a deeply ingrained habit. You also seem calmer about your role in this life, at least early on. It's like a dance you've done so many times you don't have to think about it; you just do it automatically, unconsciously.

You eventually have four children and soon you are in your glory taking care of them. You have one son you are especially fond of. You have great expectations for him. He is a very refined, intelligent, articulate boy. You are proud of him.

Though a little too stuffy and ornate for my taste, your cultural setting in this life is very pleasant and stable. It would definitely get the Good Housekeeping Seal of Approval. And although somewhat overritualized or rigid due to your social values, your relationship with your husband is more compatible in this life. I suppose actually the somewhat repressive morals kept the flame of love between you at a controlled level so it did not threaten to override the prime objective.

As I look to see what happens after your children are grown, I see that one of your daughters is crippled. I get a sense that she has come into this life to be with you so you can continue to have a child to care for throughout the life. I'm suggesting a co-dependent type of relationship taking place on a soul level. At any rate this ingenious solution does prevent you from going through the same neurotic withdrawal you experienced in your previous life.

Your special son does go on to become a well-respected and influential person in the political domain. This brings you great satisfaction and pride.

When this life is over, you have the feeling of a job well done. It's like coming home from a good day's work and just wanting to relax when you cross over to the other side. While you're kicking back, your guides come and try to talk with you, but you turn a deaf ear toward them. Once again your instincts are on automatic pilot. When conditions are suitable, you are drawn back to the planet.

As I begin to focus on your next life, I get a sense that your guides have intervened and arranged a life where you are born in a male body. You are an only child, born to parents in the countryside somewhere in Europe. It looks like Germany to me. While your soul is resentful for the intervention of guides, your incarnate personality enjoys the experience of being in a male body and growing up in the country. It finds satisfaction in performing physical labor on the farm. The smells of the earth, straw, and animals; the changes of nature; the vastness of the sky and rolling pastures all provide a pleasant sensual experience. You feel vital and so much alive.

Being free of the mothering instinct allows you to enter a whole new world, and as a man there's a certain innocence and sense of adventure you have while exploring it. As you near adulthood you are consumed with wanderlust and long to see what lies beyond the horizon. But this causes tension in your family, because they need your help to run the farm. Your father is less understanding than your mother. After all it's mainly his work that will increase once you leave. Nonetheless, your mother is genuinely more sympathetic to the longings stirring within you. It's due to her support, albeit silent, that you finally make up your mind to leave your family.

As I see you walking along a country road, it reminds me of the image of the young man on the tarot card of the Fool.

You are carefree, innocent, and ignorant about the world you are heading to. You have never been to a large city, and your first encounter is somewhat appalling to you. After the initial excitement, you are amazed at the squalor and disrespect you witness. Not having any money, you fall into the company of beggars and thieves who live on the streets. Their morals, scruples, and social interactions are very confusing and disturbing to you. You're not streetwise. It turns out to be like a bad dream, a dream you finally escape from by leaving the city and taking to the road again. But your innocence has been shattered and it takes many days to sort out the experiences you have had. In the end you are left very confused and leery of what the future might bring.

You sleep while nestled in a stack of hay, but you are hungry and the nights are starting to turn cold. You come to a small village around noon the next day. Your first concern is getting something to eat. The people in the village are wary of you, a lone traveler on foot. At an inn you manage to find someone who will feed you after you clean the stable. In fact, the man and woman who run the inn are happy to have someone to help out, and you stay on with them for awhile. You chop wood and care for the animals of the guests and do other odd jobs in exchange for room and board. The older couple is not altogether unkindly and you enjoy meeting the people passing through who stay at the inn. With cold weather approaching, you are thankful for your position and decide to stay on throughout the winter at least.

Before winter is over, however, you are struck with another fit of wanderlust. When a traveling merchant stops at the inn, you approach him with the idea of accompanying and helping him. This merchant is a rather shrewd man and considers your proposition carefully. You are a stout, energetic young lad, and quite naive. He decides, it might be worth his while to enlist your services, as he is getting on in age. In the morning you pack the few extra articles of clothing you have acquired and climb aboard his wagon for your new life as a traveling salesman.

Unfortunately, your first destination is the large city you had visited before. You are afraid as you approach it. This makes your employer suspicious, as you are unable to hide your feelings from his keen eye. Nonetheless, once in the city he leaves you at a stable with the horses and wagon while he goes to inquire about business opportunities. You are to watch the wagon and guard against thieves. This makes you quite nervous because you have some experience with how ruthless and sneaky thieves can be.

You are relieved when he returns quickly, having decided to only buy a few things here and move on. Well, before this turns into a novel, let me just say that you end up traveling in this manner for a number of years. After venturing into other countries, as far south as the Mediterranean Sea in southern France, your appetite for adventure begins to wane and you feel a pull to return home to visit your parents.

Your father is very ill when you return, and your mother is delighted to see you again. You feel good about returning to the place of your childhood and taking on the duties of the farm. You end up staying with your mother after your father passes on. In fact, you remain on the farm for the rest of your life.

Throughout this life you never got involved with a woman. You were shy and not comfortable in a man's body regarding sexual matters. The opportunities for you to overcome these inhibitions were not plentiful either. In your later life there was a nebulous sense of emptiness inside you didn't understand, but it was swept under the rug while you engaged yourself with the duties of running the farm.

When you leave the body this time, it's with a vague sense of confusion about the emotions you have stored away. It's like waking up from a dream when you return to the inner planes and back to your familiar identity. After you get your bearings, you are not quite sure if you are angry at your guides. Your life as a man has given you a new outlook, and you can't help but see that it was valuable. The Great Mother in you is incensed, but this recent experience as a man has given you a little autonomy. You have begun to create an identity that is separate from her. Now your guides can come to you and discuss things.

Your guides show you the patterns in your past lives, and how you have been dominated by this Great Mother aspect of yourself. They help you understand that there are many kinds of experiences and identities, and that it is important for you to explore new possibilities and learn new things. You decide to follow their suggestions for your next life.

Along with your guides you decide to come back as a woman again, to try to expand yourself in that form. I see you in Italy, the northwestern portion. Early in this life you marry, following your pattern of having lots of kids. But your husband this time is not a very good provider. He's kind of a lazy slob and you're always getting mad at him. You're a fiery Italian woman with quite a temper. Eventually you get so fed up with having to take care of the whole family, including your husband, that one day you walk out on the whole scene. You just up and leave your husband and your three children. It gives you great satisfaction to think that he will have to take care of the kids now.

You have a sister who lives on the Mediterranean Sea, and you stay with her until you get a job in a seaside cafe and save enough money to get a place of your own. This is around the turn of the 19th century, and what you are doing is a radical thing for those times. Your sister is totally astounded, but you're so angry at your husband that you have simply closed off your heart, forcing yourself not to think about the children. You work very hard and save your money, thinking you'll go back and get them sometime.

Several months pass and you start to weaken. You really begin to miss your children and worry about them. One day a charming man who owns a big yacht comes to the cafe and becomes infatuated with you. He starts coming everyday and tries to win your favor. Eventually you agree to go for a sail with him. Though you are becoming increasingly anxious about your children, you find yourself flattered and enthralled with this man. Your excitement mounts as the appointed day for your sailing trip approaches.

The day of sailing aboard his luxurious yacht is like being in a fairy tale; you feel like Cinderella. However, that evening after a splendid meal on board, he tries to seduce you. You become furious with him—you have quite a temper—and order him to take you ashore. You march off in a huff once he rows you to the dock.

You feel let down after this, very depressed. You can't stand to be away from your kids any longer. You pack your things and return to your village. When you get out of the carriage, you don't know what to do. You end up renting a room in town. You're afraid to go to your children, because you think they will hate you for leaving them.

When you finally get up the courage, you find your family is no longer living there. Asking around, you discover that your husband has moved back to his parents' house in Milan with the children. You weren't clear about what you were going to do once you got back, but now—all of a sudden—you become vehement about taking the children from him.

You aren't prepared for the war with your mother-in-law. She is outraged by what you have done and will not let you in to see your children. Several times you stand outside her house yelling and pounding on the door. She yells back just as loud. You hear the children crying inside, and you get more furious at the old woman. After a week you see that it is hopeless. You go back to stay with your sister and work in the cafe again. Your life becomes very dull and routine, and you avoid getting to know any men. It's like torture to be estranged from your children. Months slowly pass by.

In about a year you return to Milan in hopes of seeing the children. You hide on the street near their house waiting until you spy your oldest daughter coming out of the house. You run down the street to catch up to her, only to be attacked by your mother-in-law. Your confrontation with her nearly turns into a fist fight. It ends with her dragging your daughter back up the steps and into the house. You feel hopeless. You wait on the street a few more days hoping just to see your children. Your husband comes and goes several times and you feel very angry at him. Eventually you return to your village by the sea, vanquished.

For you, to be with a man means to have children. Because of what has happened you can't allow yourself to have more children, and therefore avoid the company of men. You grow old in that life without seeing your children or being with another man. You more or less live in an emotional vacuum. Ultimately you resign yourself to your fate, not feeling overly guilty, but thinking you more or less deserved what happened to you for your impulsive and rash actions. Later in that life you become more and more whole within yourself, and find a certain peace in that.

You're not quite sure what to think when you leave the body and return to the other side. It's not as if you had any great adventures or exciting breakthroughs. It was actually a rather dull life. Nonetheless you do feel more centered or self-possessed. Your guides are basically pleased with the way in which you carried out the life, and you are open to conversing with them regarding your next life. Together you decide it would be good to try to balance your involvement with family life with your need to develop your own interests. You also spend a brief period in a temple of spiritual learning on the inner planes this time. You were very much interested in pursuing this field of endeavor once back in the body and make plans to meet with a few key individuals to help you in these matters. Your present life is the result of this plan. I'd say at this point, your life is right on schedule and is a successful attempt to balance these considerations.

My only advice is to relax more. Whether it be your family life, or your spiritual work and interests, you get all keyed up and anxious, running around tyring to do too many things at once and thus being less effective. Breathe, relax, and just concentrate on the task at hand. Give it your complete attention, letting the energy move on calmly at the appropriate time. Everything is really all right! Really. Especially when every task or situation is met with love and compassion for yourself as well as those around you.

TOM

Tom is middle-aged and divorced. He has his own architectural business, does some painting, plays guitar, and enjoys Oriental martial arts. With his white-grey hair and stalwart physique, he sat in his armchair like a country gentleman on the front porch of his southern plantation while I did this reading for him.

C: To begin with, is there anything you would like to focus on?

T: Livelihood and creative self-expression. And maybe those things that are in my way, blocking me from release from the wheel of life and death. What work needs to be done for liberation? That, to me, is the ultimate goal.

C: I want to start off with a metaphor that helps me tune in to your soul. I'm getting the image of an old man with a cane. He is a deep thinker and rather staunch. He really wants to nail down how reality works and get to the bottom of things.

There's a sense of his working hard at developing this awareness, this philosophic endeavor. The downside of that, of course, is being too serious and having unreasonable expectations.

Your ideal is to attain this perfect level of mastery and awareness—enlightenment, shall we say—and you tend to judge yourself against this ideal. When you don't match up to it, you become critical of yourself and get frustrated. You introvert this frustration into a kind of self-punishment and get very demanding of yourself. I would say this underlying dynamic is one of the core patterns holding you back from achieving your goal. Can you relate to this at all?

T: Yeah, yeah. The feeling of being very old. Not necessarily old physically, but in terms of spending a lot of lifetimes circling.

C: In this old man as metaphor, there is a connotation of a mental process with a marked absence of feminine qualities such as emotional richness or fulfillment.

T: I can't relate to that because I'm very emotional.

C: Would you say you feel emotionally fulfilled as a being?

T: Well . . . I don't think emotions are to *be* fulfilled. By virtue of their nature there is always a new emotional factor that needs to be addressed.

C: Can you visualize two people, one emotionally fulfilled and the other maybe with a lot of feelings who doesn't feel fulfilled? [At this point Tom got very defensive and irritated with my questioning him. I was trying to point out a blind spot he obviously did not want to see. His final definition of emotional fulfillment was being able to remain dispassionate no matter what happens. I left it at that as he only became more and more angry as I pressed him on the issue. My sense is that he felt his ideal image, which included this yogic dispassion and denial of desires, was being challenged. And of course it was my intention to show him how this was one of his main obstacles to the liberation he "desired."]

I'll just end it with these two extreme images of old men. One is very serious, well-read, sincere, and studious; an individual who thinks about things deeply. He's somewhat rigid and lacks emotional warmth. The other old man has returned to childhood, in a way. He's really spontaneous and has a twinkle in his eye. He's very playful and open-hearted, kind of in love with life.

T: I thought you were going to look at my past lives.

C: Well, why don't we move on to that now.

I'm seeing you in a life in Egypt, around 2000 B.C. You are a scribe for the Pharaoh. You are very diligent in performing your duty, just as you are when you do your woodworking now. You have a desire to be very exact and meticulous. You're intent on keeping precise records of what goes on in the kingdom and of replicating the sacred texts that have been handed down from antiquity. If I scan through that life quickly, I get a sense the main quality is one of being adamant about living according to the letter of the law, to do what is right in the context of that social and religious environment.

This life seems to be your introduction to spiritual teachings. In addition to being a scribe, you are an initiate in the temple. The religious training in Egypt was fairly strict, including exacting morals, diet, celibacy, etc. And these qualities add to your intention of doing things right. Hence, there is a severity you begin to develop in your character.

When you die in that life, you're expecting some kind of journey. In your religious training there was the concept of the soul taking a long journey after death. You are looking forward to this journey, so there is a high level of awareness. However, you are somewhat disgruntled to find out you have to come back to the planet. I'm getting a sense here you are still operating within a group karma instead of your personal karma at this time. I see the guides you're working with saying, "OK, this group is going here next."

I'm getting images of Peru, an ancient spiritual community like the one at Machu Picchu, for example. This is actually the remnant of an old Lemurian outpost, a very ancient and esoteric culture. There is a carry-over here from your life as the scribe having to do with your integrity, and hence, ability to maintain the ancient teachings. In a sense you were acting as a medium in which those teachings could be contained and preserved. In this life, as in your Egyptian life, you are involved in a collective drama and purpose, not so much personal. Again, this is a rather monastic community with an emphasis on moral fiber and spiritual ideals. I'm seeing that you, and the group of souls you are part of, spent several more lifetimes carrying out that function in Peru. During these lives there is not much development in an individual sense of identity or building up of personal karma.

Before you come back into the body after these lives, your guides inform you it is time to move on to another level of development. You interpret this as meaning a higher form of spiritual work, when they in fact are talking about the need to become more individualized, i.e., more typically human.

I'm seeing a primitive existence in Africa perhaps. There are black-skinned people and mud buildings with thatched roofs. But you're not a black-skinned person, you are brown-skinned.

OK, you were born on an island, and within your life-time your people sailed to new lands. I see you coming to the southeast side of Africa from somewhere in the South Seas. Your people integrate into the native culture. The main thing I see regarding your life is a sense of confusion over trying to understand and adjust to the morals and rules of this new culture. You are placed in a situation where you have to ex-pand your known world—this is the metaphoric meaning of this life. This emphasizes your individuality, because you are the fulcrum and the point of translation between these two collective realities.

This is also the first life in which I see you living outside a monastic context. You mate with one of the black women from the new culture and produce children. This is one way you are trying to become like them and understand their ways. For these reasons this life creates some interesting emotional dynamics. Your mate is really a strong-willed woman. In the relationship with her, you acquiesce. You let her have her way and repress your own emotional needs. This is one of the most important results of this life, this emo-tional imprint or pattern of repressing your emotional needs. On the other hand, it is a real positive experience for you to have children. You have an especially close relationship with your son. These are the main aspects of this life; I don't see anything else that is significant.

The overall tone after you leave that life is one of satisfac-tion, but you are somewhat confused as to how this life re-lates to your ideals of spiritual advancement. Your guides encourage you not to worry about that yet. They say you'll understand eventually.

T: Who are the guides?

C: They are beings on the inner planes whose role it is to teach and help you. It's as if you are in school here on the planet and they are your teachers.

T: Where are they from? Are they old souls who have graduated from the class of humanity? Are they from Venus or another star system? Are they angels from God?

C: Well they could be any of those, but the guides who are working with your soul group are not beings who have graduated from the Earth plane. The closest thing to what you said would be angelic beings. They are old wise souls who have been functioning on other dimensions.

I'm getting an impression that you were involved in an experiment of some kind. It's as if they took a group of human souls and put them in special conditions. This explains to me the nature of your early lifetimes, the monastic and spiritual orientations that you were in. These were protected and controlled environments, whereas most souls seem to have been more on their own in primitive conditions. So you have been guided and watched carefully.

Your guides are pleased after your African life; they feel you did very well. I'm getting a definite sense that there is a scenario they are planning for you. In your next life, you are taken out of your soul group and venture out on your own. I see you growing up in a village in India. Your father is a merchant. He has a stall on the front porch of your house. He is a sandal maker. You grow up in this crosssroads of civilization. All walks of life pass by your front door everyday as you are growing up.

One of the things that fascinates you as you're growing up is the Hindu holy men, the sadhus, who come begging and preach in the streets. These holy men awaken the memory of your spiritual training from your earlier lives. One of the main messages of their teachings is the seeking of liberation, with an emphasis on transcendence and the attainment of an ultimate level of consciousness. This part of your childhood makes a deep impression on you.

When you grow up, you make acquaintances with some of these holy men. You travel with them to the jungles to meet their teacher. You live in the ashram, again returning to a monastic life style, a rigid system suggesting the absolute necessity to transcend the instinctual, baser inclinations of human nature. Your focus becomes purification and meditation practices, an almost compulsive fixation on performing yogic rituals for purifying your body and mind.

You don't travel like the other sadhus, you prefer to stay at the ashram with your teacher. You are dedicated to your purification practices, and you achieve deep meditational trance states. However, you judge your progress against the ultimate goal of reaching Brahman status, the godhead, and you are continually dissatisfied. You conclude that you need more severe purification and discipline. At the end of that life you are frustrated because you have not achieved your goal.

You have started to develop a crystallized conceptual framework. There's a sense that you know what's right and a rigid idea about what you need to do. Once out of the body, this creates a communication breakdown between you and your guides. You are less available for their counsel now. You choose not to follow their suggestions for your next life and come back once again to the Hindu culture. This time you come into a family of a higher caste because they are privileged and can attain more spiritual teachings. The Vedic religion is very strict and you are trying to do it right, to follow the letter of the law, to be completely orthodox, in other words. So even in your childhood you take part in religious training and rituals, since this religious viewpoint is your main focus.

Instead of becoming a yogi who lives in the jungle, you grow up to be a priest in the temple and indulge yourself in the socialized aspects of the religion, as if that will compensate for the deficiency you felt in your previous life. Unfortunately, you soon become disenchanted with this course of action. You still don't feel you are achieving your goal, even though you're performing externally everything you are supposed to. It seems too empty to you, almost like a charade. This causes a conflict, because your belief system tells you it's what you're supposed to be doing.

The part of you that is disenchanted and frustrated gets repressed and becomes a shadow-figure because you keep trying to uphold your conscious beliefs. You never allow yourself to express the irritation or the anger you feel. That's totally unacceptable to you. You repress it with your yogic willpower, creating tremendous tension within yourself because strong emotional reactions have a bad connotation to you, something akin to the devil.

When you leave the body this time you can no longer deny your feelings, and this makes you more vulnerable, i.e., less sure of yourself. You are angry because you have failed. You communicate with your guides again, but you're rather demanding. You want them to tell you what you need to do so you can go out and do it. They're trying to get you to relax and take things a little slower. But you're impatient with them, you keep demanding they just tell you what to do. You just want to get it over with.

T: So are these guides always the same?

C: Up till now I would say so. One thing to keep in mind is that from their perspective, each of your lives is like watching a movie on TV. In other contexts, we often have different teachers as we grow. But because of this special-interest group we spoke of earlier, you are still working with the same guides at this point.

And you're really putting them on the spot, so they don't know quite how to respond to you. You want to get on to the ultimate thing you have to do, and they try to distract you from that by laying out several options. They encourage you to decide which of these options you would like to do. You look at the options and demand to know how each one is going to get you to the ultimate place. When they try to explain that you need to go through many small steps to get to the ultimate goal, you don't want to hear that. You can't understand that. They finish the conversation by simply saying, "Well, here are your options." This leaves you in a huff because you don't want to accept any of the options if they aren't going to satisfy you.

One of the options does appeal to you more than the others, and you finally get drawn into it by default. You incarnate in the Orient to become a samurai swordsman. There is a very rigid code of ethics and morals, as well as the connotation of being a spiritual warrior. This is the metaphoric resonance with your attitude at that time. In your last life you repressed your frustration and anger, in this life you act that anger out. In your conscious mind, it's your service as a samurai swordsman that aligns with your past needs for discipline, etc. But the intensity of your pent-up frustration is released through acts of violence in battle. Another carryover from your Hindu lives is the ongoing battle against the lower drives of human nature—instincts, desires, etc. The will that you exercise in your training as a swordsman and spiritual warrior has a symbolic implication that you're acting out or projecting externally through overcoming the enemy. The samurai were the good guys protecting people from bandits and working in the service of the emperor. They were similar to knights in shining armor. You really throw yourself into this role, indulging yourself in the emotions of being a warrior.

I see that you have one major love relationship in this life that causes you great confusion. It's difficult for you because as a warrior your orientation to problems is to overcome them through force and with your skill as a swordsman. The warrior stance doesn't work very well in an emotional relationship with a woman. You are very secure in your identity as a spiritual warrior in all the other areas of your life, but in this one-to-one relationship with a woman you have great difficulty being vulnerable to your feelings. This really threatens your *macho* self-image, and you don't have any skills to help you stay centered. You feel disempowered by your emotional vulnerability, and more or less out of control.

Your mate is the stereotypical Oriental woman: receptive, loyal, self-effacing, etc. So your difficulty certainly doesn't stem from her being confrontational, demanding, or controlling. It might have been easier for you if she was, because your difficulty is feeling the depth of love and sensitivity you feel with her. The problem for you is how to go out on the battlefield and be a big strong warrior when you are feeling all romantic and in love.

What you feel for her is deep and abiding, and you fear the pain this might bring. And you don't know how to protect yourself from these fears.

This life ends in battle; an honorable death by your standards. You feel good about this life upon leaving the body, and you have a sense of accomplishment because you feel you did what you were supposed to do. But after you reflect on this life for awhile, you begin to wonder about what you actually did accomplish. As "time" goes by, you compare that life to your previous values on a soul level. You really did have a feeling of accomplishment even though that life didn't satisfy your ideals, and this really intrigues you.

Your guides don't interfere at this time, because you are in a process of learning and growing from your experience. They are pleased to see you in this state of contemplation. This problem is like a mystery, like your Zen koan.

As a soul, you are now awakening to the options for your next incarnation. This is the beginning of your taking a more active role in choosing these options. Because you're fixated on trying to understand the results of your previous life, you choose to be a knight. This is in medieval Europe—England. I keep getting the impression it's around the time of King Arthur. At first I thought it was just a familiar image, but it does seem to me that you are actually one of the Knights of the Round Table. Once again you're following the theme of the spiritual warrior. The knights uphold the law of the king, and there is also a spiritual side. This was the period when Christianity was conquering the pagan world, thus the implication of a spiritual mission.

You are totally involved with the idea of Camelot, and hence you are a very loyal and devout knight. However, at some point you become very disenchanted with King Arthur because you feel he failed to do what he was supposed to do. Because of the scandal with his wife, King Arthur allowed his emotions to cripple his kingship. You are really angry at him for his weakness and blame him for causing the spiritual mission to fail. This adds another dimension to your frustration, because your inability to accomplish a goal has become dependent on another person. You live out that life trying to fulfill the mission you had set out to do, but you have to battle the inner feelings of hopelessness and your anger at the king.

You're rather bitter when you die this time. You wallow in feelings of sadness and regret over not being able to fulfill your intentions in that life. There's a hint of wanting to just give up. You had entered this life with the intention of trying to understand your feelings of satisfaction from the samurai life, but this life left you feeling hopeless. So now you're more confused and feel even more thwarted. You don't want to meet with your guides; you've just had it. But the problem does not go away, and eventually you turn your attention to considering your options again. You do, in spite of your frustration, accept the process of life. Believe me, there are many souls who don't and spend numerous lives in rebellion. You are fortunate that, underneath it all, you accept the necessary task of development. I guess we could say you actually take it too seriously, for this is the source of your frustration.

You surrender and show a willingness to try something different. I see you coming back in England several hundred years later around the beginning of the Renaissance. I'm seeing you as a petite blonde woman walking down steps in a castle. You're the wife of the lord and live in relative luxury. You're not a woman who is vivacious and outgoing, but you're not withdrawn either. You have that same old acute mind and philosophic awareness, but it's not a dominant part, just an undertone. It's interesting because your mate is the kind of man you have been in your most recent lifetimes, the *macho*, domineering type. I want to say that you tolerate that.

Childbirth is a profound experience for you. It puts you face to face with the mystery of life, that feminine instinctive/mystical closeness to nature. This is all somewhat unsettling, too real and too close for that yogi part of you. This causes you to develop a certain amount of reserve. As you grow older, you put more distance between yourself and this sense of immediacy to life. Even with your children you are somewhat numb and distant.

As a woman you have a different attitude toward wars and other barbaric aspects of the culture. You don't really react to them, but again you are just reserved and remain focused on your protected life inside the castle, safe in your ivory tower.

After that life, you realize there is much more to this process you are involved in than you had believed before. You are starting to lose some of your anxiety, gaining an appreciation and interest in the complexity of life. It's starting to take on the quality of a puzzle rather than a great mission that you as a warrior must complete. You're intrigued about going back into a male body after your life as a woman. How will that be different now? Again there is not much communication with your guides. They feel you are doing fine work, and there is no need for intervention.

I'm seeing you playing with a dog. You're a boy. There's a lake, forest, and log cabin. This image evokes a Swiss Alpine feeling, but your mother is blonde and looks Scandinavian. She is vivacious, good natured, nurturing, and you have a close relationship with her as you grow up. In following up your exploration of the feminine energy theme, you chose her as your mother. You spend a lot of time alone with her in your early life. When you get older, you spend more time hunting with your father. This evokes some of the old warrior aspects, and you become a good hunter.

When you become an adult, you feel a need to seek out more social relations. I see you moving to the nearby village to be next to a woman you have fallen in love with. You don't like living in the village; you miss the world of nature you grew up in. You have a job harvesting lumber. Your love for this woman is very deep and she becomes your whole life. This is the same soul you were with in the samurai life. In that life you weren't able to allow yourself to feel the depth of your emotions. In this life you've almost swung to the other extreme, and this polarizes her somewhat because she has some leftover hurt and resentment from your previous life together.

There's no way for either of you to understand these dynamics in that life. The nicer you are to her, the more anger she feels. You don't understand what is going on and it causes you a lot of confusion. You get hurt and frustrated again. You want to have this relationship with her and it's not working. This evokes the old warrior technique of trying even harder. But the more forceful you get, the more she resists and pulls away. This is tragic, because neither of you is able to enjoy the depth of love between you.

She dies first, leaving you with a great sadness. You carry this grief to your grave. I would say the grief takes *you* to your grave. The whole focus of that life was your relationship with her, and at the end you feel once again that you have failed to accomplish a task. And now there's a new dimension to that feeling of failure—grief and remorse. After this life, that old feeling of wanting to give up comes back to you. Hopelessness and despair are now tinged with grief. Negative thoughts like, "It doesn't matter what I do," start to haunt you. The whole process feels out of your control. You're trapped now, feeling more and more tangled up in it as you lose hope of ever getting back to your original ideals. You're becoming increasingly confused about what it's going to take to be victorious. Nonetheless, there is still that underlying willingness to go along with the process. But all these intense emotions are weighing on you and pulling you back to the planet.

This next life is as a woman in the Roaring Twenties in America. There was a feeling of life being like a party, an aura of affluence, etc. This life for you is an expression of those feelings of giving up, of feeling out of control. You act out of your frustrations by adopting an attitude that it doesn't matter what you do.

I see you hanging out in bars, smoking, indulging in escapism. You are acting out a desire to escape from the seriousness of your quest and the metaphysical dilemmas of your spiritual ideals. In this life you're venting your emotions and escaping from your sadness, grief, and frustration. It's a life of partying, alcohol, sexual promiscuity; indulging yourself in the baser human instincts. You don't live very long in this self-destructive life. You die around the age of thirty. Do you by any chance have difficulty with your lungs in your present life?

T: Yeah, I have asthma. It was worse when I was younger.

C: The reason I ask is because you smoked a lot in this lifetime as the woman. When you drank you would become very morose and sad. It's the grief that kills you again in this life. It's some kind of lung disease that you die from. I don't know if you are aware of this, but in Oriental medicine the lungs are associated with the emotion of grief. So it's no surprise to me that your lungs are weak in your present life.

When you leave the body this time, you want to remain in a drugged state, comfortably numb and unaware, like when you lose yourself in a dark and smokey bar. That's the kind of environment you're hanging out in on the astral plane. You want to just hide there. Your guides come and give you nurturance and encourage you to rise up from the stupor that you're in. They try to talk to you about how what you think and feel create your reality.

After you kind of sober up and look back on that life, you see what a valuable lesson it was. You really saw the subpersonality you acted out in that life, and this caused you to feel some compassion for yourself. It deepened your appreciation for those parts of your character, and awakened you to the need to be more conscious of how you deal with them. In the past you have been, for the most part, working on the old yogic ideal of trying to go beyond the emotions and be dispassionate. In these most recent lives, you've been learning about what happens if you don't take these emotions into account.

After this lifetime, you want to take a rest. There was a healing that took place from the acceptance of your emotionally founded subpersonalities. This allowed you to let go of— to some extent—that old rigid system of ideals that has caused you so much frustration. Based on this, it now became an option for you to go to school on the inner planes before coming back in the body. You chose to attend the Temple of Wisdom.

There is a feeling of freshness now. You are once again enthusiastic about learning and growing. You're intrigued by the mystery that keeps unfolding and increasing your awareness of things you never dreamed of within the confines of your old system of beliefs.

I have a real good feeling about this. Compared to the other readings I do, I'd say for you there has been steady growth, and each life has taken you one step forward. You've learned from your experiences and worked hard to succeed, often too hard.

After your sojourn in the Temple of Wisdom, you have come back to put into action those things you have learned. You have returned at a time when there are many spiritually minded souls coming together to bring higher understanding to the race in an attempt to guide it onto the next step of evolution. You've come in to be part of that movement, but there is no particular mission for you. The old karmic patterns of being rigid and frustrated are with you in this life, but you are confronting them with the new understanding you have acquired in the Temple of Wisdom. This life is one of reconciliation, of facing your oldest and deepest patterns in the light of your new insights.

In terms of your questions about livelihood and self-expression, what you do isn't as important as the kind of meditation you practice, such as doing tai chi. It's a centered orientation where you are neither pushing nor pulling the energy in your life. It's being sensitive to the flow, rather than the old warrior attack on life.

Your work in architecture is a metaphor for that part of yourself that understands and has an interest in how things work. Architecture is the science and art of creating a blueprint or the framework, the underlying reality of a building. This mirrors your fascination with the foundation of reality and how it works. From your sojourn in the Temple of Wisdom you also became interested in the artistry of life, assuming a creative role in the elements of physical reality. Designing homes is a metaphor for designing the place where you live, your home base for life. In this life you are working on how to articulate your psychic energies, and how they create the context you live within—your psychological home, so to speak.

These external considerations are not as important for you as your task of developing a healthy relationship with your feeling self. You were married to the same woman we talked about in the readings, and you are still working on the emotional issues pertaining to her. The other relationships you've had, and will have, are proving grounds for this emotional healing, as is your relationship to yourself in the absence of external relationships. This is the most important work to be done in this life, and could very well be a topic for at least one more session.

ANNE

Anne is 37 years old and works as a therapist in a mental health clinic. She also writes grant proposals and designs special education programs for juvenile delinquents. She came to me with two issues she wanted to work with: asthma and problems in her relationships. She had already done a lot of work with her asthma, including orthodox and alternative approaches, all of which she says have helped a little. She has identified feelings of depression, loneliness, and a sense of uneasiness associated with her asthma attacks. There are a few lifetimes of tremendous grief that point toward the origin of her asthma in this reading, but we chose to focus on her patterns in relationships.

C: Can I ask you to define what in your experience has brought you problems in relationships? What, specifically, do you have problems with?

A: I'm not sure. That's part of the problem. I'm clear about the outcome, but I'm not clear about the problem when it occurs.

C: What is the outcome?

A: I leave them because I don't feel I get my emotional needs met. I seem to involve myself in relationships with people who need to be fixed.

C: You feel you need to take care of them?

A: Yeah.

C: Is it a co-dependent pattern? Are you a rescuer or savior?

A: Yeah, to a degree. Some of that fits and some of that doesn't. But generally the men I get involved with don't have the ability to respond emotionally, and I end up feeling, well, "This isn't very fair," and then I leave. I haven't been in an intimate relationship for about five years. Some of that is my own choice.

C: OK, let me take a look and see what I can see. The first thing I sense is an uneasiness on a core level of your being. What you might call anxiety, but I call a lack of feeling comfortable. I don't feel you are rooted in your own sense of self. What I'd like to do is get in touch with that on a soul level.

I want to go all the way back to the birth of your soul. There was a tremendous sense of confusion about what was happening. It would be best if you regressed back to this time and experience it yourself. For now I'll say you were confused about being separated from the Great Oneness and cast out into a feeble existence. You didn't understand why you were exiled. You felt alone and abandoned. The core feeling is of being alone, an anxiety about feeling unconnected and therefore not feeling whole or confident.

You carry these feelings with you as you go through the phases of a young soul growing and learning, so you're not fully involved in the process. You're caught up in the process, but not a part of it. There's not a strong sense of unity or awareness. You're just tumbling through these experiences, but they don't stick because there is no strong sense of who you are. A nucleus needs to be there, a stronger sense of self around which your experiences can be magnetized. Because there is no center of focus, your experiences are not organized with any sense of purpose.

I see you coming to the planet back in the cave-man days. You seem like a lost little girl. I get the same quality of tumbling through experiences during those primitive times. You don't have much of a sense of yourself. You're always looking to others for your cues and just go along with the tribal group. There's no sense of your own personal goals and desires. This is basically a "first chakra" existence. There are a lot of life-threatening situations, and your focus is dealing with protecting yourself from animals and the dangers in the natural world. I don't see you having any trauma in this life, but there is a coloring from having to deal with a dangerous and threatening environment. This reminds me of the sense of restlessness you were speaking about earlier. There is an underlying need to be vigilant, ready to move or protect yourself.

This life ends with a traumatic death by some animal like a mountain lion. You meet the animal and there is a moment of eye contact. You know the animal has power over you and you die with that feeling of powerlessness. My sense is, that fear of powerlessness generalizes. There is an imprint of lack of power.

In between lives, you are frozen in that state of fear and there is no sense of guidance. You are stuck in this fear you died in. After a long time, you come back in that same state of fear.

I see you coming back in Africa as a male child. There is a trauma associated with an initiation into manhood. There is ritual, a rite of passage, and you are fearful of your ability to perform the necessary tasks or pass the tests. Your father is a strong man, a hunter, a very solid figure, and you feel you must grow up to be like him. You feel a need to perform properly and meet all the cultural expectations. The fear you brought into this life with you is a handicap, and you over-compensate by becoming an overachiever. You have some-thing to prove to yourself, so you really tackle this endeavor of becoming the hunter. You have to pit your consciousness and prowess against the beast; your sense of identity and self-esteem depend on it. When you are successful in becom-ing "the hunter" it gives you a sense of pride.

Outside your role as hunter, you are still insecure in your interpersonal relationships. I don't see you having a mate in this life, since your whole focus is hunting. Your death is somewhat confusing to you. It is caused by problems in the digestive system. You spent your entire life fortifying your-self against the dangers in the natural world outside of your-self, so to die because of internal conditions tends to threaten the sense of strength you have developed through your hunt-ing prowess. The result is that you want to cling even more desperately to your external strengths.

In between lives, there is a struggle with your guides. Your predilection is to resume where you left off and they want you to move on to new experiences. You've become fix-ated with the idea of being the *macho* hunter, and you don't want to listen to them. There is a power struggle going on here. The guides don't have the power to force you or tell you what to do, but you don't know that. There is a pre-sumption that you should do what they are asking you to do. Because of that you give in, you go along, but you do so with inner conflicts.

You come into the Orient, in China. I see a female child in a peasant setting—a feudal social structure. It seems like a big family in a positive social environment. Going back to a feminine life, you are stripped of your *macho* hunter identity. As a woman there is a sense of just going along with what's happening again; no strong sense of identity. It seems the culture is very strong, and there is a very well-defined role for male and female. You are learning the woman's role in this life, a role that deals with other things than struggling against nature. It's a very solid, agricultural base, so your guides are trying to strengthen that feminine identity by putting you in a secure social situation.

There remains a sense that you are still not able to relax. You have to do everything perfectly to feel safe. In this culture, there is a very set, ritualized way of doing things. Somehow that fear you're carrying over is generalized into performing ritual duties in an exact way. It's like being the hunter in an overachieving way. The fear in this life is caused by the threat of shame if you do not do things right, but it's your own inner fear that is really motivating you. It's a free-floating, generalized fear that reflects your not having a strong sense of self. The ability to perform ritualized duties, therefore, becomes the basis for your sense of self.

You are married, but the emphasis of your relationship with your husband is not emotional. Your attention is focused on performing socially prescribed roles and duties, not on emotional support of each other. I don't feel any emotional vulnerability. There is even a sense of regimentation with your children.

Your husband dies while you are still young. Bandits stab him in the chest with a sword. You don't allow yourself to grieve. There is a sense of stoicism. You never allow his murder to affect you emotionally. Your overdependence on social structure and external values substitutes for a strong sense of self. If you allowed yourself to feel the power of your emotions, you would risk your sense of self, so you immerse yourself in social duties to maintain your sanity.

You leave the body thinking, "I've maintained. It was hard, but I succeeded." Through great effort and a certain emotional callousness, you were able to hold yourself together. There is some approval energy from your guides, and you feel you are making progress.

You feel exhausted after your last life in which you had to struggle so hard to keep yourself together. Your guides attempt to show how you don't have to try so hard, and they help you begin to balance your masculine identity. They strive to give you a sense of what it would be like to relax, but you don't understand what that means. You still don't want to come back soon. When you are ready, you come back as a man in India, a man different from the African life. This is a rather reserved man working the land. You have a wife and children. Your personality is withdrawn, introverted. Your wife is a strong, dominating person who runs the domestic scene. You spend most of your time in the fields and not much time relating to your family.

Without the *macho* hunter image, you don't have a power base in this lifetime. Your father was a strong male energy figure, but as a child you were a loner. You didn't feel as if you counted much because there were so many children. You were somewhat lost in the middle of the pack, with no real sense of self-esteem. Something about your father polarized you. You see him as a model (which is what your guides intended), but judge yourself and feel inadequate by comparison. He has a strong moral fiber, an inner strength, and you don't know how to be that way. It's not external like hunting, it's internal, and you don't know how to work on this. You withdraw and just go through the motions, tumbling along through this life. You acquiesce to your strong wife, doing your work in the fields. You feel depressed, sad, a quiet sort of melancholy. You feel weak and powerless, not knowing how to develop your inner qualities to compete with the strong personalities in your life. The withdrawal is a defense that prevents you from outwardly competing, and protects you from feelings of failure and inadequacy.

As you grow older, you withdraw more and more. In general you feel there is no way for you to prove yourself in this life. There is nothing external for you to excel in. You have no sense of self-worth; you simply don't *feel* worthy. Your wife is angry at you for being so remote after she has taken care of you emotionally and physically for so long. When you die—because of a lack of will to live—she has a lot of resentment toward you.

When you pass over, you remain in this lethargic state and blame it on your guides for sending you into such a drab life. You feel resentment toward them and want to rebel. It's all very infantile, very stubborn, based on frustration created by your inability to compensate for lacking a sense of self. Ultimately you are not cooperative with your guides and, you end up coming back surrounded with your frustrations.

I'm seeing a woman in a very Spartan existence in northern Europe. It could be the Saxons, Visigoths, or something like that. It's an aggressive, warring culture dominated by male values. It's a nomadic life style, one that combines the domestication of animals, agriculture, and nomadic hunting. I see you mated with a man who is a leader. He wants to go to war with a neighboring tribe over infringement of hunting grounds.

You have chosen your mate because he's the kind of man you'd like to be. You adopt a subservient role to get his protection. I don't get a sense of love: it's more like a business arrangement. He drives a hard bargain though, making sure it's balanced. You're at a "second chakra" level now. Both your physical and your emotional survival are dependent on this arrangement. You fear his being killed, because you will lose your protector and emotional security, *not* because you will lose love.

Eventually, he is killed in battle and you get captured by the enemy. There is a drunken orgy after the battle where you are gang-raped and fatally beaten in this nightmare of lust and violence. You view this experience as proof of your powerlessness. When you leave the body you are angry. The male side of you wants revenge. You reach back to the male image as your only resource in coming back to the planet. Communication with your guides is out of the question. You exist in this red aura, wanting only to come back and vent your anger and revenge.

You come back into Mongolia in a warring culture as a male. Basically, this life is nothing but blood and guts. I see you cutting off people's heads, killing just to kill as a way to get your anger out. This gives you a sense of empowerment. You don't have a mate in this life, you take any woman you please from among those people you plunder. Often you slay the women after you have raped them.

You die in defeat when three or four men attack you, which undermines all you thought you'd achieved with your strength as a warrior. You are despondent when you pass over. Your guides come and you listen. They show how you generated a lot of violent karma in this life, and aside from the catharsis, you can see it wasn't a productive life. Being stripped of your *macho* identity by this awareness leaves you in a vulnerable state. You don't know where to go from here. Your guides set up the next life for you.

You come back as a woman, spending a lot of your time by the ocean in Greece. Your husband is a fisherman. You are attracted to the sea because of the soothing, calming effect. You have a child. You have an emotional bond—a positive nurturing bond—with this child. Your husband is gone to sea a lot of the time, and even when he is home with you, there is not a lot of warmth between you. He is independent and self-contained, and you are reluctant to become too emotionally vulnerable because of experiences in past lives (the woman in China and the woman mated to the Saxon warrior). You harbor a fear that some day the sea will take him from you, so you don't allow yourself to feel and express the depth of your caring for him. He is basically a good-natured man, and quite accepting of you. He doesn't attempt to draw you out of yourself.

You take great joy in watching your son grow up, but you also fear that one day he will go to sea like his father. You don't have much contact with other people in this life. You keep to yourself and spend a lot of time with your son.

One day when your son is about 10 years old, your fear about the sea taking your husband is realized. When he doesn't return when he is supposed to, you know what has happened. Suddenly you feel all the love for him you had been repressing. You feel deep regrets that you hadn't shared it with him when he was still with you. You nearly go crazy with grief. For the rest of this life you continue to grieve. You don't have much support from others, and you never realized how dependent you were on him, even though he was gone a lot of the time. After his death you feel terribly alone. You even pull back from your relationship with your son and withdraw once again into yourself. This grief and sense of loneliness affects your lungs, and you die of tuberculosis.

This sense of grief is moving into a deeper level of your being. In this last life there was a genuine opening of your heart, with both your son and your husband, but it was associated with grief and loss. When your guides come, you only half listen to them. They try to encourage the seed of love in you. Part of you understands what they are saying, but you are submerged in grief and its heaviness is pulling you back to Earth.

The area looks like the Mediterranean coast of Italy. I'm seeing cobblestone streets, tiled roofs, and pushcarts. You are an older woman, midforties, slightly overweight, and live alone. Your father was a fisherman; you've been drawn back into a context similar to that of your previous life.

Your mother was the kind of woman you turn out to be; a busybody, insecure about material and emotional issues, somewhat manipulative. While growing up, you tended to separate yourself from your younger brothers and sisters. You spent a lot of time walking along the water immersed in your melancholy. The sea reminds you of how it took your husband, not consciously, but on an emotional level.

You shied away from boys and men while growing up. You felt too vulnerable and feared sexual, romantic energy. Your mother was tough, and you patterned yourself after her and don't let the feelings get to you. When you have grown into a woman, you stay to yourself. You sell produce, which you get from farmers, in the marketplace.

When you leave that life, it is due to a disease in your lungs again. As you look back at the life you just lived, it's as if you wrote a story about someone who was alone and sad, and you lived that theme out. You are looking for guidance now, feeling stuck. The guides are trying to show what you do while you are in the body and how it affects you. What you believe is what you become. They are trying to tell you that you are creating your experience by what you believe. You are trying to get a sense of consciousness about it but don't really understand how to get out of the emotional patterns you feel stuck in.

I'm seeing a life now in which you become a monk. We're back in the European culture; the early Christian Era in Germany. This is around A.D. 800. You grow up a male in a farming area. Your ambition is to become a monk and act out what your guides were trying to teach you about becoming what you believe. When you become a monk, you have the overachiever approach, as you did as a hunter. You seem to have a self-condemning, strict, punitive attitude as you attempt to live by the Christian morals and values. Your motivation is to purify yourself. Your problems assume the quality of "the original sin." You see this life as a cure, and want to redeem yourself by pleasing the external authority figure of the church, i.e., God.

The Christian ideal is a stringent system, and there is the Germanic influence as well. You turn this severity on yourself similar to the way you had turned it outward in the hunter and warrior lives. The life is basically austere and emotionally cold. You are very hard on yourself and those around you.

You die in that lifetime hoping to go to heaven because you've been so strict in your Christian life. You die expecting to see angels. You've believed in that vision your whole life, so you are angry when things turn out different on the other side. You feel cheated, and you feel like a fool. Your guides try to show you how you set yourself up for this. As a result you feel confused. This feeling reminds me of how you felt when you were first born as a soul and didn't know what was happening or what to do. You just spent an entire life trying as hard as you could to do what you thought you were supposed to do, only to find out that it wasn't the right thing. This leaves you feeling hopeless, and resonates with all the lifetimes in which you felt defeat.

In your state of hopelessness, you agree to go along with your guides again in setting up your next life. I'm getting a sense that they want to create an easy scenario for you. This life seems to be somewhere around the Black Sea. It's a rural environment, stable and secure, like in the Chinese life. You are a man. I see you working the fields, making stacks of hay and working with a sickle. You live in a situation with other people who work on the farm with you, but you keep to yourself. You're honest, hard working, and a deep thinker.

This is the first lifetime in which I feel you have a good sense of yourself as an individual. You have a comfortable relationship with the natural world around you and there is something very grounding about working on the land. Books are hard to come by, but you manage to get your hands on a few and have taught yourself how to read. These books are on religion and philosophy, and you spend a great deal of time pondering them. You're trying to understand what life is about. None of the people you work and live with can read or are as deeply interested in these subjects as you are. Your private mental world becomes a haven for you, and you are not particularly aware of your emotional needs.

When you die, I see your guides helping you look at the emotional void in your last life. They are telling you that you need to go back and work on fulfilling your emotional needs. In looking back at your karma, they suggest confronting the wife you had in the Indian life. You know that it's going to be difficult, but you feel you are ready to learn more.

This next life happens in Holland. You're a man again. I see you on a canal poling a boat. You feel strong and virile and pretty self-assured in your physical strength. You are a young man and I see you falling in love with a woman who still lives with her family. I get a sense that you feel you need to prove to her family that you will be able to support her. She seems young and shy, but very emotionally demanding. She isn't very clear about expressing herself, and tends to be very contradictory in her demands. Being rather new to this whole realm of emotions, you become frustrated and confused since all you really want to do is take care of her.

Not only is the young lady emotionally complex, she is also the same woman who had some pretty strong anger at you from your emotional detachment in the life in India. She feels she has given a great deal to you emotionally, and that you gave nothing in return. This has become one of her karmic themes, so you are confronted with the task of trying to satisfy a person's emotional needs who has a charged belief system that says she can not be satisfied emotionally. It seems to you the harder you try to please her, the more you fail. In other words, the more you try to please her, the more you support and validate her feelings that she is not satisfied. This becomes a vicious circle that often pushes you to the brink of anger, at which time you go off by yourself. You feel it's impossible to satisfy her. But the good news is that through your experiences with her you are learning about emotions.

You stay together throughout the life, and underneath it all there is a core of genuine love and nurturance, though it never reaches a level of good communication or give-and-take on an emotional level. When you leave the life you are frustrated, but feel you have done your best and weren't a failure. Your guides are very pleased with how you handled your karma with this woman, so they encourage you to continue to work on old karma. You feel pretty self-assured after your success in that life and don't pay too much attention to the particulars of the life they set up for you next.

I see you coming into Germany as a German soldier. You are completely against the violence and atrocities all around you, but you can't speak against it for fear of your life. You work as a guard in one of the concentration camps. It's a very painful situation because you witness what happens to the prisoners and feel responsible for it. You end up falling in love with a woman who is a prisoner. This woman is the reincarnation of the fisherman you were married to in Greece. What you feel for her is very strong and you focus your empathy for the Jewish people onto this one woman. Things come to a head when you try to help her escape. You get caught, and of course you get executed.

There you were in a lifetime in which you were facing the karma from all of the horror and bloodshed in the Mongolian life. You chose to do what you could to try and make amends, risking your life to do so.

When you leave the body in that life, you're in shock. The extent of evil you were involved in was overwhelming to you. When you meet with your guides again, you make a vow to work to help rid the world of that energy. I get a sense that the work in your present life is focused on healing that energy by working with people who were either victims or perpetrators of that kind of energy in past lives.

In these lives that we have seen today, there is a complex pattern of relationships. In the beginning, it seems for the most part you were dependent on others for your sense of identity and security. In order to warrant their love you felt that you had to please them, or act in a prescribed manner. There wasn't any sense that you deserved to receive affection and support simply for who you were. Your frustration came from feeling you had fulfilled your part of the bargain, but failed to get your sense of security and sense of self validated. You were never really satisfied with achieving a sense of identity because it was always determined by your ability to fulfill someone else's criteria of who you should be.

There is also a pattern of fear based on depending on someone who might die or loving someone and losing the person you love. There's a tremendous amount of grief from those experiences that you still carry with you. The depression, loneliness, and uneasiness you say is associated with your asthma attacks is the way this grief is manifesting itself in your current life.

I might ask you to look at your definition of emotional nurturance, what you feel you're not getting from relationships in your present life. Are you simply looking for validation for your sense of identity now, as you have done in the past, and experiencing the same old frustration?

A: Well, I can relate to the part about my sense of self being defined by what I do. And that's how people frequently relate to me, out of what I do. I can see that especially at work, and I'm comfortable with that in my professional life. But in my personal life that doesn't apply. I can see that I don't have as much sense of myself there.

C: And so, do you think you are looking for that in your personal relationships?

A: No, my immediate reaction is that I find people with less sense of self than I have. So, at least I have some identity in comparison with them.

C: Well now, that's interesting, isn't it? Do you think it's possible that this life is set up so you will not be able to find someone who you can depend on to validate your sense of self? Could this be a life in which you have to fall back onto yourself and look within yourself to develop a strong identity and sense of security?

A: Yeah, yeah. That would seem accurate. But maybe you'll have to take me a few more lifetimes into the future to figure it out though.

C: In the past you have, shall we say, used people to attempt to gain your self-esteem. In your current life you are experiencing the other side of the coin. You have to be the strong one now.

A: Yeah, well I've looked at it in the negative way of finding people that I feel superior to. You know, "I don't have much, but at least I have more than you." It's been this one up, one down, kind of thing. It doesn't seem too positive to me.

C: Yes, you have been looking for people who are superior so you could latch onto them, especially when you have been a woman. So you have resentment when they turn out to be more dependent than you. You resent being the one in the superior position because you're not getting the security and validation you want.

If we consider the male lifetimes we've seen, it seems in all except the last two you were emotionally detached. At the beginning of the session today, you complained about the men in your present life being emotionally unavailable. Do you think at your present state of development you might be beginning to integrate your male and female sides? In doing so you may be confronting that part of your own maleness reflected in the men you are attracting.

Because of the trauma and sense of loss around love in the past, both as a man and a woman, I feel you are also unwilling to be really vulnerable in this life. Instead of meeting an equal person in a state of openness to love, I feel you want to go back to a safer, i.e., dependent form of relationship. By attracting men who are not suitable for this kind of relationship, you are successfully avoiding really being in a relationship. I'd like you to think about that for awhile and really search your heart to see if what I'm saying might have some truth to it. Looking at your fears and researching the necessary resources and steps to prepare yourself for a genuine relationship would be a good topic for another session.

DAN

Dan is 41 years old. He's a skilled and meticulous finish carpenter. He has been married for twelve years and has three children. As Dan sat across from me to start the reading, his facial expression and posture reminded me of a dog that had just been scolded. His wife and he had been having hard times and he was having the reading at her, shall I say, request. I got the impression she browbeat him regularly; she was not at all pleased with his performance as a husband and lover.

C: What would you like to focus on today?

D: In terms of intimations of my past that I've seen in dream images, there have been both monks and warriors, so there seems to be quite a dichotomy there. There are specific geographical indications, but I would like to see what you pick up before I say any more.

C: I don't know how much I am being influenced by your imagery of the warrior and the monk, but I'm seeing an image that seems to be a metaphor for these two parts of yourself. You are on a battlefield following a battle contemplating the aftermath of the rage that you have been in. The heat of the battle and the seething anger have been spent, and there is a post-battle reflection. The destruction is there, the emotions have been vented, and there is a quietude and pensiveness. It is as if you are sitting on a hill overlooking the whole scene. There is a combination of disgust—not a vehement disgust— and a quiet cynicism about the activities you have been involved in. There is also a sense of relief as a part of you feels a certain righteousness in having expressed your pent-up frustrations and hostile feelings. I definitely see a strong conflict between these two parts of yourself: on one side the part that feels righteous at having prevailed on an epic field of battle, and on the other the part that feels disgust at the hideous waste of human life and the incomprehensibleness of the bloodthirsty and seemingly maniacal dark, barbaric forces lurking in nature, indeed, in human nature.

I just looked for a life to tap into, and went all the way back to a real primitive lifetime. I'm seeing you almost as an animal, with watchful, hunted eyes—acutely aware, listening for signs of danger and threats from predators. This is really a struggle for survival of the fittest. This is the initial imprint on your being: there is a sense of identity with that struggle— that you have to fight to live, against real and formidable enemies. I don't see any one particular trauma or event in that life that is important, but the survival theme is a fundamental quality of that life, and it has left its mark on you.

I'm seeing you in another life now, you are walking. This isn't necessarily in chronological order. This seems to be much later—a Gypsy life. There's a horse-drawn Gypsy wagon. It has a broken wheel. You are with your wife and two children, who you have to leave in order to find someone to help repair the wheel. You are quite paranoid about having to leave them behind. The watchfulness and wariness from your earlier life is apparent here. It is very much present as you walk along looking for aid. This is Europe, a peasant setting. You are walking and asking those you meet for assistance, but no one is willing to help because you are a stranger. You keep walking, sure that there will be someone to help since this is farming country. Eventually you come to a village and get someone to help you. But all the time you were away you worried about your family.

I want to go back in that life to see why you were on the road. It wasn't a drought. I think you were from a region where the soil had been depleted, and it was becoming more and more difficult to eke out an existence in that area. You decided to pack up and try to find another place. It was a difficult thing to do in those days. This is after the feudal lords. It is definitely Europe.

OK, the important thing here, the idea that is being impressed in your mind and in your belief system, is that life is really hard. It was very difficult to eke out an existence where you were, it was equally difficult to find another place, so we have the reappearance of the "struggle to survive" energy. This time it is not so much wild predators, but rather the economic conditions of the social structure. As I see your soul leaving that lifetime, there is a sense of heaviness—a weight about you. Life is a burden.

The next thing I'm plugging into—apparently we're going back in time now—is a life as a Roman soldier. It's a life where being a soldier was one of the most noble things to do. In the context of the Roman Empire, it was one of the most meaningful things you could do as a man. There is a sense of pride and self-esteem associated with your position as a soldier. You appear to be a sergeant in the Praetorian Guard, with superiors and subordinates. You're very trustworthy, responsible, a very good soldier. Expanding the horizons and conquering new worlds for Imperial Rome was exciting to you. The teamwork, esprit de corps, and the precision of the way the army functioned was satisfying and engaging.

You were able to ignore the blood and gore of battle by focusing entirely on the idealism of the empire. You were able to shut it completely out, most of the time, and disassociate yourself from it. But you were not able to do that all the time. There were periods of weakness when you succumbed to grieving, and went into deep melancholy over that part of your life.

There was a dichotomy between those two aspects of being a soldier. One side was real positive, and the other real negative. It was very hard for you to integrate those two qualities, because you perceived that you had no choice as to an alternative life style and career. So you attempted to ignore and repress the negative side.

I'm seeing you at an old age. You're lying down, and you know you're dying. You're still dressed in your uniform, lying on a granite slab or table of some sort in front of a monument. Here at the end of your life, you feel that all of the great imperialistic adventures you have been on have really come to nothing. They have lost their meaning for you as an old man looking back with regret and disillusionment. You've lost the will to live, and all that you had lived for. You had believed the empire was bringing culture to the world, but looking back you realize that what you had done was barbaric—crushing, destroying, and dominating other cultures. You feel as though you had been duped by the government. Serving Rome had been your whole life, and ultimately you die regretting that service.

Dying with those realizations in that life was a spiritual turning point for you. In between lives your soul begins looking for a deeper meaning in life. I can see in your next life you are attracted to the Christian movement. I see you involved in the Crusades. There are several lifetimes intervening between the time as a Roman guard, and the life in the Crusades, but the Crusades are jumping out at me now, strong. I see you thrusting yourself into the Christian movement with the same zeal that a Roman soldier went to war with. There is a transference of that passion, the brave, noble, and philosophic quality of being a warrior. Like a samurai, there's a certain posture toward life, and you put that energy into the Christian Crusades.

I see you on a road with a horde of people. You're a real motivator. You're very animated, keeping everyone's spirits up, and moving the troops so to speak. You view yourself as a knight in shining armor fighting the holy wars. There are many hardships, many deaths, and zealous, fanatical mobs of warring faiths. What a mess it turns out to be.

In the end you are appalled. Once again you are overcome with total disillusionment—you believed you were fighting for a noble cause only to have it end in utter barbarity. You do return to your homeland with a small group of people, but with a marked difference in your outlook—complete confusion. God has forsaken you. Once again you are back to eking out a hard existence, a peasant living off the land. Your God has failed to save you.

When you leave the body this time, you are subdued, but not as disenchanted as before. You're not as crushed; there is an intuition that there is a spiritual aspect to life, more than just a hope. There is an inkling it is not something you do in the outside world. The seed of an inner life is germinating.

I'm seeing you born in India in the next lifetime, really pursuing this aspect of religious feelings, this going inward, as a Hindu yogi. It's the same kind of warrior energy, the disciplined soldier turned inward. You're fascinated by the Hindu philosophy and seek Brahmin, the ultimate reality,

with all the zeal of a fanatical crusader. Only you're very austere, very rigid in your beliefs and goals. You travel sometimes as a sadhu, begging and preaching on occasion. But
you prefer to live in the jungle, fasting, or living on herbs and
berries.

Nonetheless, you feel you are not getting anywhere in
this life, you're not realizing what you think you should be.
But, as in the life as a Roman soldier, you don't think there is
any alternative. This is the path that is supposed to take you
where you think you should be going. The more dissatisfied
you get, the more driven you are to put your nose to the
grindstone and keep treading along that path. It almost becomes a bit masochistic in a way—the more dissatisfied you
get, the more unfulfilled in your search, the harder you drive
yourself. This path is very dry for you. It alienates other
people, and you have become emotionally dry and hard.

I hadn't thought of this before, but looking back on your
other lives there seems to be the theme of struggle and of not
being aware of, or not being able to take care of your emotional needs; your need to be loved and nourished. There's
always this yang, male driving quality, whether it is a warrior
or an inner warrior, a quality of being driven, and not taking
the time to allow your feminine side to blossom and be fulfilled.

Toward the end of this life, I can see you are pretty successful at controlling your mind and emotions, and can go
into deep trance states, but this ability has only made it more
apparent that there is a lot of restless anxiety within you that
has not been satisfied by your quest as a yogi. So there is a
tension at the end of this life.

So far all the lives we've looked at have been in a male
body, so I want to see what the feminine side of your being
has been like. I'm starting to get an image of you as a woman;
you have dark hair and are quite attractive. I see you in a
dress, which is kind of straight with ruffles along the hem. It

seems like the early 20th century in the United States. You're not very comfortable in a woman's body. You feel too vulnerable. This is not your first life as a woman, nonetheless you feel very much like a man trapped in a woman's frail body in a social environment that doesn't permit you to express any of your masculine traits—a very strange experience for you. You don't know how to react to men and just keep them at a distance with a psychic barrier. I see one relationship with an aviator in World War I. He is a very sensitive person, very patient and understanding with you, but you are intimidated by the whole aspect of interpersonal relationships—especially being a woman. It's hard for you to be in your body in this situation. There is a lot of confusion.

He ends up going off to war, and you wait for him. You feel more comfortable writing to him, and during the two or three years in which you are apart, you grow close to him in that distance, through letters. You find yourself opening up, and when he does come back, you're quite changed: you're very vulnerable. You latch onto him and abandon yourself. You become totally dependent emotionally and physically. I see one child, maybe two, one for sure. You enjoy being a mother, having a son. This seems to be a safe relationship for you, and eventually you become much more secure in your role as a woman.

I see that you stay married to the same person and have a fairly happy and healthy relationship for that day and age, but you are by no means a "liberated woman." You spend a lot of time reading. The world of the book becomes your world. There you can express the adventurous part of yourself. This balances the rest of your life, which is just a traditional, orthodox, feminine role in that time. Oddly enough, I'd say this life is a big step forward in terms of your soul's progress. From what we've looked at today, it has been your most satisfying life; you were more at peace with yourself. You weren't a mindless woman. You read and thought about things very deeply. The warrior and monk were still there, but weren't dominating you. I think this was the life just before your present life. When I see you leaving this life, I see there is a certain peace, a calmness.

I am getting the impression that the lesson in your current life is to learn how to integrate that sense of peace and emotional fulfillment as a man, because when you plug into the male body the struggle to survive and the male/warrior aspects come forth. So, how can you overcome the masculine inclination to drive yourself, to struggle toward ambitious goals and just *be?* How can you say "timeout" and allow yourself to simply exist in a timeless emotional state of peace and well-being? It seems to me you get there sometimes when you play with your kids.

OK, now I'm jumping back in time again. There's something calling me. This is some kind of village life again. It's African. I'm seeing domed thatched huts, made of sunbaked mud. You're a big, tall, black man. The first thing I notice about you in this life is your pride—the pride of being a hunter and a warrior. There is a lot of dignity in your bearing. The hunting and fighting skills are highly articulated. Again it goes back to the wild animal quality—the acuteness and almost extrasensory perception that comes from being in the world of nature. It is a very psychic place—very alert, very aware, and tuned in. The stalking of game is almost like Samadhi, you're so attuned to what you're doing, so at one with the animal you're hunting. This is an incredible dance. It is the same when you are fighting other tribes too. There is great skill involved, and you exist as if in a trance state while doing it.

Even though you have a mate and children in that life, there is an aloofness—a dignity and pride you cloak yourself in. You are not available or vulnerable to an emotional relationship with your mate and children. That same quality expressed itself through you when you were a Gypsy farmer.

Even though you were taking care of your family, your attention was so focused on the struggle for survival that there was a certain dignity and aloofness as a result of being the one who must carry the burden—shoulder the responsibility—and you feel alone in that. It's the manly thing to do. But it separates you from the emotional relationship as an equal with your family. And that inhibits you from any emotional symbiotic flow where you can get nurtured, and where you could give a kind of nurturing that you are unable to in this other role. You are so committed to being a provider in a material way, that you fail to provide hardly any emotional nourishment at all.

I'm scanning now to see if there are any other patterns that jump out. I get the sense that we have talked about the main patterns, and that the other lives that are coming up are merely repeats, more of the same. If you imagine a life line going back through history, there is one area that is kind of muddy around the early Middle Ages. It's just drudgery, total drudgery. One life is as a woman, scrubbing floors as a servant in a castle—you are old, haggard, totally bereft of joy, beauty, or fulfillment. I also see a life as a medieval blacksmith. You have a wife and children, but your life is a struggle. There is a quiet inner knowledge in those lives, but there is no avenue, no way to approaching that inner something that would bring meaning and happiness.

Even though it seems most of these things I've talked about this evening have a weighty feeling, when I experience the energy of your soul, there is still, in the midst of all of this drudgery, hardship, struggling, and fighting, a kernel of optimism and joy. Despite all this other dismay, there is a spark that hasn't been tainted or squelched. But, as a soul, you haven't found a way to feed and fan this spark—to express it—and really live it here in the physical dimension. You haven't given up the vision, but it's kind of the light at the end of the tunnel. You know it's there, but there's almost a resignation regarding the conditions of the world and your inability to reach the end of the tunnel. But your spirit hasn't been vanquished. There's still an intuition of potential, of what is possible; the seed of spiritual awareness is there, but you haven't found the secret ingredient that will bring it to life for you.

I think the secret is to touch the feminine side, to just be and allow the emotional waters to flow and nurture the seed. Put aside the aggressive, mental, disciplined approach for now, and learn to trust the spontaneous, chthonic forces of being. Make friends with your feelings, accept them, allow them to live. At any rate, it seems as if that's what's on your schedule for this lifetime.

Do you have any questions or comments? I feel I'm really starting to fish now, nothing is jumping out at me.

D: No, it just seems like a long string of miserable existences!!! Thanks a lot. (laughter) Wasn't it Emerson who said, "The mass of men lead lives of quiet desperation"?

C: One thing I'm beginning to understand, relating to this project of how karma works, is that what we see is what we get. I did a reading for a friend the day before yesterday, and I have been scrutinizing his lives. I'm beginning to realize it's what we decide to believe, and how we perceive things, that determines how we continue to perceive and experience life. But how do we change our perceptions? That's what I'm interested in, because the mirror of my life isn't that rosy either.

Somehow we need to look around or beyond our projections—through the dreams of our lives. I'm not talking about denial or avoidance, some idealized spiritual panacea, or ego-powered plethora of positive affirmations. I'm talking about seeing things clearly, for what they are in their suchness. This is the hard part—to see without making judgment, to see without prejudices and preferences, to see without saying this is bad or good, real or unreal, spiritual or evil. We have to learn how to see as if our minds were like a clear mirror. Then there is no attachment or reaction to how we embrace the world with our awareness. There is no identification with what we perceive—no belief system about who we are and how the world is treating us as a result of our experience. Hence, there is no karma created.

I have this working hypothesis that if we quit believing in our projections and judgments, their power to manifest the realities we have instilled in them will gradually dissipate like ripples from a pebble tossed in a pond.

Maybe we can have tea together in a few lifetimes and I'll let you know how my theory is doing.

DIANNA

Dianna was married to Dan (the subject of the previous reading) at the time this reading was given. A few intense weeks later they signed their divorce papers.

When I met Dianna, she already had been steaming with frustration for years. Her body was plagued with arthritis, which she claimed was due to the repressed anger she harbored from her long relationship with Dan.

When Dianna met Dan thirteen years ago, she was involved in a major restoration project (having done most of the work herself) on a classic wooden sailboat she had named Tantra. Personally empowered and mostly detached from the idea of being in a relationship at the time, Dianna became preoccupied with the notion of having a baby. This made Dan attractive as did his enthusiastic willingness to join the work and plans in progress on the boat. After the birth of their first son—almost within a year of their meeting—and the eventual completion of work on the sailboat and a second pregnancy, the couple found they were hopelessly incompatible cruising together on the boat. They soon concluded it would be best to sell the beloved vessel and try life in the mountains of West Virginia where their second child was soon born. But with the loss of her sailboat, and the lack of a satisfactory sexual relationship, she lost the capacity to envision and actualize a happy life together, and her resentment for Dan began to grow.

Soon after I did the reading for Dan, Dianna became infatuated with another man. As her heart opened to the "love of her life" (who characteristically avoided getting involved with a married woman), and her conscience tied her to age-old co-dependence patterns with Dan, she pleaded with me to do a reading comparing the history of her relationships with these two men. The usual, somewhat mischievous, but oh so spirited sparkle in her eyes was eclipsed by her inner conflict and the gravity of the decision she struggled with—a decision that involved more than just her motherly concern for her husband, Dan, and the intensely deepening respect and love she was feeling for Robert. She now had three children and no viable source of income, not to mention the weight of reactions from parents and in-laws. Dianna was distraught the day we sat upstairs, away from the noise of the kids playing downstairs, to do this reading. Though still perhaps the most difficult thing she has done in her life of forty-odd-years, this reading provided her insight and gave her permission to follow her heart.

C: Let's begin by going back to your first lifetime with Dan. You are a woman and Dan is a man in a matriarchal setting. You have a considerable amount of responsibility and a leadership role, which means there are a number of men you oversee. You have a certain number of men—I want to say three or four—who are in your personal service. Dan is one of these men, and he is like a puppy. He follows you around wagging his tail trying to please you. You have a certain fondness for him because of his loyalty and amiable character. It is very much like having a pet, in the sense that people often talk to their animals and become dependent on their unconditional love. Your other men are kind of unruly and rebellious. They don't appreciate their oppressed condition. But Dan is always there, eager to please.

In this life you are very much like your present self. Your energy is easily scattered and you are under constant stress because of all the things you are trying to accomplish and keep together. Dan is a comfort to you; his is a nonstressful relationship.

There is another element involved in your relationship with Dan. I'll have to digress for a minute here. Your soul is from another dimension and you came to this planet to help the influx of souls that arrived during the Atlantean era. Dan is an Earth soul, and you fell into a motherly role toward him. He's like one of your Earth children on a soul level. So this element was there in that matriarchal life. I don't see you as lovers in that lifetime. He is just one of your wards. That's how you relate to him.

Okay, let's jump ahead to another life with Dan. I see you as a teacher in India, again as a woman in a matriarchal setting, an ancient Tantric setting. Your energy is much more focused in this lifetime. It's very grounded. The Tantric practice and philosophy give you a more nonattached attitude. On a soul level, you had a tendency to be overconcerned or take too much responsibility for your wards—to be too attached to the results. But in this Tantric life you are merely channeling energy, and the philosophic context makes you less attached to the results. You are very grounded and very centered.

Dan is one of your devotees; you have initiated him into the Tantric path. But he is not so much interested in the Tantric path as he is in being your servant again; he is carrying forth that same karma from the earlier relationship. He is not there to really do spiritual work, he's there to hang on to your skirt. In this particular lifetime you are irritated by that. There is a tension between the two of you. He basically wants you to take care of him, and you simply refuse to do it. You were using him in a way before, as a confidant, in the earlier matriarchal life. Now you are uncomfortable with the way he feeds on your energy. The more you reject him, the more he clings, and it becomes a test of power.

You end up sending him away eventually, but then the mothering tendency is activated again and you start worrying about him. So you continue the karma, you carry on the tradition of being overly concerned about his welfare. You have your spies keep tabs on him for awhile, but then you lose touch with him. He passes out of your life completely in that lifetime, and leaves you with a lingering sense of guilt. You wonder if you have done the right thing sending this poor helpless man off into the world by himself.

You harbor this guilt for the rest of that life. It's something you repress: those kinds of feelings are not resonant with your conscious identity in that lifetime. You have your beliefs and your Tantric philosophy, but this guilt slips right into your unconscious. Because that co-dependent pattern is already there within you, your sense of guilt in this life ties into it peripherally.

Dan leaves feeling rejected. He has no understanding of what has taken place, only the emotional reality of being abandoned. To continue his life, he has to repress these feelings and do the best he can with this crippling emotional insecurity.

I'm seeing another lifetime now. Looks like you are a man this time, and he is the woman. I see you as a young man, tall and lanky, in his early twenties. You are working on something at this long bench-like table in what looks like a log cabin. I think you are working on a clock. I'm getting the sense that you repair clocks. It is so tedious, you get real flustered.

D: I know this life. The clock is analogous to my mind. I have the sense there is something coming into my life that is a force I can't turn back and I am really frightened. I know that it is the end of my life. I just can't turn it aside. What it turns out to be is exploiters. It's men who are cutting down trees; they have a whole army of men cutting down trees. And I have this sense that this is intruding upon me. There are a lot of men and there's a lot of force. I first become aware of them when they are at a much further distance. I know they are coming when they are a couple of mountain ranges away. Now they are coming closer, close enough that I can spy on them and see what is going on. They are bringing something to this area that I have never seen in men before. I don't know who these men are; they're not from far far away, they are not very exotic looking, but they are not the kind of men I know. They are bringing a kind of coarseness, and a very bad feeling.

I draw this analogy to the watch: I'm very frustrated. It's like I have a premonition; I know how to fix the watch, but this watch isn't going to be fixed probably. I have been observing them for a very long time and I have come very close and I am standing within the site and among them. I am not getting this right now, I have known this for quite a long time. A tree falls on me and I am killed. I remember saying to myself as I am leaving my body, "Thank you, for I can leave this life and this body without any sense of guilt." I have thoughts of Dan as my wife and particularly for the children, and I have no feeling that I have responsibility to them. They will be OK. I don't have a feeling of guilt about leaving them and I leave my body with a sense of gratitude, because compared to the life that preceded it, it is a blessing.

C: Do you have a sense of what your life with Dan was like in that lifetime?

D: It was nice. It was good. There wasn't stress in the relationship; it was very loving. Dan was sharing and it was a good relationship. Quiet, low-key . . . log cabin sounds very right . . . modest, humble, easy life. No conflicts at all until the advance of these men. You know I still can't tell whether it was a railroad or what, but it was like a path or a swath being cut through the thick forest. There are these big wagons and timbers they have built. This big machine with iron and timbers—something that wasn't built at a farm, but at a place where there was real enterprise. There was this feeling that it was not about to be turned away. In a way abdicating and dying at that moment was extremely important to me in order that I could experience an untarnished life then. To have a simple life. I didn't serve anyone but my family in that life, not any schools or initiates, any apprentices or hierarchies.

C: The way I see your relationship with Dan in that life was really similar to how you spoke about it. I see you very dedicated to your family, and as a woman he's really self-effacing and dedicated to you and the kids.

D: I never thought of this woman as Dan before.

C: Shall we go on? I'm not quite sure where this is yet, but I'm seeing you again as the woman and Dan as the man. It's a difficult life; the image I'm seeing right now seems to be of you having to sandbag for a flood to save your land. It appears to be flooding waters. You feel you're the responsible one, more responsible and more concerned than he is. You have to push him to keep going. You resent that. You feel as if the responsibility is all on your back.

This is just the image I'm seeing right now, I haven't really connected it with anything else yet; I don't know where it is. It could be Australia. It's an outback kind of survival life. There is a ranch setting with lots of fences. I think it is a cattle ranch. Dan just drags his butt around and doesn't take on any responsibilities. You're the foreman and he is just some kind of uncommitted worker. You are man and wife, but he is just not as engaged as you are. He's really dependent on you. He is not like a man, an equal partner.

He's almost like a child in his emotional dependency and his inability to do his share. You have built up a lot of resentment about that. For you in that lifetime it seems there is no alternative. You just go through that whole life maintaining the same pattern. You're in the outback. You don't even think of getting rid of him or leaving him. Life is so hard. Back in those days you didn't move around as much; there wasn't that freedom. Do you know what I mean? You're just locked into it.

A lot of the energy from that life is coming into your present life with Dan. There is a real similarity to what was going on then and how you relate to Dan in this lifetime. I feel in your present lifetime, Dan is trying to do more of his share of the physical work and take more responsibility—that was the area of imbalance experienced in the life in the outback. In that life, you were so caught up in the struggle for survival the emotional issue wasn't particularly apparent. So the physical level was the primary bone of contention. What's different in your present life is that the imbalance is more on an emotional and spiritual level.

In this life in the outback, there's the old pattern of dependency; Dan clinging to you, and you using him as in the matriarchal life. You needed someone to help and he was there, so there is a kind of symbiotic relationship going on.

I'm starting to get an impression of another life where the same patterns are prevalent. I see a stream, a stream that's coming down from a mountain. It's not a big mountain—it seems like the Ozarks or the Alleghenies in Virginia. Someplace in the East. I'm seeing you as a woman. It's before cars—somewhere between cowboys and cars. You have on a long dress and work boots. It's another life of survival; a farm life. I'm seeing a white house with skip siding. You are alone in this lifetime. I think the house belonged to your parents who are gone now. You inherited the family farm and work it by yourself. I see chickens. I think you have a still, too. You are a saucy young woman, hard as nails. You like to give the boys in town a hard time. You have a horse and a cart and I see you selling moonshine to supplement your income.

I think Dan is in town. He's one of those young men stepping on his tongue when you walk by. It's hard keeping the farm together by yourself; it would be kind of nice having a man around. But the men in town are generally narrow-minded and crude. Dan is, at best, the least of all evils. He still has that puppy-dog ambience about him and seems relatively harmless compared to the other men. You have a hard time keeping most of these jokers under control. So you string Dan along for awhile, kind of testing him out.

Well, he ends up out there living with you on the ranch. I'm seeing that you become lovers, but you don't really give your heart to him. You let him service you so to speak, but you don't really let down your defenses. You keep him at a distance, and you keep him in his place. It's your homestead, and you're the "matriarch."

Then you have kids. I'm seeing you don't really like that in this life; it's more responsibility; it's more struggle. You resent having gotten into that position because taking care of the children is considered woman's work in this society. The children become an additional burden while you threaten and cajole Dan to keep the place up, but he isn't able, or willing to pick up your share of the load. I see you ending up with a situation that you never would have chosen and you aren't really pleased with.

Do you think you have enough insight into your basic patterns with Dan? Shall we change the subject?

D: Yes, it all sounds too familiar. I want to hear about Robert and me.

C: The first thing I see about your adventure with Robert is that what you are really responding to in him is his energy on a soul level. He really resonates on the same kind of spiritual level that you do. He is from another dimension like yourself.

I'm definitely getting the feeling that you two knew each other before coming to the planet. He's a kindred spirit from the same soul group. It's like family. As souls you were being trained together. There is a history that you share on that level. He is almost like a big brother to you. You look up to him and there's a real camaraderie.

I'm seeing that in this pre-Earth relationship you are more dependent on him than he is on you. He is more self-centered. I don't mean self-centered in terms of being selfish, but he is more self-contained, more complete within himself. He's a well-balanced being, very centered and not searching outside himself. He's not dependent on others emotionally, so although there is a caring on his part, it tends to leave you feeling a little unbalanced because you want more from him than he wants from you.

It seems that in your early training as a soul you developed feelings of inadequacies about yourself. The work you were doing on the inner planes—and what you felt was expected of you—seemed like a monumental task. You were not confident about your abilities to perform well. I'm seeing this as the beginning of your scatteredness, of an uncenteredness that you have. It's based on a lack of self-confidence. You get anxious about having to do things well and because you feel there is so much you have to do, you start running around trying to do everything at once. This causes you to spread yourself too thin. Thus you act out your fear that you will not be able to accomplish what is expected of you.

When you knew Robert before coming to the Earth plane you looked up to him because he was someone who was very confident and very capable, so you began to project the part of yourself that is capable and confident onto Robert. You expect him to give that to you. Does that make sense?

D: I can't relate to that being true of myself, but I can see what you are trying to say. I think that is something I should pay attention to, even though I disagree. I'll have to study it.

Well, I guess one thing I see when I look at my current relationships with men—when I see Robert—one of the very first things I said to him was "I see your equanimity." Just seeing his equanimity and the fact that it looks so good, lifts me and makes me feel all right. You know I see it embodied in another soul and it's beautiful. It kind of makes me feel like it's a stronghold.

C: So what do you mean by equanimity?

D: Equanimity? Evenness in temper and evenness in mind; uncluttered. Centered and calm.

C: Judging from the intensity of your emotional response, it seems to be an important issue. I sense you have experienced a lack in your other relationships with men. Let's imagine that you had become dependent, and therefore expect the kind of relationship I'm suggesting you had with Robert before coming to the planet. Then you came to the planet and suddenly you are forced to be the responsible one. The men you related to didn't have the same strength and equanimity that you had found in Robert. You would experience a greater lack. See what I am saying?

D: Well I can certainly see that I am frustrated now and for a very clear reason. I'm just looking for someone that is a little bit older, a little bit wiser. Why is that? Because I think I can grow that way. I think that I don't want to be constantly on call to serve quite so many people, or to take care of a man. I just feel I have served enough and the greatest service is not to be there to serve. You know, it's old, it seems to get in a stalling pattern and so I just need to gracefully remove myself.

So what would I like? You know I have been seventeen years without a spark in my relationship. And I say to myself, "I would like that spark back, I'm ready, I'm worthy. Get back that spark. It's okay to get it." You know, maybe just to experience it once, would carry me through more decades, without it. . . . I've been complacent about it, I've been complacent.

C: Well I would say your feeling for Robert is definitely genuine; it's coming from a really deep soul level. I think we should go on and look at some past lives between the two of you here on Earth.

I see a life in Greece where Robert is the one who is all business, and you're the emotionally dependent one. Robert is a priest and you're a priestess in a Grecian temple. He's very centered and dedicated to his role in the temple. He's very aware of your energy, but he doesn't react or support it—he just totally accepts it. It's really beautiful, the place he's in, neither pushing you away nor bringing you closer. *Equanimity* is a good word for him.

The temple setting is very idyllic. In this environment you feel a great deal of love for Robert and long to have a more personal relationship with him. But the context of your social roles does not allow for this more personal relationship to flourish, and Robert is the one who makes sure the social mores are respected. You tend to fall into a daughter/father, little sister/big brother dynamic, looking up to him for guidance and approval. That pattern seems to remain fairly constant throughout the rest of that life. It's pretty straight-forward.

Let's go on to another life. Atlantis, Atlantis . . . there's a relationship; apparently it's a relationship as equals. It's one of your first lifetimes on the planet and you really had to stay focused and get your act together. You had this job to do on the planet and felt you had to live up to it. You were probably trying twice as hard as you needed to, and you became pre-occupied. There wasn't time for you to have a personal life; you really hadn't manifested any emotional imbalances yet. They were undoubtedly there in seed form, but it took more lifetimes on the planet to bring them forth. Your main focus at that time was on the work. You didn't give much credence to the feelings, you just mowed over them. There wasn't re-ally that much happening in that life between you and Robert except as two souls who were involved with many other souls in doing this group project. Just his presence was sup-port for you because of the past you shared—the spiritual en-ergies you shared together. The fact that he was there was support for you, even though you weren't drawing on it. Do you know what I mean? I think it's important to know that just that quality was significant there; it is kind of an under-lying theme.

So far these lives with Robert have been all business, spiritual business. I'm seeing another one like this. This one has a lot of energy. Can you see yourself as a nun?

I'm seeing Robert as a Catholic priest. He may be a bishop. It's a very prestigious position in the church and he is grounding a lot of spiritual energy; he's really being a spir-itual conduit. But by this lifetime you are really an emotional basket case. In the earlier part of this life you are taking all your emotional disappointments, your sense of lacking suf-ficient nourishment and support during your many lifetimes on the planet, and you are projecting it onto God—expecting God to save you. In this life, your projected God image becomes everything a man has never been for you, and more: the perfect father, lover, male friend, and authority figure.

You have a very difficult time with the patriarchal structure of the church. It really grates against your matriarchal background. All of the confinements and inhibitions, all the patriarchal aspects of the church, cut across the grain of your inner sense of essential spirituality. It's a double bind for you, almost torture. You end up judging yourself for having all these out-of-control desires and feelings and thoughts. You feel guilty about it, so you punish yourself and do penance and pray harder. It's a pretty sick scenario.

To throw another monkey wrench into the situation, here's Robert, this beautiful spiritual being who you feel so much love and respect for, in a position of power in the church. So you have all the incongruities of the church, and at the same time you have this beautiful being that you really admire as a figurehead. He is your main spiritual source of nourishment in that life, but on a personality level he has become more distant from you. He is less unconditional than in the Grecian life. He shies away from your emotional intensity and irrationalism. It's not very pleasant for him, and causes friction with the punitive aspects of the church which he is obliged to uphold. And so in this way you become a thorn in his side.

In your turmoil you want to go to him to gain his support and consolation. But the nature of your social roles and your positions in the church are such that you cannot go to him and be an honest emotional being. Instead, you pull on him psychically, in an insidious way. You're very dependent. First you pull him, then you punish yourself for doing it. It's almost sadomasochistic. He is being affected by all this on an unconscious level and doesn't really understand what is happening. You don't have the kind of personal relationship where you can sit down and talk about it. He doesn't come in and say, "How are you feeling today?" The environment in

which you exist is very constrained—the amount of intercourse a priest can have with a nun is very limited, and suspect.

There is a long list of taboo subjects, and that list happens to incorporate most of the things you are going
through. But beneath all the external constraints and sup-
pressed emotions is the integrity of who both of you are as
beings. So there's not a real negative outcome; it's just kind
of weird and very unconscious. This was all mostly taking
place on a psychic level.

Even though he became irritated, Robert never lost his
spiritual center or his compassion for you. And in a strange
way this encouraged you to seek that more sublime part of
yourself, even though the Christian dogma was not really a
viable means to accomplish that end. The end result was the
reawakening of the necessity for you to achieve your own inner equanimity, your own spiritual connectedness. That was
the underlying tone. Remember I said this life had a lot of energy; well this is the main energy—the determined attempt
to reconnect with your spiritual center. In a sense it was a life
where you were there with Robert, but there wasn't as much
personal contact as there had been in other lives because of
your roles in the church. And so you were forced to seek in
yourself those qualities of strength and equanimity you had
previously projected onto him.

These lifetimes don't seem to be coming to me in chronological order, but rather along the lines of certain themes. I'm
seeing a life now that is more concerned with a personal relationship. It looks like Japan. In this life I believe you and
Robert are married. He has some position in the court; an official in the upper echelons of government. Once again there
is that self-contained equanimity. He is very good in his role.

As his wife, of course, you must be completely subservient to your husband. He totally accepts this Japanese custom
without exploiting it. He just accepts it. You, on the other

hand, have some trouble with it. This male patriarchal repression is repulsive to you, and at the same time you are totally humbled by your love and respect for your husband. It's a very interesting juxtaposition. The depth of your love and the depth of your anger and frustration are equal and focused on the same man.

There are times when you are a little bit larger thorn in Robert's side than you were in the Catholic setting because there is less of a buffer; there is closer contact and he is more vulnerable to what is going on with your energy. He never retaliates either psychically or verbally. There are occasions where he will leave the premises rather tight-lipped until domestic peace has returned, because you do bounce your anger off him. That is one of your main patterns, lashing out at authority figures that represent the systems you feel victimized by. So in this life with Robert, your heart is on the line along with the other issues. It is an intense life for both of you.

I would say the outcome is very positive. I feel you chose your heart again and again; the other side, your anger and frustration, never wins. At the end of that life I see that what remains is a deep respect, a deep love for one another. His feelings for you are becoming more personal. He definitely has deep, abiding feelings; he cherishes and cares for you. Your love has deepened mostly because it has been allowed to flow into the channels where you want it to go. There is a release of pent-up energy and the satisfaction that it brings— the satisfaction of having attained what you have longed for, for so long.

Let's look at another life. Seems Polynesian, the South Seas. Robert is the leader of a village or tribe. I believe you are a man in this lifetime. You are one of the sailors. I'm seeing that there are journeys taken in boats to other islands. There's commerce and some kind of spiritual meaning. These journeys have some religious purpose. I'm seeing that there are certain people on these boats who are in leadership roles, but you are not one. of them. You are some sort of significant person though. You are Robert's son.

He's very wise. He doesn't give you any favors. You are left to the ways of the people to earn your way up in social status and find your place in its structure. You have the deepest respect for him as a person, as a father—the ultimate father, the wise king. There is some kind of spiritual transmission that takes place between the two of you. He is much more of a spiritual father than he is a biological father in the strict sense of the words. I still don't understand what the spiritual significance of these journeys is, but it involves following the currents of the ocean and the path of the stars moving through the heavens. There's some sense of synchronization and attunement with cosmic forces. These sea journeys are in some way prophetic. The amount and type of fish that are caught on these journeys is considered an omen. In fact I see that the journeys are often not taken from island to island. You go out into the middle of the ocean and then turn around and come back at the appropriate time, depending on the omens. It's a way of communing with the cosmic forces by being out on the sea. There are creatures below the water and there are creatures in the sky. Spirits are surrounding you and guiding you. The messages you bring back to Robert are prophetic and are taken into account when he rules. So there is a symbiotic relationship in that sense; you are working together in a spiritual function.

You develop into what would be a medicine man, a shaman within that life. That's your calling as you get older. So in a way you are functioning as a pair. You are very much in a feminine role as the shaman receiving messages from the spirits. He is the outward Logos, the organizer, the male. You are the inner, receptive energy. There's a real nice balance.

It's very hard when he dies, because there's such a close bond between you. It's heavy for the whole tribe when the king dies, because the king really embodies the whole spirit of the tribe. He becomes a deity when he passes over and so you maintain a connection with him, which helps you with your own pain at his loss. You maintain that spiritual connection as part of your role and position in society. It helps a tremendous amount, since you have the support and responsibility to remain in contact. So the real essence of your relationship remains.

I'm seeing another life now, I think it's in a far corner of the world. It seems like New Zealand. It's really easy to pick up on Robert's energy; he's right there, same as usual. I'm seeing him dressed in one of those khaki shirts. Something to do with wildlife. Some kind of government official and something to do with concerns about wildlife. We'll see what we get here.

I'm seeing that Robert's married, but his wife is not there for him; it's not a good relationship. Well it's you who is the home breaker this time. The two of you meet in some kind of professional setting. You are involved in management of natural resources, or something like that. You both fall in love and this puts Robert in a double bind. His integrity gets challenged in this lifetime. He feels he should be loyal to his marriage. This is the first time I've seen Robert sweat. But the connection you feel for each other is really strong, and he eventually leaves his wife to be with you. It's much more of a mundane relationship than any of the ones we've seen so far. I'm seeing you go through periods of being emotionally distraught, but he's always there for you. You're caught up in trying to protect nature from the onslaught and abuse of modern civilization. Looks like it's the last life you had before this lifetime.

. . .

Well, so far there is a happy ending to this story. Dan has met another woman and has moved away to live with her. Dianna and the children are living with Robert on his sailboat. Ironically enough, within a month of their union, Robert and Dianna were hired to go to the Fiji Islands to pilot a sailboat back to the United States. So their honeymoon, so to speak, took them back to the tropical water of the South Seas.

TINA

Tina is the mother of two teen-age children. She has been divorced for four years. At 43 she was in her fourth year of a college program to attain a masters degree in counseling. She had been a nurse for most of her adult life and wanted to be more helpful to families and patients undergoing the emotional stress and healing that occurs in life-threatening illnesses. She herself was involved with a therapy group for the healing of the inner child, endeavoring to overcome the co-dependent patterns in relationships, especially with the men in her life.

Free from the narrow confines of her marriage to an orthodox physician, and being in the intellectual environment of a university, she is in the process of searching beyond the boundaries of her Christian background for what she calls the Absolute Truth. All through childhood Tina had planned to enter the convent and be a nun. Her plans were diverted when she and some of her friends were suspended from high school for not complying with the strict dress codes. This was a very traumatic event, and a devastating blow to her image of herself as a model Christian. As a result of what she felt was cruel and unjust punishment by the principal of her school, she became disenchanted with the church until many years later.

During her fourteen years of marriage to a doctor, she had what she calls a spiritual rebirth. In a state of rapture, she heard a voice tell her that "I am the way, the truth, and the light." It also told her that all she needed to do was follow it. Because of her religious upbringing she naturally assumed that the voice belonged to Jesus, hence she threw herself back into the Christian religion, finding herself in the charismatic movement. Her fanaticism alienated her husband, and he finally pleaded with her to give it up so they could try to bridge the increasing abyss in their communication. In a last-ditch effort to save her marriage, she gave up her involvement with the charismatic movement.

Tina has spent more than one life believing that God was going to save her. All she had to do was be good, i.e., perfect, and she would be magically swept away to heaven. After our initial visit, I loaned her Ruth Montgomery's book, *A World Beyond*, hoping the accounts of the disembodied Arthur Ford—a Christian minister while in the body, writing on what happens after death—would help free her from the oppression of Christian dogma.

When she came back for a reading, she told me that the possibility there might not be a personal God who was looking out for her and would someday swoop her up to heaven if she was good, was terrifying to her. The idea that she was responsible for her own salvation was overwhelming. She was moved to tears, insisting it wasn't fair that we are punished for patterns that are unconscious.

I presented her with many anecdotes from my experiences with doing past-life regression for clients to illustrate how the beliefs and emotional patterns we acquired in other lives affect our present lives. I was particularly keen on helping her discover her spiritual lineage and why she was so riddled with fear and apprehension.

C: Do you have anything you would like to focus on in the reading?

T: Well, when I see people doing things that I don't like—you know, that are evil—I can't believe that they are consciously doing it. I'm convinced that they aren't conscious of it.

C: Are you implying that if a person does something wrong without being conscious of it, it's all right?

T: It may not be all right in the way things work out, but what about the soul and responsibility? I don't see how we can be responsible for unconscious motives. It's not fair. I'm learning that it's really our unconscious motives that are running things. So I don't know what to do.

C: So you feel you've done everything you're supposed to do to be good, but you don't get your rewards because you have unconscious motives that you don't feel you should be responsible for?

T: I would like to try and reach these unconscious things so I can do it right, see it all, and make the kind of changes I need to make. I've really worked so hard at it. So I'd like to know what else I need to do.

C: OK, so we can get a more complete picture of who you are and where your difficulties stem from, I'm going to begin by describing an image of your soul before you came to Earth. When I gaze upon your soul, I see an image of a little girl in a big world surrounded by powerful beings. You feel very small and insignificant. You can't imagine how you're ever going to grow up and do all the important things these other beings are doing. You can't envision how you are ever going to grow up and be what you *think* you're supposed to be.

Metaphorically, I see your soul now at an adolescent stage of development. Hence, there is also a quality of naiveté and idealism, and you judge yourself based on this idealism.

I see you in a celestial realm where light beings of angelic status reside. You are a being of splendor who is veiling her light with a layer of anxiety because you have this predilection to compare yourself with other "older" or more developed beings. In your mind you always fall short by comparison. You adopt a whole catalogue of "shoulds" and "shouldn'ts," becoming your own worst critic. Afraid of acting out your own negative judgments of yourself, you instigate a soul-level pattern of not allowing yourself the freedom to express your innate capacities. You create a core belief that you are small and insignificant and that you will never be able to do all the spiritual work you are supposed to do.

T: That was my choice to believe that way?

C: Yes. That was your response to your environment, your interpretation. Because you feared proving to yourself that your core beliefs were really true, you have inhibited your development as a being and become a severe and punitive parent to yourself. You tend to project this punitive parent or authority onto men: your father and your husband, in your present life, for example.

I have a feeling this pattern can be traced back further. I'm seeing that when you were "born" as a soul out of the Great Spirit, you were stunned by the magnitude of the experience. The power that pushed you out left a deep impression in your being. It left you feeling hurt, shocked, and confused. In that state there were unvoiced questions leaving their imprint on the tabula rasa of your virgin awareness. "Why have I been exiled from the Great Oneness?"

You felt rejected. You felt it wasn't *fair*. You concluded that you must have done something wrong to have been exiled from the Great Oneness. The resulting sense of guilt became the matrix for your individual sense of identity. But you don't want to address the implications of these core beliefs. Your internal logic reasons that if you have done something so wrong that it caused you to be cast out and to experience so much pain, then what's going to happen to you. The consequences seem too frightful, something akin to eternal damnation. So this whole complex becomes a generic fear, whose cause you desire to keep unconscious and avoid at all cost. This is the starting point of your identity as a soul.

So it's easier to understand how later in your development as a soul you could look at the beings around you and think that there is no way for you to grow up and be like them. How can you envision becoming the angelic being that you are destined to become if at the foundation of your being you believe you have done something terribly wrong? Something you can't even identify, and therefore something you can't fix.

This initial thought of yours has a lot of resonance with the Christian dogma of original sin. This primordial, or pre-conscious, judgment has marked your soul and on some unconscious level you believe you will never be able to overcome this flaw. This nagging core belief is expressed through the "critic" that dominates a large portion of your conscious psyche. It's always demanding you to be perfect as an attempt to compensate for your "original sin," and berating you when you fall short of its standards of perfection.

Until you go back and erase the core belief that you are guilty of some mysterious crime against the Creator, you will continue to live out the frustrating dynamics of your internal logic. Meanwhile the purity and beauty of your spiritual loving self remains fixated in an infantile, i.e., helpless and dependent stage of development.

This "inner child" never gets any positive support from the punitive parent part of you. It has no self-esteem or any reason to believe it can do anything. This conflict on a soul level was so crippling to your development you were not able to remain with your soul group on the inner planes. Your guides could see that for you to remain in this angelic realm surrounded by seemingly perfect beings was only exacerbating your condition. No one can really help you as long as you maintain those beliefs about yourself. Even those beings with all their wisdom were unable to dissuade you. So they sent you into this realm to live out the consequences of the beliefs that are inhibiting you from fulfilling your destiny as a soul.

When they sent you here to Earth, you took it as proof that you were bad. This is an example of how once we have created an identity we are driven to validate that identity, regardless of whether it is a positive or negative identity. Even though they tried to communicate to you that it would be best to come here to a low-pressure situation where you could learn certain skills and outgrow your inhibitive patterns, you chose to interpret their actions as proof of your unworthiness. It's by taking small tasks and completing them that you will gradually come to believe in your ability to learn and to do things right. That's why they sent you here.

I can see now why the Christian paradigm has been so powerful for you. The myth of original sin evokes one of your core beliefs, and the male deity who embodies the Absolute Authority parallels your own inner critic. Throughout the history of your soul, you have labored under the belief that salvation was dependent upon your ability to satisfy the dictates of the "critic." In a similar way, Christians need only satisfy the commandments of "God," to be saved from their original flaw. Let's go on to see what's happened since you came to planet Earth.

Before you incarnate here, you're like a little girl who has come to a big city. You're fascinated by the new experience. There is a guide showing you how things work. It's like a shopping mall or a fair, and you're going by all the little shops or booths intrigued by what you're seeing. The guide is helping find an area you would be interested in. You are drawn to helping people. You and your guide then discuss an overall plan for your sojourn on the Earth.

Before you come into a body you feel anxious. You have trepidation about your ability to perform well. You came into a female body in a primitive culture. The first image I have is of you bathing a baby. The mother of the child is watching. You are a shamaness. You have black skin and wear only a loincloth. Your breasts are not bound. The buildings are circular mud huts with thatched roofs.

Your mother was the medicine woman for the village. You chose her so you could grow up and take her place. This was the custom in the tribe. You express a lot of nurturance in this life. I might just add here that different souls perform specific functions in the cosmic scheme of things. The angelic being that you are, embodies the love and compassion aspect of creation. This first lifetime on the planet is a good example of your innate soul qualities.

The child you are working with dies. This is very traumatic for you. You feel that you did something wrong, that it was your fault because you were supposed to heal it. So right from the beginning, you project your negative core beliefs into your physical identity.

You wanted so much to save the baby, and when it dies it really hurts you. This resonates with the pain you experienced at the birth of your soul. The "why" question overwhelms you. You don't understand why there is pain. You don't understand why the baby has to die, why the mother has to feel the pain of her loss, why you must suffer the pain of wanting to save the child, etc.

T: Instead of just accepting the pain I feel like I should have done something to avoid it?

C: Yes. It's as if pain is a cosmic evil and you feel powerless against it. As you go on in that life you develop a fear of doing healing work, afraid others will die or feel pain. You think that because you're the healer, you should be able to save them from the pain. If you can't, that means you're not a good healer. Your belief systems create a situation where you cannot develop a sense of self-confidence.

You leave that life feeling you have failed because you were unable to save people from pain. You're afraid to meet with your guides. You assume they will judge you as harshly as you judge yourself. So you cloak yourself and avoid communicating with them. You feel you must come back to the planet and prove yourself before you can see your guides again. Now you are setting up criteria whereby you must satisfy your inner critic before you will accept any help from your guides.

As you reflect on the life you just left you don't understand why you have failed. You decide that you just have to go back and try harder.

I see you as a tall African woman. You're standing outside a structure in which some ceremony is taking place. It seems you're standing guard. It's like a healing ritual. Your job is to keep evil spirits away. The person ends up dying and you think it's your fault for not keeping all the evil spirits at bay. The people who were involved in the healing ritual don't talk about it afterward. You don't tell anyone you think it's your fault, and no one tries to talk you out of your thoughts. You just go on thinking it's true.

In this life there is a collective belief in evil spirits. Your own fears have drawn you into this cultural setting and you are projecting them into the fear of evil spirits. This life assumes the quality of a nightmare in which you have to watch for and fight the evil spirits. These evil spirits are what you have to overcome in order to do your healing work. Your fears grow into a severe paranoia in this life. You neurotically and compulsively engage in rituals to keep the evil spirits away.

When you leave your body in that life you carry the fear of evil spirits with you. You're so preoccupied with looking out for evil spirits that you're once again unavailable to guidance from your guides. Because you were so preoccupied with looking for evil spirits you were drawn to denser areas of the astral plane where deranged and inimical beings reside. This is a hellish world full of demons. You are so fearful of these "evil" spirits that you escape and come back to the body as soon as you can.

It seems you came back as an aborigine. Your father in this life was the head of your tribe in your previous life. He is a being you trust and look to for protection. He is a very good father and treats you with much kindness. This helps you feel safe. This culture has a sophisticated system of altered states referred to as "dream time." They also have methods for divination and you become a good oracle. You are a man in this life and under the tutelage of your father you develop a good self-image.

When you leave the body from that life you feel good about the progress. At that point you are willing to address your guides again and go on with your learning. There are two beings who help you choose the next lifetime. Your guides are encouraging you to do something different in this next life.

I'm seeing you observing your new mother; you feel anxious. It's an American Indian life. I see you traveling with your parents when you're still a baby. It's a small group of Indians and you are going to the winter camp of your people. Your mother is carrying you in some kind of backpack.

As you grow up, your father is very patient with you. He is highly tuned to the forces of nature and he is teaching you about that. Your father really wanted to have a son, so he teaches you about things that are taboo to teach women, like the different kinds and properties of wood. You want to please him so you become sort of a tomboy.

One of the things your guides wanted you to do different in this life was to have a love relationship. You do fall in love when you get older. You're very shy, but he courts you, and when he wins your heart, he takes you away from your family. This is difficult for you. In the lifetimes that we have seen so far, you have remained within the family unit throughout the life. This is the first life where you leave the security of the family, and you feel very insecure about being on your own.

After you have your first child, you begin feeling more secure because you have a focus for your attention and energy. Because your mate is a brave who is infatuated with his own bravado as a hunter and warrior, there is not much of a heart connection between the two of you. You act out a subservient role where your duty is to please your spouse. This might sound unhealthy, but remember that until now you have had a need for approval. So in this life you are projecting those dynamics into a love relationship in an attempt to gain that approval. Within the confines of your belief systems, to successfully please your mate is a form of progress that gives you a sense of accomplishment.

Your second child is a girl. You end up feeling closer to her than to your son because he aligns himself with his father. He removes himself emotionally from you because he senses it's the manly thing to do.

When your son reaches manhood, your spouse is killed in a skirmish with a neighboring tribe. You're somewhat confused as to how to respond. You don't feel a significant emotional loss because you weren't close to him emotionally. You're more concerned about trying to understand what is appropriate behavior in terms of your social surroundings. You wonder what your new social role is supposed to be.

Your daughter in that life is your present daughter. After your mate dies you begin living vicariously through her. Hence, you become emotionally dependent on her and she becomes your whole life. Eventually she falls in love. When she begins to live with this man she takes you with her, but she transfers a great deal of her emotional energy to him. You feel abandoned and find yourself tagging along after her. Now you have lost the two major external supports for your sense of self. You feel lost and confused.

At the end of this life you feel very much alone and frightened. Your tribe has beliefs about a journey that must be made after you die, and you fear you will not be able to go by yourself. You're so emotionally dependent on your daughter that you can't bear the thought of having to go and do the things you are supposed to do as a spirit after you die.

After you pass over, you're surprised when your guides come to you. Slowly you remember and feel relieved about not having to go on the horrendous journey you had feared so much. Your guides are perplexed; they're not sure of how to help you get out of this emotional dependency pattern. You're not very coherent after this life, and you just go along with what they suggest for your next life.

Your next life is somewhere in Europe. I'm seeing a big rushing river. I'm seeing you as a boy in a rugged land, maybe in Russia. You are traveling with a small group of people dressed in fur coats. Your father is a trapper. He is a big, coarse, strong outdoor type, but you are a frail, sensitive boy. Your mother is a strong peasant type also. You live in a log cabin of sorts. It has one big room with an openhearth fireplace and a table made of split logs.

As an older boy, I see you trapping with your father. You're very timid and always keenly aware of what your father thinks about you. He's not very patient with you, and not very pleased with your timid, frail manner. There is not a lot of love in your family. Both your parents are rather silent, stern, and serious. Their main focus is coping with the hardships of life. Even when you grow up, you still live with them in this one-room cabin. There is not much social contact at all.

There is a village where you travel with your father to sell furs and get supplies. You like going to town and seeing other people. There's a woman in town that you look for, but you haven't talked to her yet. You seldom see her, but you admire her from afar. One time she is in the store when you and your father are there. You want to talk to her, but you're afraid of your father's reaction. Eventually you develop a relationship with her and you move to town. You work in the store and eventually marry her, but you feel you betrayed your father because he wanted you to be a trapper like him. You feel intimidated when he comes to town because he is angry with you.

Your guides had set up a life in which you were inspired to leave your parents. Even at the risk of losing their approval, you made a life for yourself. This was a big step for you. Moreover, your relationship with your wife is a sincere heart-to-heart connection. One based on real caring and nurturance. You have several children, but your wife dies in childbirth. This leaves you in a state of grief for the rest of that life suffering from the loss and your emotional dependency on your wife. This part of what your guides had set up for you was not successful. You failed to regain yourself after the loss of your wife. It was so painful for you that you even closed yourself off from your children emotionally. They reminded you too much of your wife. Again the old pattern of being unable to accept pain surfaces. You wallow in feelings of it not being fair that your wife died and left you. You get angry at life for making you feel this pain. This becomes more of a passive aggression.

When you leave your body in that life, you feel mistrustful of your guides. Confused as to what to do, you refuse to speak to your guides and you resist incarnating. You're like a child that has gone to its room pouting. When you tire of your self-proclaimed incarceration on the astral plane, you come out feeling vanquished. Instead of agreeing to work with your guides and having a positive attitude about learning, you just resign yourself to what you feel is a hopeless situation. You therefore take no conscious part in choosing your next incarnation. You are thus subjected to a life that is determined by the raw forces of the karmic patterns that have been building up.

As a baby you cry a lot. You're acting out your frustration and sense of hopelessness. Your mother tries to comfort you, but to no avail. It's a lifetime in Europe. Your father is a coal miner. He works very hard in terrible conditions for little pay. In this life you are living out how you feel about life on the planet; life is a struggle full of hardships, heartache, and pain. No matter how hard you try, you make little or no progress. As you grow, you despise your life and your surroundings. You want very much to escape your lot in life. The only available avenue of escape is the church. At an early age you become a nun.

Being within the cloistered walls of the nunnery, you feel protected from the hardships of life. Like a traumatized or autistic child, you retreat into a fantasy world inhabited by your imaginary friends, Jesus and the angels. Your history of emotional dependency gets focused on your personal relationship with Jesus. If we stripped this relationship of its religious vestments and looked at it through the eyes of a psychotherapist, it would look like a co-dependent relationship with a fantasy character. I have already spoken about the way in which the Christian dogma resonates with your core beliefs; I will only say here that you project into your relationship with Jesus your desire to be saved from frustrations and responsibilities as a soul. You place these outside yourself with the conviction that he will do it for you. You place all your trust and hope in him and ardently convince yourself that he will take care of everything.

I don't want to sound entirely negative about this; there are other factors playing into your fascination with the church. The core of the Christian teachings was, for the Western world, the most profound vehicle for spiritual truths. Christ's teachings on love evoke the deepest aspects of your soul. Though his teachings have been twisted and misused by human beings down through the centuries, the essence of his truths awakened in you your destiny as a soul. Neither of these factors—your neurotic relationship to a magical fantasy saviour nor your attunement to the wisdom of spiritual love—precludes the other.

Because of your own psychological makeup, and the dualistic dogma of the church, you become compulsive about your spiritual purity in this life. Hence you repress a great deal of yourself. To acknowledge or accept any part of yourself that did not fit into your "pure Christian" image of yourself carried the threat of damnation. Here we see a profound culmination of the internal conflicts you carried with you from the earlier period of your pre-Earth experiences on the inner planes. You leave this life as a nun with a highly charged split within you. You have damned to the unconscious any and all aspects of yourself that threaten your Christian identity, and hence, any chance for salvation.

You die young. The monastery is cold and damp, and due to your severe asceticism and lack of concern for your body, you die of pneumonia. As you leave the body you are sure you are going to heaven to be with your beloved Jesus. You are confused and then alarmed when your guides are there to greet you instead. Seeing them is a shocking dose of reality. Slowly you realize that you haven't escaped. So despondent are you that it is difficult to listen to your guides. They are pleased with you for having chosen the religious life while in the body, but they try to talk with you about your motivations for doing so. You do not want to hear what they are trying to tell you. You are not happy about your fantasy bubble being popped. You are not pleased to learn that you will have to return to the Earth. It's with a heavy sense of resignation and reluctance that you do so.

You are still very attached to your Christian beliefs and you come back to a life where you once again become a nun in Europe. Your guides did manage to encourage you to be more involved with helping people instead of being a cloistered nun. You work both with orphaned children and the sick. You enjoy your work, feeling that you are doing something worthwhile and at the same time assured that you are living a life that satisfies Christian morals and values.

Throughout this life you maintain your personal and emotionally dependent relationship with Jesus, your fantasy lover/saviour. You rarely leave the convent, feeling secure and protected from the hardships of the world only within the stone walls of your religious sanctuary. Because of these two factors, this life appears to be one in which you achieve a good level of self-confidence and self-esteem. All things considered, it seems to be your most balanced life of those lifetimes we have looked at so far.

You live to a ripe old age this time. As an elderly woman preparing to die, there's not a doubt in your mind that you are going straight to heaven. You have lived a strict, charitable, and pure Christian life; surely your saviour will embrace you at the gates of heaven when you pass over. You die in peace with your rosary in your right hand.

You have your mind set on heaven and don't even look back as you leave your body. When your guides come to greet you, you mistake them for angels. They congratulate you on your progress in that life and begin to discuss your next life before you finally realize they are not there to take you to heaven. You go into a mild state of shock. Confusion, anger, and fear stir within you, but you remain paralyzed. Your guides gently try to help you see why you need to return to another life.

One of the things they point out is how you disassociated from your emotional self when you were a nun. Though confronted with the emotional and physical pain of the orphans and sick people you worked with, you shielded yourself like Pollyanna in a fantasylike world of angels and your beloved

Jesus. You were numb to the pain in the world around you while repressing your fear of pain from previous experiences. Your guides also want to show how your fanatic indulgence in the Christian religion was supporting your predilection to deny the realities of life and your responsibilities as a soul. You did not want to hear that. You refused to listen to them. Neither did you want to go back into another body—and you didn't until your present life.

The theme that seems to run through all these lives is the fear of pain, especially painful knowledge or awareness, and the self-defeating attempt to avoid it. Though you are still riddled with fears, it seems that you are making great strides in this lifetime dealing with them. Your work with healing the inner child, and your choice of professions appears to be perfect for you and what you as a soul are endeavoring to accomplish.

T: What an incredible illusion to be going on throughout time. To think I can, and should, really keep trying to avoid pain. That feeling, too, of life not being fair; how strong that has been in me. I can see how I adopted rigid rules and a critical/savior God to help me feel secure. It helps me to hear you say that I'm making some progress in this life. Whatever else happens to me in this life—and I believe that much will happen, as I intend to let it—I know I'll be more open to my guides next time and will make more careful choices.

EVIN

Evin is 42 years old. He's divorced and lives on a sailboat in the San Juan Islands. He's somewhat of a sophisticated water rat, a great photographer, and a "middle-aged man in search of himself," as he put it. While listening to the reading he maintained what seemed to be a characteristic smirk.

C: I'd like to begin with an image that symbolizes a general undercurrent throughout your lives. I see you walking along a shore, alone. It's a soft, misty, grey day. A somber-hued sea moves against the shore, not in waves, but in languid surges. There is a gentle sadness, the sadness of a heart that is capable of appreciating the sweetness and beauty of life but is appalled by the hostility and abuse that takes place on this planet.

The mood is a soft melancholy, a melancholy that washes over you. In that submerged state, your essential nature is divorced from you. You have memories that haunt you, memories of what it is like to be united with your true and spiritual self. It's almost like the love of a beautiful woman who has gone out of your life. She is gone, and you don't know where or how to find her again. And now you don't even believe that it is possible to find her again.

As I follow your past lives back through time, I see that you came to the Earth from another dimension. You were a wise, mature soul, calmly abiding in peace and harmony in a nonphysical reality that I have come to call the seventh dimension. Perhaps the common idea of the Angelic Kingdom is the closest concept I can draw upon to give you some idea of what I'm suggesting is the origin of your soul.

Back in the times of Atlantis, there was an imbalance on the Earth plane and there was a large number of beings who came down from the inner planes to help get the Earth back on course again. Your soul had matured to the point where it was operating on a transpersonal level. You didn't really decide to come to this dimension. It's more like you were pulled down automatically as the forces of the higher dimensions began responding to the needs of the ailing Earth plane.

You and your co-workers brought a great deal of spiritual knowledge and technology to the planet. Using the Earth's magnetic pathways, you used crystals and pyramids to do what might be called "interdimensional acupuncture" on the planet. At the same time you were seeding the mental plane with conceptual structures, creating models for further development of the races.

It caused you tremendous grief when you witnessed the results of your work. The information and technologies were disseminated freely, without a full understanding of the greed and ruthlessness of some of the power-hungry souls on the Earth. Eventually these souls who lusted after power—as well as some of those higher-dimensional beings in your own group who had problems with power issues—misused the knowledge in an attempt to overthrow the theocracy that you and your co-workers had established. The great civilization of Atlantis was destroyed.

This was your initial experience of being on the planet, and you died in the destruction. Out of the body, after that life, you were totally amazed and confused at what had happened. You judged yourself by the outcome. On some level, you blamed yourself and drew a shadow over yourself—a cloud of self-judgment and doubt.

The Atlantean project was moved to Egypt. The work was carried out there on a much smaller scale. I'm seeing you as one of the head priests. You're making sure everything is kept under control. The initiation procedures were very strict, almost punitive. You didn't want to make the same mistakes as in Atlantis. Your doubt inhibits you, so you're not able to be there in your full wisdom and brilliance as a being. This shadow of doubt separates you from your spontaneous, intuitive, knowing connectedness to your higher self. You are becoming a dense separate individual who mistrusts the higher powers that flow through you. You feel a need to control them, and you are burdened with a weighted sense of responsibility.

It's very interesting for me to observe this process as you begin to cloak yourself in a dense individualized identity. It's happening without your being aware of it as you start to think and make judgments from your earthbound perspective.

I'm seeing you now as a very old man. There is something about the pyramid energy, a special diet of herbs, and the monastic life the priests live that enables you to live to a very old age. You've maintained a clear awareness into your old age, but your body is not able to hold the vibration of your consciousness any longer. It's worn out.

As I see you leave the body, I sense this overwhelming heaviness. It feels like guilt to me. It seems you still feel responsible and guilty for what happened in Atlantis. Can you identify with this sense of guilt? Ah, it's more like you feel you should be doing more to make things better.

E: Sure, I'm always getting down on myself for not doing more.

C: Well, you started doing that way back here. You made the judgment that if you would have done better, the terrible things that happened in Atlantis would not have occurred. So you blamed yourself, and since that time you've been plagued with a need to compensate for that judgment. For some reason you weren't satisfied by your work in Egypt. Ah, I see. It was on too small a scale to do what you know needs to be done here on Earth. So you were frustrated, you felt a need to do more, much more.

I have this image of you pacing back and forth between lives now, trying to figure out what you're going to do. You eventually get sucked back into a body before you come up with a game plan. You are so involved with your dilemma that you are pulled automatically back with the group of souls you are working with. I see you in a secret community in the Andes. It's an ideal society, like one the gods would create on Earth. You were working mainly with balancing the Earth's subtle energy in this life, rather than focusing on working with social structures. This life is like a vacation, or a trip back home to your native dimension. But this did not eclipse the sense of guilt. I see that you still carry it with you.

E: Yeah, I do feel that guilt is pretty well instilled in my being, one way or another.

C: There were many beings and forces coming together to create what happened in Atlantis. You're not omnipotent; it wasn't just your fault. I want to say there is nothing for you to feel guilty about, but there is. There was another being of equal status who was pushing things too hard. You have a tendency to be more passive, and acquiesced to this more aggressive person. The case you have on yourself is that if you had stood up to this person, things might have turned out different. If you had followed your own instincts, you would have been much more careful and taken things slower. So you judged yourself for not standing up for what you knew to be right.

Because of who you are as a being, you think you should be perfect. The idea that you have done something you consider to be less than perfect, creates a dissonance in your belief system.

E: I was raised by two perfectionists in this life.

C: Well that's a projection of the internal punitive parent within yourself. You need a paradigm for how you can be perfect and still make mistakes. That's your Zen koan to work on.

OK, after your vacation in the Andes it's time for you to get back to work. I see a lot of activity near the Mediterranean Sea. Mesopotamia. I also see you as an Etruscan. You spent quite a number of lifetimes in this area, enmeshing yourself in the cultures that were developing there. You found this to be very limiting, and hence frustrating, because there weren't systems of spiritual thought that offered you a good vehicle to do the work you wanted to do.

For example, I'm seeing one life where you were a statesman, a local governor, or something like that. The cultural setting is a proverbial Babylon. You're at your wits' end trying to bring law and order into this hotbed of greed, pettiness, and licentiousness. You have a wife who is basically a demanding and self-serving shrew. In short, everything in your environment is out of your control even though you're supposed to be the sovereign. This life was a representation of your growing feelings of being powerless to make the changes here on the planet that you came to make.

I want to take a moment. I feel there is a pattern here concerning your experience with women. I'm wondering what has drawn you to such a woman. I'm going back to a life in which you were a man in a matriarchal culture. This setting is like the Amazons the early Greek writers wrote about. This woman who was your wife, lorded over you in this earlier matriarchal life. You were scarred by the hostile and abusive treatment you received in that life. It left a black picture of the feminine sex smeared across your unconscious.

You don't begin to feel good again until the Grecian experience. The mystery schools and temples of Greece finally offer you a sense of satisfaction for all the work you've been trying to do in the Mediterranean cultures. It's like you can take a breather now and relax. The sense of beauty and harmony, the balance of spirit and physical realities you have helped create in Greece is a major accomplishment. You spend several lifetimes enjoying the fruits of your labor, only to watch it be devastated by the Christians.

After this life, I see you walking away shaking your head in disbelief. You're totally amazed by the mess those who followed a being like Jesus could make of his teachings. At first you're just stunned, and then later you get angry. But your anger translates into a clenched-toothed, tight-fisted resolve to go back to Earth and work even harder.

What's really hard for you to believe is that a being like Jesus was unable to do the kind of work you felt you needed to do on the planet. So even though you've made a resolve to work harder, you also start to feel more hopeless about your ability to make a difference. This was hard on you, because you still had a need to prove yourself, to redeem your inaction in Atlantis, so the tension within your being was heightened. It also plunged you further into your dilemma, i.e., what's it going to take to get things right here on Earth so you can finish your job. The answer to your dilemma is starting to assume the quality of a quest now.

This quest gets played out later in a lifetime with King Arthur. That period was the next major group effort of the beings who had worked with the Christ Force, and you chose to align yourself with them. The image of the knight in shining armor represents this need you feel to manifest the truth and the purity of your being. The whole aura of magic that surrounded Camelot shows how desperate you were becoming to conquer the darkness on the planet. It's as if you were naively retreating into a fairy tale to carry on in your quest.

You were one of the knights of Arthur's Camelot. You were steadfast and loyal and took great pride in riding forth to employ "might for right." In this life there was kind of a karmic replay of the struggle between those beings who were prominent in the Amazonian culture, and the male beings who finally rebelled and overthrew the power structure of the matriarchy. A lineage of matriarchal energies was carried forward through the Druids and their nature-worshipping practices. The patriarchal orientation of the Christian world was at war with the ancient Druid social structures prevalent in that part of the world.

Another one of your karmic patterns becomes evident in this life. There is one major and one more minor affiliation with a woman that ended in you choosing your quest and duty as a knight over your love for the woman.

E: That sounds real familiar. I've done that a number of times in this life.

C: I'm seeing that you have created this boundary in your mind between personal love and universal love. And due to this split you are forced to make a choice. It was also a convenient way for you to avoid being too vulnerable and getting hurt in love.

E: Hmm, the plot thickens.

C: I see you dying in a bloody battle in this life. When you are out of the body, you gaze down on the scene and feel disillusioned. Actually you're disgusted with the whole process, and with yourself for being involved in such a barbaric drama. Your resolve to get out there and make greater efforts is undermined. Your enthusiasm turns to depression and melancholy as you repress it. You're unwilling to play the game anymore. You reason that if you don't play you can't lose again.

In your next several lives you retire to the sidelines and watch. You're the philosopher watching from afar, but you don't get involved. Your quest gets altered becoming a search for transcendent truths. The transformation of your quest is an expression of how far you are separated from your essential nature and the wisdom you possessed before entering the human arena. Your quest now becomes a subtle form of escape from the chaos on the planet and the dilemma you have set up for yourself; the belief that you have to make things right here.

I see you incarnating in a European setting, maybe Germany or Switzerland. You are working within the church, but not as a priest. You are a financial advisor or administrator. You take care of the business end of the church. This shows you still have some hope in the Christ energy, which has you karmically bound to it. You still hope it might be able to do something constructive, and you don't know of anything else at the time to align yourself with. But when you are in the body, witnessing the manifestation of the Christian church, it's not satisfying you. In this life you just observe, and you're critical of all the corruption in the church and the way they warp the truth to fit dogma. Your search for truth is on a much deeper level, and hence you feel even more alienated.

You have a wife and children in this life, but you are not very emotionally connected to them. You live mostly in your mind. As you grow old in that life, you feel more and more alienated because you have this inner sense of what the truth is, but there is nothing in your environment to support and validate your inner knowing. This creates another self-image, another layer of karmic fabric to further cloak you from your essential self. You become so despondent that it actually kills you.

When you leave the body this time, you are ready to give up hope in the Christian group. You turn your attention to the Tibetan experience. Some of the beings who you had been involved with back in Atlantis and Egypt were there in Tibet. They were establishing a very powerful and focused energy. The Tibetan lives for you were like another reprieve, they went a long way toward satisfying your quest for higher truths and union with your higher self. You spent three or four lives there in a row. You gave yourself to these lives with great abandonment. But in a sense they were an escape, an escape from the rest of the world and its problems. You really just wanted to be a hermit. You weren't even very active in the structure of the Buddhist monasteries. You spent a great deal of time as a recluse, living in caves, etc.

I see that you weren't able to stay in hiding. You were nudged back out into the world, and you resented it. Especially when you realized that you really hadn't escaped any of the karma you left back in the world. It was there waiting for you. This is interesting for me to see that just getting away and reconnecting to the spirit doesn't automatically eradicate our karma.

Now I'm seeing an image of you as a tall lanky pioneer out on the prairie. You have a wife who is damn hard to get along with. You're fighting constantly, but she does a good job of keeping your feet on the ground. There's not much time to meditate. You eventually have three children—two boys and a girl. Your house is made of mud and straw. You raise sheep and have difficulties with the cattle ranchers. Everything about this life is a struggle. It's a concentrated version of all that you despise about the Earth.

You're really sad at the end of this life because your wife dies, and you regret having spent so much time fighting with her instead of sharing the love you really felt for one another. By the end of this life you're polarized back into your mundane identity.

You incarnate next in southern France, again in a rural farming environment. In this life you develop a sense of humor with a cynical twist. It's a defense against the pain and hardships you lived through in the life on the prairie. This life has more warmth in it, but you don't experience it because you constantly have your guard up. You don't marry in this life, and you're kind of the village trickster. But beneath your mask, you are very lonely and sad. You become what is called a *vieux garcon*, an old little boy. This is an older man who lives alone because he is so difficult to get along with. You're like a little devil challenging the authority of Earth-side reality. You live to be a plump old man. When you die you're rather amused; you think you've won. You had set up this game you played with life—you didn't allow any-

thing to get close enough to your heart to hurt you. You felt
that you had tricked life and won.

E: That's really interesting. I traveled in France several times.
Twenty years ago I wondered if I had lived there in my last
life. I especially felt at home in southern France.

C: It does seem that you came into your present life next. I
get a feeling that all you repressed in that life beneath the
mask of humor is coming out in this life. It's as if you're acting out now what you polarized by your avoidance in that
life. You're much more serious and melancholy in this life.
You've also had some very painful relationships with
women.

E: Yes, I'm a very serious person.

C: This life is serious in the sense that you are confronting
many of your major karmic patterns.

E: How am I doing?

C: I'd say you're doing pretty damn good. You're staying
with it and taking one thing at a time. You're very fair in the
sense that you consider what's going on, and you're definitely there relating, responding, and adjusting yourself to the
changes. Can you hear the "but" coming?

E: Yeah, let me get in first, I believe that's right. Now bring in
your "but."

C: You feel a resentment about having to do it; you're bitter
about it. It's almost like a matter of pride. What you haven't
accomplished, and what could be a pivotal factor, is the ability to open your heart completely. You're withholding.

You've been hurt, you're bitter about it, so you're defending yourself. Your heart is closed. So you're resigned to facing the hardships of this life, but you're still resisting them. I'm seeing how imperative it is to be able to open our hearts and bring ourselves completely into these experiences. That's what's going to release the karma, that's what's going to heal us. We must be able to completely accept—without any judgment and resistance, but with compassion—all that we have reacted to.

E: It's interesting that you mention the heart, because I am more cerebral. But when I have opened my heart in relationships, I get stomped.

C: I thought you said you had a habit of leaving relationships to go on some quest?

E: Well, I have done that, but I've also been stomped on too many times.

C: Well, you'll need to learn how to keep your heart open right through the stomping. From what I'm seeing right now, that's what it will take to overcome the belief system that keeps pulling you into those kinds of experiences.

E: It is hard sometimes to open the heart, and it really shouldn't be.

C: Ahhh.

E: Yeah, back to guilt, right?

C: Yeah, it's hard.

E: But why is it so hard?

C: I guess for me it's because I'm angry and I have resentment. If I can get beyond that, it's not hard because it does feel good to open the heart. And we're the ones choosing to close the heart by holding onto our hurt, and our anger.

E: Oh, I don't hold on to my hurt, but a . . . a yeah, oh I don't know.

C: Then who is?

E: Yeah, right.

C: What strikes me about this reading, Evin, is how powerful our thoughts and beliefs are. I'd like to leave you with some questions to ponder. How would your life be different if you let go of your judgment on yourself about what occurred in Atlantis? How would you be different if you didn't believe it was your sole responsibility to save this planet? In other words, how would it alter your ability to be fully here manifesting your "true" self? And finally, what resources or skills do you need to develop to allow you to open your heart? Can you spend some time imagining yourself in the future after you have answered these questions and get a strong sense of what it would feel like. If you can, and you like how that feels, you can look backward from that imaginary future to reexperience the changes you went through to get to that comfortable place.

ANDREA

Andrea lives and works in Harpers Ferry, West Virginia, as a fund raiser for a nonprofit land stewardship organization, the Appalachian Trail Conference. Andrea is an attractive woman in her late 30s with long auburn hair. She has the appearance and demeanor of the Hollywood stereotype professional woman, say a lawyer in New York City. She has been married for ten years. In her words it is "a remarkably successful marriage."

The first time I met Andrea she had come to my home in the country with her husband. They were on vacation visiting some friends of mine who happened to mention me to her. I didn't have a phone at the time, so she braved the mud of my winter driveway to forthrightly request a reading. Once she was inside my small house, I suddenly felt as if our beings were larger than life. The walls could not enclose the energy resonating between us. I was extremely affected by this; she did her best to ignore it. An arrangement was made whereby I would join her and her husband and my friends for dinner, and we could do the reading at that time.

She sat next to me at dinner. It was her that I turned to when we all laughed at a joke. It was her I engaged in conversation. My attention just naturally was on her. Once upstairs in a private room to do the reading, she was feeling increasingly uncomfortable with the dynamics between us. In her mind she was interpreting the intensity in terms of a sexual attraction, and she was doing her best to repress it and conceal it from her husband. Knowing that she didn't want to address this issue, I avoided bringing forth past-life connections between us as I progressed through the reading.

After Andrea and her husband returned home to the East Coast, we corresponded for awhile. In general, she was unhappy with the reading and felt I must have had my feelings for her mixed up with the information that came through. To satisfy my own curiosity, and to help work out whatever karma we might have together, I wrote and asked her if she would be interested in my doing a reading that focused on our past together. She let me know in no uncertain terms that she would take it all with a grain of salt, but yes, she would.

The reading that follows is a composite of the original reading, and the subsequent reading that I did tracing our past lives together.

C: I've found there are a good number of souls on this planet who were not originally part of the Earth's evolution. Many of the people I have worked with have come onto the planet from other dimensions. There are different levels or gradations that make up the cosmic organism. Hence, there are nonphysical dimensions, and there are beings that exist in those dimensions. I see that your soul is one of those beings. How you came to be here really sets the tone for your experience on this plane. And your experience of being here is going to be different from someone who began her life as a soul within the evolution of this planet.

The metaphorical image I see for your soul is a businessman in an office. The mode is "full speed ahead." There are many papers and constant phone calls. You're totally involved, plugged in, busy, busy. So I'm asking myself, what is the motivation? What is the driving force? I'm seeing that you're a being, for whatever reason, who accepts a lot of responsibility. I don't know if this helps, but for some people, I get a feeling they are "old souls," but from you I get more of a sense that you're a "young adult," full of ambition and drive. You're gung-ho!

Are you familiar with the seven rays? The principles of the seven rays as elaborated in the Theosophical literature?

A: The chakras?

C: No. The seven rays could be related to the chakras. We could say that each chakra is the vehicle for one of the seven rays without making a gross error. In short, the theory states that there are seven fundamental articulations of the primal energy of the cosmos. And the various interactions of these seven rays create all aspects of the phenomenal worlds. Hence, each soul will be composed of all seven rays, but each soul will have a dominant ray that it is expressing. The ray that is the main aspect of your being is the ray of the Will of Creation. In a sense you might say your soul is an expression of the will. It's like a brain cell in the cosmic organism.

Souls are like cells in the cosmic organism. Each soul has a type of function to carry out, and therefore possesses innate abilities and destinies that coincide with those abilities. So that's the really busy part of your being. That's who you started out to be. I think at the end of the reading you might be able to understand what I mean when I say you don't need to be so busy. The "will" energy can be channeled in a focused calm manner, rather than just scurrying around. There's a way you can flow and let things happen, rather than to identify with the process—to think it's *your* responsibility. Do you understand so far?

A: Umm, yes.

C: It's interesting, I used to work with a lot of souls from other dimensions who had inhibitions and learning disabilities. Either that or they had some problem with power and authority, and that was why they were sent to this planet. But you, you're like a person I just did a reading for. It's as if you signed up to come. There was work to do, and you were out the door!

I'm seeing that you and I were part of the same soul group. It's somewhat like being in the same school or being in the same class in school. You were a very good student, an honor student who followed all the rules. I was more eccentric, bored and restless within the confines of the prescribed curriculum. I longed for more creative and farreaching pursuits. I was a dreamer, a romantic, and had no regard for details or protocol, so to speak. This rubbed you the wrong way. You didn't approve of my irreverent preoccupation with freedom and creativity. I doubt if even today you would admit it, but I sense you were jealous. There's a part of you that would like to come out and play, that would like to have a vacation from the great taskmaster within yourself. I see that I sort of teased you, challenged you to lighten up.

Are you familiar at all with Atlantis? There was a large group of souls that came to Earth during the time of Atlantis, and you were part of that influx. The group of souls that came was made up of souls like you, as well as souls that had learning disabilities, problems with power and authority. It was quite an involved project. There were certain forces on the Earth that were hindering the evolution of the race. Also, many of the inner-dimensional souls were arrested in self-limiting patterns. By coming to this slower vibrational system, which offered more concrete feedback for their actions, they would have the opportunity to solve their individual problems while helping the denizens of the Earth plane. And for other souls, like yourself, it was their first assignment: "in the field training," so to speak.

I came to the planet in the same group of souls that you did. You of course were eager to get to work. Prior to coming down to the planet, I was not at all happy with the assignment. I judged it as a degrading, almost punitive effort on the part of our mentors. I wanted to be involved with grander, more rarified endeavors. To me the Earth was backward, a hellhole. My attitude was careless and arrogant. This only caused you to be more rigid and strict in your relationship to me and our work together. Are you familiar with what happened in Atlantis?

A: Well, I have questions about it. If so many people with talent and those with a higher mind were part of Atlantis, what went wrong?

C: First of all, we weren't that cognizant of human nature. Where we came from, things were how they were "supposed to be." We didn't realize how primitive it was here. We didn't have any concepts of the greed, deceit, and aggression. We were pretty naive. We came in and set up this theocracy. We set up educational systems, and began disseminating spiritual knowledge. The mental bodies of the human kingdom were only beginning to develop at this time. We were using some pretty sophisticated technologies to raise the consciousness of the human kingdom. We were broadcasting, using crystals, pyramids, and geomagnetic grids. We were sending out seed thoughts, setting up structures in the collective psyche. It wasn't like creating, it was more like translating these mental structures from the higher dimensions. By tapping into our own higher selves, we would bring this information down onto this plane of existence. It was mostly done in pyramids, charging crystals with these thought patterns, setting up energy fields, and using geomagnetic lines of force as carrier waves. This is what your main focus of work was.

A: I've been told before that I was a communicator in Atlantis.

C: I'm seeing you were definitely involved with the communications project. Once in the body, you and I worked closely with one another. It was a huge undertaking. Once I got here, my creative juices were stimulated and I was more interested in the project. In fact, I became quite complacent with my relatively prestigious role. In spite of this, we had a great deal of regard and respect for one another, and worked well on the tasks at hand. Our main source of tension was over the amount and intensity of information and energy to be disseminated. With some reservations you agreed with me. Looking back now I'd have to agree with you; it was too much, too fast. I was in a hurry to get it over with so I could return to the inner planes.

We were very optimistic—and very naive—about the work we were doing. We didn't suspect that some of our own group would rebel, and we were not particularly concerned about the Lemurians' souls who were reincarnating in Atlantis and whose power was being threatened by our project. What happened was that some of the souls in our group had problems with power prior to coming to the Earth, and they aligned themselves with some of the Lemurians who wanted to undermine our work and take control. They began using the information and spiritual technology that we were implementing to serve their own end. There was an incredible psychic war. They used the power of the Fire Stone, a huge crystal, to perform a sort of black magic in order to try to control our minds and block the work we were doing. They were using the Earth's magnetic field as a carrier wave and it was so powerful that it disturbed the subtle energies of the planet causing great magnetic storms. The Fire Stone finally blew up causing great earthquakes, which destroyed most of the landmass of Atlantis.

So the work you were involved in was directly related to why things started to fall apart, but it was not your fault. However, you did feel you should have been able to do something to avert the rebellion, and this frustrated you. You were angry about what happened, about those who misused the power. You were also angry at yourself and at me. You assumed the responsibility for what went wrong because of your position as overseer. Consequently you made a vow to yourself that you were going to buckle down and work harder in the future.

A: Not to back you up, but how does Lemuria fit into all of this?

C: At the very beginning of life on this planet there were inner dimensional beings sent here to help create the life forms. Also, they were beings who had been insubordinate in another realm of existence. They were sent here to curtail their activities in that realm and also offer them an opportunity to rectify their behavior. The resentment they were carrying got bred into the animal life forms and became part of the lineage of the planet. To express their frustration at the work they had to do, they used animals to vent their aggressions. It's like they were sitting up there on the ethereal plane and using the animals like roosters are used in cock fighting. Their karma was to incarnate into those animal forms in order to evolve into a human form.

The biblical legend of Lucifer is a racial memory of these Lemurians. They were the fallen angels, inner-dimensional beings at odds with the Divine Plan who were sent here and given an opportunity to realign themselves.

A: But you feel their job, their intent, was to create Earth?

C: Well they were working with the etheric body of the planet to mold structures for the developing life forms. That was their job, that was their function, and many of them are still actually here, incarnate and still working off some of their karma. Not all of the original Lemurians remained rebellious. A great many realigned themselves with the Divine Plan and have returned to the inner planes where some of them are still working with the etheric energies of the planet.

A: An image I have is of the amount of love it must have taken to create our planet!

C: Well there are two sides to it. They were creators, but they had "fallen" in another situation, and they were sent here to make up for their mistakes, for the good of all, for the good of themselves.

Shall we return to your own progress? After this first major destruction of Atlantis, I see you plugging away in Egypt, getting right to work. Like you've just gotten a new office, organizing everything. I'm trying to get exactly what you were focusing on there. I'm looking at it to see if you're a man or a woman, and your energy is so balanced I really can't tell. I'm getting that you were both, in different lifetimes. There is one that I see, being a woman, and working just with other women. The women were trained more as the seers, receiving spiritual information from the inner planes. There was a lot of information that you were still trying to bring in from your work in Atlantis. Really fascinating work. It was the next step. You concentrated on this for a couple of lifetimes, not too unlike what you did in Atlantis. You were also working with the development of methods to record or depict this spiritual knowledge. A language of symbols was devised, and used in conjunction with crystals and gemstones to embody the information. By using these implements a person could learn how to tap into the level of consciousness where the spiritual knowledge existed.

In the life as a man, you and I worked more closely together. We were setting up and overseeing the initiations that took place in the pyramids. While you had been focusing on bringing in the spiritual knowledge and developing ways to encode that information, I had been concentrating on techniques for preparing the human nervous system and bio-psychic organisms to channel the increased amperage of cosmic energies. The initiations in the pyramids were a combination of our two fields of endeavor. This work was very intense; some people actually died or went crazy during the initiations inside the pyramids. For those who were successful, it was a big step in their spiritual unfoldment. The spiritual technology we developed in ancient Egypt was probably the most advanced and effective spiritual training ever employed on Earth. We had learned a great deal from our folly in Atlantis. Our work in Egypt was on a smaller and more focused scale. In some ways we might have overcompensated; the training in Egypt was very strict.

I'm seeing another life now. You spent some time in a matriarchal society, first as a shamaness. Many of the power-hungry souls from Atlantis incarnated as women in these matriarchal groups. Because you felt so responsible for what happened in Atlantis, you came to these matriarchal cultures wanting to help balance the power structure. In the first life you were a shamaness, but left that lifetime feeling you didn't have enough impact on the society. You came back in another lifetime as a man, trying to help the men evolve within the power structure.

A: I've always had a memory of a life like this. This is the life-time where I was killed by a spear.

C: This was a very difficult task, and there was some satisfaction because change was created, but the fabric of the culture was destroyed when the men finally rebelled and gained their freedom. Originally the matriarchal culture was fairly egalitarian. You came in when the power structure began to be unbalanced, when the souls from Atlantis began to dominate it. The same people in Atlantis were also key players in these lifetimes, so you had karma with these people. We were men together in this life—actually for several lives—and joined forces to eventually overthrow the power-hungry souls incarnated in the women who sat at the pinnacle of the matriarchal hierarchy. And yes, in your first life as a man in this context you were killed for speaking up against the abuse that, as men, we were subjected to.

The next life I'm seeing is in ancient Greece. Your goal was to create a spiritual balance between humanity and nature, to create a social structure that would reflect that bal-ance and embody a sense of the sublime. It was a beautiful culture, but of course it changed with time and devolved into a more philosophical or intellectual sterility with the stoicism of the Greek philosophers, until it was literally destroyed by the Christians.

In this one life that I'm seeing, you were a priestess in a temple. The setting is very beautiful. The temple is on a mountainside and there is a sense of refinement and harmony in the way the priests and priestesses lived. It was like a monastery, and we only mingled with the common people during religious festivals and ceremonies. You were somewhat rigid and strict; it reminds me of the way you were in Egypt.

I was a priest who was caught up in the romance of the idealized beauty and harmony of the cultural setting. I tugged at you to "let your hair down" and open your heart more. Though we were celibate, I had fallen in love with you. Intuiting the sublime qualities of our celestial home and past together, I was projecting the inner spiritual love and beauty onto you. The more I did this, the more rigid and business-like you were, thus creating a "forbidden fruit" dynamic, which only spurred my love for you.

Due to your extensive background in various religious systems, you had an innate predilection to repress your human "instincts" and keep yourself busy to avoid your emotional nature. It seems like this vehement repression of your instinctual nature goes back to Atlantis and the destructive results of human emotions and drives you witnessed there. You worked hard in Egypt and other religious lives to rid yourself of these "human" qualities. Meanwhile, I had spent lifetimes in the Tantric tradition in India where sexuality and human emotions were employed as an integral part of religious practices.

What I'm seeing now seems a little strange. I feel self-conscious or embarrassed to admit it. I am so overwrought with my "love" for you that I challenge the tradition. I'm someone who has a lot of power in the temple. I reason that the gods and goddesses on Mount Olympus have mates and, under certain circumstances, when blessed by the gods the priests and priestesses ought to be able to mate. I stage a ceremony to petition the approval of the gods. I see myself looking up into your eyes as I sacrifice a goat. You are not condoning this; I've placed you in a very uncomfortable situation. Soon after the goat is sacrificed, the sky clouds up, and it begins to thunder. This is interpreted by all present that the gods are showing their approval.

In public you feign our "marriage," but in private you completely resist it, physically and emotionally. For me it is very painful. Aside from my self-centered investment in my desires for you, my love wants to feel you open. In a way it is like the spring sun shining on the buds of a beautifully flowering tree. I want to share in your blossoming. It's like when I used to play with you on the inner planes before we came to Earth trying to get you to lighten up. From your side, you feel forced, and resent me for using my power to invade your private life. And we live out the rest of that life in a stalemate.

The next life I see is a rural setting. Looks like Europe. I'm seeing a scene where you are a teenager or young adult working in a hayfield. There is a boy you work with that you are close to. It's your present husband. Don is very playful. He charms you with his warm and friendly nature. He is very playful and seduces you into playing with him. I see an image of you and him fooling around in a big stack of hay in the field.

Through Don's warmth and gentle loving nature, you allowed yourself the freedom to become a woman, a mother, and a wife. The conflict between accomplishment on the planet and indulging yourself in the emotions of a woman was the issue here. But you were long overdue in exploring this side of yourself. As a woman in that life you enjoyed your role, but there was a drive within that you could not realize within the cultural setting, a drive that you did not really understand in that life.

In your next life you are a man, a minister in a small village. Here you are overbearing and plagued with the feeling that it's your job to save these people. This causes you much frustration. Things seem insurmountable, since you have lost a conscious connection with all the knowledge you brought with you to the planet. All you have to work with is Christian dogma, and you use great effort trying to make it satisfy your hunger for spiritual knowledge.

You have a family life—a wife, a daughter, a son—and your life is very regimented. I think this was a reaction to the dichotomy between your responsibilities as a spiritual being and a physical being. You don't allow yourself to be vulnerable to the feeling side of yourself in this life. The part of you that is strict is projected into the punitive aspects of the Christian religion.

The plot is beginning to thicken now: your human identity is getting denser, thicker. You're in Holland. A man again. By now, being a man is beginning to become associated with being in control, while being a woman is becoming associated with feelings and instincts. You have something to do with printing books, printing "The Word of God." You are a devout religious man. I see you praying a lot and taking your religion very seriously. A little bit of distaste here from having to be a minister the lifetime before. You feel inadequate to do what you think you need to do. You need to feel you're being effective. You don't get that need satisfied, no matter how hard you try. Printing Bibles is the only thing you can come up with. But you're still not happy with what you're doing. I see this really becomes a problem for you. You're very aggravated; it eats at you. I see you drinking alcohol to let the pressure off, and afterward you feel more disgusted, creating even more frustration, creating a cycle.

Again there is a family, but you're caught up in this process, and you're not available to them. You die in that lifetime with remorse that you weren't more available to your family. Your wife was very loyal and you regret not having been more loving. Interestingly enough, you don't seem to regret not having been there for your children, just not having been there for your wife.

After you die in that life, something happens in between lives. Some kind of communication breaks through your Earth identity from your higher self. Like a puncture. I see that you function on this level in setting up for your next lifetime. You need to get out of the Christian dogma and gravitate toward the East. Life as a man. You become a Tibetan recluse. Early in your life you live in a Buddhist monastery, but later you go into a cave. We are together again in this life. I am your teacher in the monastery. In this context I am able to express the love I feel for you in a "spiritual" way. That is satisfying for me, but you have mixed reactions. The love between a student and teacher in the Tibetan tradition is a very important part of the spiritual transmission that takes place. As such it has become an integral part of the myth and ritual. So here you are again in a situation where you feel you are being forced to love me. Your reaction in this life is affected by our life together in Greece. You do allow yourself to feel the "spiritual love," but you are still somewhat guarded in our personal interactions, which in this life are minimal, and I am much less attached to the personal aspects of our relationship.

When you leave the monastery to live in a cave, you spend the rest of that life reconnecting with your higher self, making it more available to you on a physical level. You get a good hit of Bodhisattva—the desire to reach enlightenment so you can better help other people. Your goal for reaching enlightenment is to help others work toward spiritual fulfillment.

After you spend this lifetime developing those abilities, you come back—again in Tibet—as a teacher, a man. And you get a reprieve from that nagging sense of having to do something, because you have a religious structure that's been going on for hundreds of hundreds of years. It is very similar to the Greek and Egyptian structures. So you're back doing the work you do best. In this Buddhist experience, there is still this segregation between you the spiritual and you the emotional being. So in this life you get rewarded for letting go, detaching yourself from the emotional side, which feels good to you. You spend three lifetimes doing this.

By the end of this time, you've managed to disentangle yourself from karmic patterns. Well actually, you've stepped out of it, gotten your breath so to speak. And you've become more focused, but the karmic energy is still there; you will still have to come back and face it.

Just getting a geographical location. I'm not familiar with it. Looks like Morocco, near Spain, northwestern Africa—is that Morocco? Hmm, nomadic desert people. I can't tell if you're a man or a woman again; I see both. I think you come back first as a woman. But there is a bleed through between lifetimes. There is an awareness, a kind of telepathic awareness with both lifetimes. I'm not sure, maybe it will become more clear as we go on.

So you come back as a woman. In this culture, there is a quality of sacredness. Life is a sacred event. In the things you do—packing tents, moving beneath the starry heavens in the nomadic life—there is harmony, a pristine quality. It's a very noble and very beautiful existence. And as a woman in that life you maintain your spiritual centeredness. I don't get a sense that you're married in the normal sense. I see you as part of the entourage. I don't know if this is a harem. It seems there's that kind of quality. If so, I don't see a strong sexual energy to it. He must respect your spiritual side. He is like the leader. It's not a love relationship. But he looks up to you, turns to you for advice. He is not anybody you know now.

In your next life, it's a little harder for you being the man. I get a sense of you looking back to that life as a woman, trying to draw support from that experience. There is some sense of alienation or power struggle with you and someone in that tribe. It's your father. I think your father in this particular lifetime is an important person in the tribe. I'm seeing you leaving on a horse, and you don't have his approval or blessing. I guess what you're doing is breaking tradition. I see you riding across the desert on this horse. You want to go to Europe. There is a nobility to your life that hasn't prepared you for some of the hardships you experience on your journey. You're doing some kind of manual labor in order to take the boat across the Mediterranean. I see you digging, moving rocks. It's very difficult for you to be treated like a common laborer. But there is something that allows you to maintain your integrity.

I see southern France. This is an experience and an adventure. I think somehow your family sent you some money. I see you now going to school. It's knowledge you're after. I see you writing. Somehow there is a way to get messages to your family. It doesn't seem like your family is nomadic in this lifetime.

In the end you go back home. There is no place for you. You didn't get what you wanted. You'd hoped for some kind of great knowledge, and you didn't get it. When you come back, you and your father have words. He says, "I told you so," and you have to swallow your pride to go back. There is this real dilemma of what to do: the need for satisfaction; the need to *do* something. Somehow your family is wealthy, so there is no need for you to work. There is nowhere to put your energy. I get the sense that you spend the rest of your life just spinning your wheels.

What I'm going to do now is see where all this goes. Umm. I see a series of lifetimes where you plug into the European culture again. You get into the church, politics. More frustration. You are bogged down in bureaucracy. I get a sense that in your present life you are still bogged down. Do you get that sense?

A: I'm not sure.

C: I'm seeing another life in America. You are an Indian woman somewhere around Texas or New Mexico. I come across you as I'm riding south for the winter months. I'm a trapper, a drifter. You're camped by a stream; you have a baby with you. You are frightened and timid when I approach. I know how to speak some of your language, and I'm dressed in buckskins nd moccasins. I've lived with the Indians and know their ways. Your people, or the small band of them you were traveling with, were killed by soldiers. You and your baby alone managed to escape their wrath.

You are very frightened, but because I know your language, because of my dress, and because of the inner knowledge of who we have been in other lives together, you have some trust in me. Because of your situation, you end up traveling with me for the winter. You and your baby ride with me on my horse. Eventually we become lovers, but I am a white man and you have an inbred hatred of white men. Your love for me feels like a betrayal of your Indian heritage. So you hold back. You're afraid you will never be able to return to your people if they find out you have been with a white man. And so here you are again in a situation where you are more or less forced to love me, for survival reasons. But the love goes against the grain of your morals and values; this sounds familiar also. I love you very much. I admire your people and their ways, and so to have an Indian woman is for me the perfect mate.

We must have been together for a number of years because I see your little boy at the age of three or four. I am very fond of him. He's a real little Indian brave. Sometimes he comes trapping and hunting with me. On one occasion I was setting a trap and he wandered off and got bit by a young rattlesnake.

You never forgave me for your son's death and decided to return to your people. I wandered the prairies and woodlands for many years filled with remorse, grieving over the loss of you and your son, who I also loved deeply.

So we have met once again. We must be making some progress because you're not in a position where you feel forced to love me, and it only hurts a little bit to feel my love for you. But I am still telling you to lighten up. I'll have to work on that some more.

What you have to express and offer to the Earth, the Earth is not ready for at this time. You see your own process on Earth go down and up. The planet as a whole has these same cycles, only it cycles much slower than you do. I myself, have the same sense of frustration and hopelessness. But it helps me a great deal to do readings like this for people. I see so much of myself in others—it's much easier to see things in others than to look at yourself. Often I see that people like ourselves are just here as a balance, we're not really here at this point to make it all better. Our presence here is like a lead keel on a sailboat. Our primary task is to maintain our spiritual center, to focus on being a ballast of light, to just be a stabilizing and guiding force while the winds of change blow.

Just remember who you are, rather than being preoccupied with judging yourself on the affect you have on the world. Can you see the difference you could make by just being in that frame of mind rather than trying to make things happen, and then becoming frustrated, when you fail to create the affect that you wanted?

A: If I've had all these spiritual past lives, how come I don't remember all this stuff, how come I can't channel this knowledge now?

C: My sense is that there is a certain level of frustration because you don't have the far-reaching affects you would like to have to satisfy your need to feel you're being effective in the spiritual upliftment of the planet. So you have cut off that part of yourself. I don't think you understand what I'm saying.

You are frustrated, and that's uncomfortable, so you repress it. Because your frustration is directly related to the spiritual part of yourself, it is being cut off and repressed also. If you become aware of the information, you'll release all the past frustrations that go with it. In this present lifetime you are hiding out because of the frustration and not knowing what to do about it. You're unwilling to realize your full potential, so you're just keeping busy. I get a sense that concentrating on your family isn't only a diversion. I don't want it to sound so negative.

A: Maybe my resolution is that since I won't work on the spiritual problems facing me, I've decided to work on the family, Earth-type problems.

C: I see you stay busy to keep the anxiety and frustration at bay. I'm getting the sense that's not as easy as it used to be. Perhaps this reading is corresponding to an inner urge to reconnect with those spiritual dimensions of yourself.

RENE

Rene is a surgical nurse and mother of a 10-year-old boy. She also plays the cello. Her husband Joe is a metal sculptor. Because Joe is home most of the time working in his studio, and because of his intense jealousy, Rene feels trapped and oppressed in her day-to-day life with Joe. One way she has dealt with her feelings was to have an affair with another man, which lasted fourteen of her twenty-year marriage to Joe.

Rene had come to me on several occasions for healing work and this reading came about as a suggestion on my part during a healing session. Rene had terminated her affair with her lover of fourteen years and was clinging desperately to her marriage, which was threatening to fall apart. She developed a severe yeast infection that later gave way to irregular or chronic vaginal bleeding. These symptoms ceased after I helped her integrate her feelings for her alienated lover and her resentment of her husband (or more correctly her attachment to the security and power struggle of their relationship) for separating her from the more emotionally satisfying and sexually fulfilling affair with her lover. Her symptoms were effectively keeping her from having sex with her husband, Rene's way of seeking revenge.

After her symptoms disappeared, she soon began bleeding from her nipples and developed lumps in her breasts. She came to me again. We worked more with her "bleeding heart" and the threat to her femininity by the emotional dynamics of her marriage and the loss of her lover. During this session she also asked me why she was so fascinated by her affiliation with an American Indian medicine man and the rituals she was learning from him. I could see she was empowered by this shaman. By aligning herself with this powerful individual, she was vicariously inflated and acting out her own need to feel powerful. I simply told her that it had something to do with her desire for power, and suggested we do a reading to explore it, and also to look at her relationship with her husband.

As Rene sat across from me during the reading, she maintained her usual arrogant and nonchalant expression, occasionally breaking into a rather diabolical laugh. She appeared to be completely unaffected by what to me would seem like alarming information in the reading. She refused a copy of the tape of the session when we were finished and departed with a cheerful smile of denial. Her reading is a good example of a powerful soul from the higher dimensions who has been sent here to learn from her misuse of power.

C: To begin, I'm going to tune into you first and get an overview of your soul, and then we'll move on to look at your relationship with Joe. Would that be all right?

R: Yeah, that sounds good.

C: As I look for a metaphoric image to characterize some of your core qualities I feel this strong aggressive energy. I see a shield and spear, and sense a real challenging energy. There's anger here. The challenging energy is your way of expressing anger. You are angry about having been sent to Earth. Let's back up here and find out why you were sent here.

R: Yeah, the very beginnings, huh? (laughter)

C: I see your soul as a young adult who has just entered the work force, so to speak. You're very aggressive, a lot of male, *macho* energy. You have a predilection to run the whole show. It's like you were being hired as a minor executive in a large corporation and you came in with an inflated sense of self-importance and act like you're going to take over the whole operation. Of course this is going to create repercussions in the system because you're ignoring the pecking order and the process of checks and balances in the power structure. For a corporation to function, there needs to be a chain of command. It's like the physical body with its brain and central nervous system. If one nerve plexus doesn't cooperate with the higher functions of the nervous system maintaining homeostasis, there will be disharmony in the body, leading to disease of the organism. So this is essentially what was happening with your attempt to express your will and dominate the larger process you were involved with on a soul level.

Those beings who were responsible for your guidance and education decided you needed some strong medicine because you weren't in the habit of listening to them or accepting their suggestions.

R: Headstrong? (laughter)

C: Yes. You figured you had your training and you had your degree, so to speak, and now you were just going to go out there and take the world by the horns. So you see there is a problem with relating to authority and a drive to have power over others.

Over the years I've arbitrarily developed a language to describe what I experience on the inner planes. I'm sure it's not true in the sense that I must be seeing only a minute portion of all that is really out there. Nonetheless, I have discerned there are various levels on the inner dimensions and there is a connotation of a hierarchical structure. A being like yourself, who I see coming from what I call the sixth dimension—near the top—has a greater influence in the cosmic organism than a being from a lower dimension. Hence, your misuse of power or use of cosmic forces for your own self-aggrandizement, has more far-reaching effects. Many of the higher-dimensional beings I have worked with are here on the Earth for similar reasons.

R: There's a lot of us being chastised, and going back to school with this. I know.

C: Yes. The physical world is very concrete. What you do with energy here comes right back to you. It's a real good place to experience the results of your actions, and learn how to articulate your use of energy.

Anyway, it angered you to be sent to this lowly world. It was a big blow to your inflated self-image. That means "war," in your way of seeing things. You were left with a lot of resentment at your mentors on the inner planes and it expresses itself by challenging authority and rebelling against them and their plan for you. One way you have acted this out is by sabotaging your own spiritual growth. There is an implication that the authority—your spiritual mentors or Universal Law—in the situation wants you to grow and evolve so you can come back to your native dimension and do your work. So you have rebelled by resisting your own growth. Can you relate to that at all?

R: No! I don't know what that implies because I have this incredible yearning to advance in that direction. So I don't see how I sabotage the spiritual growth.

C: Maybe we will see it when we move on to look at your past lives. Obviously this rebelliousness and sabotaging is an unconscious process, a shadow figure in your being. So it's possible that because you have been exiled from your native dimension there is a part of yourself that longs to return, but there is this other part of yourself that is angry. Let's see how this might play out as we look at some of your past lives.

There was a network of beings who came to the planet during the Atlantean era. For some of the beings it was an expression of their desire to help the planet. For others, like yourself, it was an opportunity to redeem themselves, a chance to overcome the inhibitions and difficulties they were having in their native planes of existence.

R: They were doing what they chose to do, you think?

C: Well, no. Beings like yourself were given the opportunity (laughter) to come here and help with the spiritual work being done on this planet. At first, you refused to incarnate here. You stayed on the astral plane and did "office work."

But once you were involved in the Earth plane you were caught in this downward spiral, so you couldn't resist incarnating here for very long. You came to the planet in the later part of the Atlantean period. (Long pause)

I feel uncomfortable telling you what I'm seeing now. If this information is helpful to you, by all means take it for what it's worth. Please don't feel there is any pressure from me to have you accept my vision.

R: OK.

C: Once in the body you were angry and rebellious and chose to throw a monkey wrench in the intense spiritual work that was being done on the planet. You aligned yourself with human beings and other power-hungry inner-dimensional souls who were attempting to overthrow the theocracy that had been established in Atlantis by the network of higher-dimensional souls. A tremendous psychic war ensued. I see you gloating over your ability to wield the spiritual powers we were working with in a destructive way. Incidentally, I was one of the beings endeavoring to maintain the theocracy and carry out the work we had come here to do.

You and your cohorts were successful in causing the demise of the Atlantean project, and after that life you felt rather omnipotent. You reveled in the sense of power it gave you. You were challenging your mentors and guides on the inner planes. It's as if you're saying, "Go ahead, try to make me behave. I dare you!" At that point your guides decided to back off and just let you act out your will to power. They realized any further attempts on their part to give you suggestions would only become fuel for your fire. You continued to incarnate into the remaining lands of Atlantis until its final destruction in 10,000 B.C.

So here you are now, firmly entrenched in the karma of the Earth. You're here in a big way. Let's see where you go next. Aside from the cultural centers that were built over a considerable period of time on the continent of Atlantis, and some of the spiritual outposts of the much older Lemurian culture, the rest of the human species existed in primitive tribes scattered over various parts of the Earth. The social structure of these tribes was based on the cycles of nature. They worshipped the forces of Mother Nature, in both her life-sustaining and life-threatening aspects.

The great number of souls who lost their lives in the final destruction of Atlantis were forced to come back into these primitive tribes or enter into the esoteric spiritual communities in such places as Egypt. As a group they mostly decided to do their own thing. There were not a lot of parents available for the larger number of souls who were disembodied in the destruction of Atlantis, but the souls who were drunk with their own power forced their way back onto the planet, eager to indulge themselves in the glory of their power. They incarnated into female bodies in the matriarchal tribes in Old Europe. The fabric of the culture of these primitive tribes was drastically altered. What was previously a peaceful and egalitarian social structure became more and more hierarchical. A warrior and hunting goddess became a prominent deity. Women, identifying with the power of the goddess, lorded over the male members of society and repressed many of the feminine aspects of the female members of the tribe.

R: The male becomes more oppressed? Umm. How could the matriarch become more militant then, matriarchal militancy?

C: The souls who were inebriated with power incarnated into women's bodies. The desire for control and power often expresses itself in a militant manner. The association of masculine energy with authority on a cosmic level was threatening to these souls who were now inflating themselves with the power and divinity of the goddess. This was acted out culturally in the abuse and oppression of men.

This lifetime finds you in your glory. Here you are in a social structure that supports your predilection to be in control and revel in a sense of power. Even though you're swollen with pride over success, I'm getting the impression there is an undercurrent of, well not sadness, but remorse. That's it. On a deeper level of your being, you know what you are doing is not right. You're acting this out and getting away with it, but you know you are doing something wrong. But when you feel this remorse, you have a defensive response. This creates a split in the identity you are developing here on the planet. One side is connected to the conscience and your true or spiritual potential and destiny, and the other side is related to your arrogance, anger, and rebelliousness. I can't help but think this is going to become the main dynamic acting itself out in your future lives.

R: The separation of the conscious powerful . . . the . . . the . . . a conscious one who misused power, from the subconscious spiritual core?

C: Yes, and as the more rebellious part of yourself feels split off from your inner, or true self, the more insecure and defensive it becomes. Although it would do anything to guard itself from the realization that it stands on shaky ground, on some level it knows its days are numbered, and it is at odds with the Way of the Spirit or Universal Law. So it has to fight hard and create delusional systems to maintain its sense of identity. It needs to be more aggressive and defensive to struggle for its survival. You see, whatever identities we assume or create are instilled with the instinct for survival.

So, I see that you have several lifetimes in this matriarchal culture, you lock into it because it's a good way for you to express what you want to accomplish on the planet.

R: Using the power issues?

C: OK. There's a positive side to this—forgive me if I'm sounding entirely negative. You got an opportunity to do things the way you wanted to do them. That's how we learn. You were one of the women in power creating the kind of situation you wanted to and that gave you some self-esteem, a sense of accomplishment, without the spiritual authority figures breathing down your neck and judging you. However, there was some internal friction with the conscience side of yourself. Nonetheless you were having the opportunity to act out these impulses and desires, that's why you were sent here, to get a chance to act it out and learn from the results. So it's perfect, it's what you needed to do.

Deep down inside, you have a fear that your mentors are judging you for your actions, but let me remind you that you are, and will always be, your own worst judge. It's your reaction to your conscience, hence the defenses and delusional attributes of your identity, that are binding you to the karma for your rebellious and power-oriented actions. The war you are fighting is within yourself, not with spiritual authority figures or the Universal Law as something external to yourself.

Well let's see what comes up next. I'm seeing an image of you by a river. You are there with other women washing clothes on rocks. It seems like Guatemala to me, a Mayan lifetime. You're heavyset with big powerful arms. You resent having to do this work. There aren't many opportunities for a woman to be in power in this culture. The men are the priests and astrologers. A few women are seers and priestesses, but for the most part the men are in control. You have a lot of resentment about that. You want to be in power. So you don't really partake in the social structure. You refuse to support it. You spend all your time in silent rebellion against the ways of that lifetime. You waste the whole life, losing the opportunity that each earthly life offers for spiritual advancement and the shedding of inhibiting habits and attitudes. It looks like I'm seeing this life as an example of the result of the matriarchal lives.

R: Just feeling stymied?

C: Yeah, let's move on and see what else comes. I'm having a little difficulty discerning if you're a man or a woman. I see. You're a woman, but you want to be a man. You're young, a tomboy, late teenager. I see you driving a 1934 Ford pickup truck in a prairie setting. You're a cowgirl. You live on a cattle ranch and have a conflicting relationship with your father. He's the strong silent type, very solid and rigid. He's like hardwood. He's not oppressive in the sense that he tries to control you, but you engage him in a power struggle. You actually try to control him, to challenge him. But he doesn't budge; he's steadfast.

You're an attractive young woman and enjoy giving the boys in town a hard time. You're a fiery little lady and you turn your encounters with the opposite sex into fights. You have all these men pursuing you and get pleasure out of fighting them off. It's like you use your sexual attractiveness to torture them. So you see, your desire for power has become a sexual issue. When you feel like it you choose the pick of the litter, but you don't really open your heart to any of them. You enjoy hurting them and staying in control.

I'm seeing later in that life that you meet Joe (Rene's present husband). All of a sudden you have met someone who is as stubborn and unmovable as your father. Your father, and then Joe in that life, were men you couldn't control, so they held a certain fascination for you.

Joe is someone who has come from out of the area. You were vulnerable to him because of previous lifetimes and he proves to be a formidable opponent in the war of love. You get married to him, but are basically at odds with one another the whole life. The struggle is very much like what you had with your father. There's something you were trying to do to him. You want to control him, but he is staunch, steadfast, and sticks by his guns. His energy reminds me of an Aikido master. Have you ever seen a number of men try to move an Aikido master when he is demonstrating the grounding energy?

R: Yeah.

C: Well Joe is like that, he's rooted and unmovable. You try to get his goat by having affairs with other men. But he's tenacious and doesn't let go of his hold on you. No matter what you do, you are unable to break his hold on you. It's like the ultimate challenge, a fight to the bitter end. Well I'm sure you can recognize these patterns with Joe, and of course this lifetime is just prior to your present life. Let's go back now and look at your history with Joe.

[I didn't tell Rene this, but I saw that Joe, in a fit of jealousy, had killed her in that life because of her wanton infidelity. In their present relationship, Joe is terribly dependent on her emotionally. Rene feels obligated to take care of him. Though she pushes it to the limit, she must feel intimidated by him, and afraid that he could take her life again if she tries to leave him. This is a good example of where the common "eye for an eye" meaning of karma doesn't really fit. Karma, as I often see it, is simply doing what we have done before. It's being stuck in a rigid way of perceiving the world and acting in prescribed manners.]

R: Yeah, the power issue seems to have developed into—

C: It's come down to a one-to-one relationship with a man.

R: Yeah.

C: As I trace your history with Joe, we will have to go back to a particular period in matriarchal times. Joe was one of your male servants, but even then you were unable to control him. You know it would be much more meaningful for you to allow me to regress you back to this lifetime. I would also put aside whatever suspicion you might have about me projecting these strange things onto you. I believe these experiences are really germane to your psychology as a woman, and it would be good for you to see for yourself. I'll just sketch it briefly, and if you want to, we can do a regression at another time.

The men were forced into a position of subservience. They were kept like caged animals for the most part and used for mating and hard work.

R: Is this like the Amazon women the Greeks wrote about?

C: Exactly, they weren't making that up. In essence the men were used and abused sexually and emotionally. In fact it was taboo for a woman to allow herself to feel love for a man. You see that would have been a threat to the power structure; it would have undermined the supremacy of the women. So the social structure deemed that a woman had to repress part of her feminine nature, and the nurturing and caring that would come into play with the opposite sex. There was severe punishment for transgressions of this taboo. I've done workshops and private sessions with women who refused to talk about what they experienced in their past-life regressions to these times because of the nature of the punishments to women and the cruelty to men. These often included castration for the man, and the mutilation of a woman's sexual organs if she was caught succumbing to her instincts to love a man. So you see, that ancient war between the sexes began here. There is a fear of women that lurks in the collective unconscious of the race from these times. Women were also punished for their feelings of intimacy and nurturance in regard to men. This is really tricky.

R: That's interesting because I've always had the feeling that Joe and I were working on healing something on a global level, between men and women, and that's why we needed to stay together and work this thing out. I thought it had to do with male energy, I never thought it had to do with female power.

C: Well, I might comment that what you are calling female power is really more male energy. The Amazon women weren't really expressing feminine energy. The power they wielded was more like the negative expression of male energy that dominates our world today. This is obvious in what I see as a resurgence of this Amazon element in the feminist movement. In general, militant feminists are fighting for the right to compete with men in a man's world and are actually devaluing feminine values. But let's not get sidetracked here.

Getting back to your relationship with Joe. You had control over his physical body, but not over his emotional and mental self. And that was the challenge, and that's the key to what has locked you into your karma with Joe. It's like a prizefighter who has gone through his career and there is only one person he has been unable to beat. So his whole career as a fighter and his self-esteem become dependent on whether he can beat this guy. And for you the issue is whether you are a powerful being or not. You have an identity based on being a powerful being and you are fighting to validate it. Joe had become the opponent you felt you had to conquer in order to prove yourself and uphold your identity.

I'm seeing that there is another aspect to your relationship. It's like being a woman from a wealthy family who marries someone from a low social standing to spite her family. Joe is not a soul from the inner dimensions like yourself. By attaching yourself to him you can rebel against your spiritual heritage.

R: Like choosing the Earth over the spiritual?

C: Yes, that's part of your fascination with Joe. And let me remind you that in these early lives on the planet you were creating the generic qualities of your earthbound identity.

So for Joe, back in this life, he had to close down all of his sensitivities and vulnerableness to survive in the matriarchal environment and his relationship with you. He becomes a tough guy on the outside, but emotionally he remains like a little boy who needs nurturing and love. These have become generic patterns in his character.

The next life I see is in India, a culture in which the women are very repressed. Joe is happy being a male and king of the castle. You are forced by social position to wait on him and take care of him, but you never give your heart to him. You concentrate your resentment for your social role on him. You do it insidiously, but you harbor much malice toward him. On a personal level he represents the oppressive aspects of the culture. You express your resentment by keeping to yourself, living an internal life.

R: Do you think this is a recent lifetime?

C: No. This is in the ninth century. One thing I see about karmic patterns is that they do not necessarily follow chronological sequences. It's like dreams. Certain themes run through them, but this has nothing to do with linear time. And this seems to be a theme in your relationships with Joe, the swinging of the pendulum of who is the one in control. In this life in India, there is no possibility of leaving him. There's no such thing as divorce, so you have no option other than gritting your teeth and putting up with your lot in life. You're trapped in a subservient role just like he was in the matriarchal life. In a twisted sort of way, your ability to stay there and hold your ground in an oppressive situation is another source of power. Your stubborn strength to bear adversity in that life is being carried over into your present relationship with Joe. Even though you feel oppressed and unfulfilled emotionally in your present relationship with him, you are trying to prove your strength by staying with him. You're going to fight to the finish, and win. Your present life with Joe is a crucial one. Neither of you is being constrained by social roles. You both have an opportunity to let go of the power struggle and go on to grow in other ways in new relationships.

The next life I see is in Germany during the Industrial Revolution. Again you're a woman, and he's the man. Joe is a metalworker, and his temperament is very rigid. You live in a small village. You're not German, you're from Brussels, or something like that. Your family has moved there. You're in your late teens and still living with your parents. Joe is older, living on his own. Your fascination with Joe is partially founded on your rebellion against your very orthodox family. Joe is a lower-class, blue-collar worker, and you are in some kind of college or conservatory studying classical music. That's why your parents have moved to this town.

You actively pursue Joe. I see you drinking in pubs and indulging yourself with him and his working-class friends. Once again, you are in a cultural setting where you want to act in ways that are taboo for a woman. Hanging out in bars and drinking a lot is one of the ways you vent your desires. In this context you're also quite promiscuous.

Later you have children, and this stimulates another aspect of your being. It brings out the nurturing and loving part of yourself that we haven't talked much about today. The sincerity and the heart begin to reconnect you with your inner spiritual self.

R: That's really interesting, I haven't chosen that at all in my present life.

C: You mean with your son now ?

R: Yeah, even before he was born, I knew that I didn't want to do that in this lifetime.

C: OK. I see that when you did that in the life in Germany, it really challenged the part of you that wanted freedom and was into power. Even though you began to open your heart with your children, being a mother was associated with orthodox values and social limitations, things you have come to abhor. And Joe once again is a target for your resentment at these constraining forces. Even though you remain married to him for the duration of that German life, you never open your heart to him and you continue to butt heads with him.

It seems we're going back in time now. I see you as a veiled woman in what looks like a Moslem life. You have dark piercing eyes. You live in this big palace with round domes on it. You are somehow related to the family that is in charge, the local royal family. In this culture you are forced to live a cloistered existence. You're not even allowed to go out into the street without being chaperoned. It looks like a perfect place for you to continue acting out your feelings of oppression and constraint. On a conscious level in this life, you more or less comply with the social norm. But inwardly you are seething.

In this life, Joe is a soldier, a horseman. I see that he has a large saber hanging from his belt. In fact, he's also a blacksmith or a person who makes swords, and this is a prestigious art. So in his own right he has a certain standing in society and is justly proud. He's like a palace guard and you see one another from time to time and exchange intense eye contact but never have the opportunity to speak. There's a great deal of sexual energy that you and he share just through your eye contact and in your fantasies. The setting is too repressive and your desires for one another are never consummated. But years of passion and psychic intensity are indulged in by both of you. Your fantasy romance with him, however, serves as an outlet for rebellious feelings and wanton desires.

Eventually your parents choose a husband for you. You hate your husband and long to be with your fantasy lover, Joe. In a twisted sort of way, in this life you and Joe experience your love for one another as you have never been able to while together because of the power struggles. Going all the way back to your first life together in the matriarchal setting, your nurturing and loving sentiments for one another were repressed and eclipsed by your defenses and struggle to control each other. In the matriarchal society you were not able to allow yourself to be vulnerable to your love because of the social repercussions, and Joe also had to defend his vulnerability in the situation. The dynamics that resulted have dominated your subsequent relationships. So the spark of love has never been allowed to burn. Only in your fantasies in this Moslem life have you opened your heart to Joe.

R: So you think that Joe has been part of the spiritual sabotage that you mentioned in the beginning.

C: Well if we agree that the purpose for your coming to Earth was to overcome your defiance and craving for power so that you can cultivate your innate spirituality and return to your native dimension to continue your work there, would you say the patterns of your relationships with Joe are supporting or working against that goal?

R: Yeah, I'm locked into this power struggle and don't have the energy to do the other. Yeah, I've been becoming more aware of that on a conscious level.

C: In your relationships with Joe, the power you hold over him is the potential of a loving relationship.

R: Yeah. I, I, I don't. . . . Yeah, he's real locked into the emotional entanglement. But I don't sense that there's a. . . . You talk about how there's been more attachment on my part to the struggle than to the love, I think that's the same for him too.

C: Well, I agree. It's come down to that. But the power you have over him is his desire to love you. Let's look at it from another perspective. You are a soul from a higher dimension and naturally carry a certain responsibility and a certain, well, light or spiritual awareness. And you are interacting with a human soul who is attracted to that light, the charisma of that light.

R: Yeah, because I provide the impetus for growth. I provide . . . yeah.

C: Yes, but you're not being very responsible with your power. You use it as bait, but you don't care about him. You just keep leading him on. You're playing with him. You keep dangling the carrot in front of him, but you never give him the carrot.

R: Well, I think he's getting what he needs out of it. He's getting tremendous growth out of his relationship with me.

C: Only in a backward way.

R: Because of the struggle? Getting it the hard way? But thinking of all the karmic things that we have had for so many lifetimes it seems like the struggle is getting easier. The progress is being made, I mean we can both see that. It does seem like there is a way to go, I mean, just a. . . .

C: What if in the beginning of your relationships with Joe, back in the matriarchy, you would have been more responsible, being a soul from a higher realm and being more conscious of the ways of the universe.

R: I wasn't aware of that.

C: On a soul level you were aware of that. If you had the desire to act on your knowledge, how would your relationship with him be different? You claim he is growing from his entanglement with you.

R: Oh, well my vulnerability would have been more evident. I suppose, yeah.

C: And how would that have affected Joe differently? How would that have affected his growth?

R: Well he may not have even been interested in me, I mean I don't know whether he. . . . Oh I don't know, it may have involved more of a love relationship than a power struggle if I had more vulnerability. Yeah, I was thinking that might not have been what he wanted either. He might have just been interested in the struggle, but I don't think so. I think he would have been more interested in the love and vulnerability.

C: So, do you think it would have been a more positive learning experience then? You know what I'd like to do? I'd like to give you a homework assignment.

R: (diabolical laughter)

C: I'd like you to write a story about how your relationships would have been different if, instead of acting out the rebellious part of your soul, you would have acted from the part of your soul that wants to evolve spiritually and accept the responsibility of being a soul from a higher dimension here on the Earth plane. Focus on what Joe would have learned from you and how he would be a different person today. Also write about your own feelings so you can decide if basing a relationship on love and caring is more fulfilling than one based on power struggles. Does that sound like a good homework assignment?

R: (more diabolical laughter)

C: You say you and Joe are learning through all of this, and yes that's probably true. But did you really have to go through all of this, did Joe really need to be drawn into your desire to act out your rebelliousness and be entangled in this power struggle with you for all these lives? I really think Joe was actually after the promise of love implied in your relationship with him. And, believe it or not, you were too.

Well, so far we've only seen relationships in which you have been involved in power struggles. Let's see if we can see any lives in which you allowed yourself to open your heart.

I'm seeing you as a man in a uniform. You are a soldier in World War I. You are tall and lanky. I see you standing by some water, looking down pensively. You're thinking about a woman, a woman you're separated from. This is just after the war. The woman you loved died while you were away at war. As a teenager you had fallen in love with a blonde woman back in the United States. In this life as a man, you were very vulnerable to your feelings. I'm seeing something here. Because of your predominant identification with being a woman, a powerful woman, there is an image of what it means to be a man in your psyche. The image of being a man necessarily has to be a weak man for your identity as a strong woman to feel secure. So in this life as a man, you feel insecure and emotionally dependent on this woman with whom you have fallen in love.

R: As a man I have no way to relate to that?

C: What? Your womanly sense of power?

R: Yeah.

C: Yes. The implication is that the man is powerless because as a woman you have to be in control of the man. So in this life as a man you feel totally defenseless. And this seems healthy to me in the sense that you were at least having an opportunity to experience your feelings of love. However, your loss of her is devastating to you. She was so distraught about your being in the war that she became ill with a lung ailment and died. You are so overcome with grief, that you do not want to go home to the United States. There's too many memories. You don't know how you are going to live without her. I see you in a hotel room there in Europe very depressed. You slash your wrists and kill yourself. When you leave the body you try to run from your pain and you come right back into the life in the prairie as the tough woman we already talked about.

The tragic quality of this life as a man indicates how much pain you have buried beneath your veneer of being a powerful being. I sense a tremendous amount of pain locked up deep inside of you, and you don't want to feel it. It's like a pearl, in that—

R: I wonder who that woman was?

C: She is someone you don't know in this life. When you are ready to get in touch with your heart again, you will probably meet her. Your love is like a grain of sand inside the oyster. It's something you are trying to cover up and push away from yourself. But in truth, it's the most valuable treasure you as a being possess. There will come a time when you will open up and discover this treasure, this priceless pearl, and realize it is not something that is trying to hurt you.

PART TWO

WORKING WITH KARMA

The Mirror of
Our Day-to-Day Lives

What can we do to break the snowballing momentum of our karmic cycles? There's an array of therapeutic methods available, but the most auspicious means of working with our karma is a mindful participation in our day-to-day lives. So often the ego-self can use spiritual practices, and even therapy, to fortify or defend itself. The ego loves to control, manipulate, and rationalize the world at large, and hence the karmic forces working toward our education and transformation. Karmic lessons are not something to skirt around or fix. They are experiences that, when lived through consciously, offer the potential for change and growth. Spiritual practices and therapy can focus and accelerate the process of psychological transformation, but it's in our everyday lives where genuine growth occurs.

In our day-to-day living we have a tendency to aggressively express our desires and will by pushing ourselves on the world. We also have a tendency to recoil from, react to, or avoid situations we have an aversion to—pull away from the world. In general we spend a great deal of time pushing and pulling. If you try to imagine psychic energy as a thick sticky substance, you get a picture of how we get all tangled up from pushing and pulling our psycho-physical energy around. Unlike our friend the spider, the web we weave about ourselves is not an aesthetic geometric mandala, it's more like a hopelessly tangled ball of gooey psychic yarn.

The image of an onion, with its many layers, has been used to describe the psyche. A tangled ball of yarn is a better metaphor. At the core of the ball of karmic yarn is our true self, or in Jungian terms, the Self. Our task is to unravel the ball of yarn to reveal the jewel of the spirit at our core. The best way to do that is to allow it to unfurl itself, which it will begin to do as soon as we refrain from our frantic pushing and pulling.

The things that spontaneously happen to us in our day-to-day lives are mirror images of who we are, i.e., the constellation of karmic factors dominating us at any particular time. They are the loose ends on the ball of tangled yarn. The awareness/attitude we bring to each situation is the key. We will either unlock the wisdom imprisoned in the event or we will suffer—and perhaps curse—our fate depending on how we exercise our "free will" and "response-ability."

Our main response-ability is consciousness. The more awareness we bring into the dramas of our lives, the less shocking and traumatic they need to be to waken us from our delusional realities. Jung points out in *Aion* that when inner dynamics (such as a karmic pattern) remain unconscious, they project externally and we experience them as fate. Hence, a commitment to self-knowledge is the first step to overcoming the suffering we experience from the karmic residue from previous actions.

I want to give an example of how the illumination of karmic patterns by the light of consciousness can alter their projection into external reality. I've studied astrological affects for nearly twenty-five years. I've watched closely the affects of transiting and progressed planets as they set off certain complexes of energy in my natal chart. Over the years I have become very familiar with these natal complexes and the genre of events they relate to.

When I have taken the time to address upcoming planetary configurations by staying alert to the karmic lessons they are triggering, I find their dramas often play out poignantly in dreams and insights in meditation. I prefer this to traumatic and stressful events in the external world. I qualify this statement often because sometimes it is necessary to experience things in the "slow" temporal mode of external reality. Sometimes we really need to surrender, to let go, or let some old outmoded part die. This can take good old time and the inertia of concrete reality. Nonetheless, the more conscious we are, and the more committed we are to the task of self-unfoldment, the less painful these deaths and rebirths can be.

In working with our karma, astrology is a useful tool because it delineates in its symbolic language our primary life patterns, i.e., karmic patterns. The birth chart is a blueprint of the soul's present pralabd. The relationship between the elements in the birth chart depicts one's talents, potentials, and basic character, as well as areas of crystallized or disharmonious psychic factors. The chart therefore points to our past conditioning and psychological patterns. Problematic areas of the birth chart indicate the lessons to be learned. The subsequent movement of the planets revolves through the birth chart energizing these sensitive areas or karmic patterns. The combination of astrological elements coming into play at these times describes the types of archetypal energies contained in our personal complexes and gives some clues as to how we can best articulate and express these energies for our growth and transformation. When we pay attention to how the movement of planets activates the natal chart, we know where we need to focus on transmuting our present modes of expression. A book such as *Transits, The Time of Your Life* by Betty Lundsted, will help you interpret the movements of the planets in relationship to your natal chart.

In *Astrology, Karma, and Transformation,* another book I recommend for those who would like to follow my suggestion of using astrology for working with karma, Stephen Arroyo emphasizes that astrology when applied to an individual's life deals primarily with transformation. He says that astrology is a way of seeing graphically the forces of change, the cycles of growth and decay that operate through the natural world. Its language of symbols describes our inner experiences of life and how they relate to our basic character. If nothing else, I find it helpful to know there is going to be an end to a difficult time, and to know approximately when that will be.

I said earlier that the best way to work with karma is to stay in the moment and be attentive to the lessons that life is bringing you on a silver platter. Astrology enables me to read the karmic menu.

Our commitment to self-unfoldment begins with a willingness to bring into the light of awareness those parts of ourselves we have damned to the darkness of the unconscious. As Jung pointed out, "We don't become enlightened by imaging figures of light, but by making the darkness conscious."

I often hear people say they are not interested in past lives because it is this present life that counts. What these people fail to understand is that without exposing the causative factors, most of which are from previous lifetimes, we are not able to deal effectively with our present lives. Milton Ericson, master of modern hypnotherapy, knew what he was talking about when he said unconscious factors control our lives. Sheer willpower is not enough to surmount the momentum of past actions and unconscious attitudes and emotional complexes. It is a well-known phenomenon in psychotherapy that what we repress becomes autonomous and gains the freedom to act beyond the vigilance of our conscious selves.

Following awareness, acceptance, and forgiveness are important steps in releasing karmic patterns. Acceptance is more than just allowing these forgotten parts to come into the light of awareness. It implies having understanding and compassion for the subpersonalities, or other selves from other lives, that acted in manners judged to be evil or unacceptable by either ourselves or society. These subpersonalities may have suffered things too painful or threatening to our sanity or present sense of identity.

We do the best we can with the skills and awareness available to us in any particular lifetime. The Buddhists say our bad karma is nothing more than folly based on ignorance. Armed with clear insight into the long-lasting results of our self-limiting and dysfunctional attitudes and behaviors, would we continue to act on them? Only in extreme cases of resentment, self-destructiveness, or stubborn defiance perhaps.

We are here to learn, and the method seems to be one of trial and error. We learn through our mistakes. One of the obstacles we face in our learning, however, is our tendency to identify and hold on to what we have known. Confronted with a situation, we respond to the best of our ability based on our present awareness and unconscious conditioning from the past. When our chosen response fails to attain a desired result, we usually don't rethink our decisions and strategies. We identify with the feeling of frustration or other charged emotional reactions, all of which serve to initiate or reinforce a belief system. In the future when faced with similar situations, we act upon our belief system and bring to bear the entire complex of emotional energies to the event. Instead of changing our thinking and actions, we normally put more energy into established feedback loops.

This is not something to feel guilty or defensive about. It doesn't mean we are failures. It just happens to be one of the factors of the psychic software we need to come to terms with. Acceptance also means being able to demonstrate that same understanding and compassion for those who have transgressed against us in this or some other life.

From that understanding and compassion we can move on to forgiveness. The act of forgiveness dissolves the fetters of judgment and resentment that bind us to others with whom we conflict. It also unties the knots within our own psyches that shackle us to the repetition of self-limiting patterns of behavior.

Forgiveness enables us to let go of the negative emotions and beliefs associated with an event. Through releasing of the blame and resentment, we open ourselves to the power of grace. Forgiveness can erase many lifetimes of negative karma. There is no need to suffer and punish ourselves for mistakes and harmful actions. An acceptance and forgiveness for the past sets us free to begin anew. What's important then are our actions in the moment. Thoughts and emotions are actions also.

Have we learned our lessons and can we think, feel, and act in a healthy and life-supportive way? This is what life is asking of us. We may come into relationships with those we have been in conflict with in the past, but we don't need to view this as a debt or punishment. It is an opportunity to actualize or test our progress in transforming old patterns.

Past-Life Therapy

Many years ago I became disenchanted with my work as a clairvoyant. I felt that even though I was able to clairvoyantly see the source of people's problems, simply telling them what I saw didn't seem to help much. I began to concentrate on therapeutic methods and explored various schools of psychotherapy and other alternative approaches. Such things as deep tissue bodywork, rebirthing, holotropic therapy, neuro linguistic programming, and hypnotherapy became my new tools. After releasing and integrating events from this present incarnation, more often than not there was often a need to dig further, back into past-life issues. The important thing for a person to do was to be able to bring into consciousness the original event, or at least the underlying logic or belief system. I began to understand that reintegrating splintered aspects of the psyche, emotional catharsis, and changing unconscious or core beliefs, were the key to healing. And for a complete healing, there was often a need to extend these therapeutic methods back through the series of lifetimes related to specific patterns of "dis-ease."

The benefits of past-life therapy are manifold. Allow me to give some examples. In many instances certain tissues and organs of the physical body are prone to dis-ease because of past-life traumas. I worked with a dancer once whose career was in jeopardy because of problems she had with her knees, specifically with the ligaments and tendons transversing the knee joint. In a hypnotic regression we explored a past life in which she froze to death. Her last conscious moments were focused on her lower legs, which had already frozen. She had carried that image of her frozen lower legs with her into

this present life in her cellular memory. The muscles and con-
nective tissues of her lower legs therefore suffered from a lack
of vital energy. These kinds of tissues heal slowly, but several
months after reliving this past life she was able to dance
without any further problems.

Another friend came to me with periodic back pains,
which neither medical nor chiropractic care alleviated,
though no physical cause was ever discovered. I regressed
him to the life just before his present one. He was a gold
miner who was waiting until he struck it rich so he could
marry the girl of his dreams, a woman who worked as a
dancer at the saloon in town. One day he hit a vein of gold
and rode off to town that evening to ask for her hand in marriage. When he got to the saloon he found her drunk and
preoccupied flirting with some seedy character. He told her
of his good fortune and pleaded with her to marry him, but
she ignored him. My friend was so distraught he didn't stay
in town that night to file his claim the next day. The seedy
character, having overheard the story about the gold, followed my friend back to his camp, shot him in the back, stole
his gold, and later made the claim for himself.

In the regression, my friend relived lying on the ground
for several days critically wounded. The woman eventually
came to find him and saved his life by taking him back to
town in her wagon. After reliving this in detail, he realized
that woman was his present wife. In his present life he was
the manager of a rock band. Hence, they traveled a lot and
spent a great deal of time in nightclubs where his attractive
wife would meet and often flirt with other men. It was during these times his old wound would flare up. The physical
wound from his last life was associated with jealousy and
fear of losing his lover. We spent some time at the end of the
session working on ways he could deal with his jealousy and
fears. From this one session his "psycho-somatic" malady
cleared up.

Some cases are as simple as this, some are not. An elderly, and very staunch, woman came to see me in a wheelchair. She was born with extremely pronated feet and had been unable to walk from birth. After a life of seeking every kind of medical help, she was so desperate that she came to someone like me. I say that because this woman was a fundamentalist Baptist, very rigid and orthodox in her beliefs. I worked with her for a grueling six months doing structural bodywork and, yes, past-life regressions!

Her story is too long and complicated to relate in full. One of the main causative factors we uncovered came from her most previous life. She was a "fire and brimstone" minister who severely browbeat the members of the parish. This woman's parents in her present life were two of the most abused members of the congregation from that life. When she was born to them in this life, she was so stubborn that she was not going to "stand for it." She was not going to stand up and face her karma in this life. But, by the end of the six months of "karmic castor oil," she was walking for the first time in this life. This was no miracle, I assure you. She fought me every step of the way.

Here is another example showing how profound the affect of a traumatic death often is. A young man of about 18 came to me with a nightmarish story of a life spent trying to strangle himself. He was unable to work or go to college as he desired because of his uncontrollable compulsions. All through his life his parents had taken him to many different therapists, but to no avail. As he told me his story, I had a stark vision of him being attacked by a bear in his most recent life. He agreed to try a past-life regression and I led him back to when he was a little girl on an outing with her family. They were picking berries when a bear came out of the woods and attacked. I had a real difficult time getting him to relive that actual death. He kept jumping ahead and looking back down at his mauled body.

It took me literally hours to get him to relive his traumatic death. When he finally reexperienced the bear ripping his neck open, he grabbed his neck with both hands and flopped around my floor like a fish out of water. This lasted a good thirty minutes or longer. The energy being released from his body was phenomenal. I myself became quite nauseated, not to mention a little worried about his welfare. This guy had been trying to strangle himself all his life! Was he going to succeed there in my house?

I only saw him for this one session. Several weeks later he called to say he was feeling great, he had gotten a job, and was making plans for college.

After I had been doing regressions for several years, I accidentally broke through to another dimension. I found myself regressing to a time before I came to this planet. What a revelation it was to me to find out where I was from and why I had been sent here. I was in my early thirties at the time and suddenly many missing pieces of the puzzle of my life fell into place. At that time I was doing a lot of teaching. One of the classes I was teaching was a three-month-long course in psychic healing. In the class we were doing a lot of past-life regressions, and it was a natural place to experiment with taking people back to the time before they came to the planet. As it turned out, nearly all the students I was attracting at that time were souls who had come here during the time of Atlantis, and who had been with me in the spiritual work there and later in ancient Egypt. Hence, it became a significant aspect of their personal healing journeys to remember what they had been doing before coming to the planet, and why they had come here.

Years later I found myself exploring a deeper area of the psyche. It began when I met a woman who I spent four years living with as man and wife. She was involved in a similar kind of healing work, and we soon found ourselves remembering our birth together as souls. Until these experiences, I was convinced that "twin flames," or "twin souls" was a metaphysical rendition of the projection of the Jungian concepts of the anima and animus. After reliving our birth together as souls, I realized that our personal imprints of the archetypes for the anima and animus are based on our relationship to our Twin Flames. In the following regressions I have included these levels to show you how germane they are to our makeup and to give an indication of how you might begin to work on them.

In the next section I also want to show the therapeutic use of metaphor. Although I have frequently stressed the importance of regressing to literal traumatic events, events also carry a level of metaphoric reality. It's sometimes crucial to work on the symbolic level for healing to occur. Indeed much of the success of modern hypnotherapy is due to its ability to communicate to the unconscious mind through the language of metaphor.

To explain the healing use of metaphor please allow me to digress. Stanislav Grof, the innovator of holotropic therapy, has coined a phrase that is useful in translating the concept of karma to Western psychology: the "COEX" (system of condensed experience). It is similar to Jung's definition of a psychological complex, but with the important addition of perinatal and past-life factors. In his book, *Beyond the Brain*, Grof explains the COEX system to be a dynamic organization of memories and associated fantasy or mythical factors garnered from several biographical periods, including past lives, biological birth, childhood, etc. This grouping of condensed experience forms a constellation around a specific strong emotional charge or intense physical sensation.

In *Other Lives, Other Selves*, Roger J. Woolger, Ph.D., a Jungian analyst and past-life therapist, explains how he has integrated Grof's COEX into his practice of past-life therapy.

By using the image of a six-petaled lotus, Woolger illustrates the way he envisions six elements of a COEX budding from a core feeling. These elements include:

1) The existential aspect, the present literal conditions in our lives;
2) The biographical aspect, genetic and childhood history;
3) The somatic aspect, physical symptoms and patterns of tension in the body;
4) The perinatal aspect, intrauterine and birth trauma;
5) The past-life aspect, traumas and complexes carried over from previous incarnations; and
6) The archetypal aspect, symbolic reflections in our lives of the universal themes in mythology and folklore.

All of these elements share what Woolger refers to as a "symbolic resonance." They all share the same feeling tone and evoke the same general emotional response when activated, either in life situations or therapeutic intervention. Woolger maintains that we can access the core of a complex through any one of the six elements. Hence, a healing metaphor that resonates with the COEX system can change a complex.

In using the motif of the lotus blossom, Woolger is rejecting the orthodox perspective of seeing a complex as a buildup of layers, suggesting that older is at the bottom or deeper. He contends that the psyche exists beyond our normal concepts of space and time. In his work with clients he has observed how the six elements of a COEX overlap or interface with one another.

Therapists like Woolger and Grof are generating a new paradigm for the psyche to replace the mechanistic and dualistic view of the body and mind functioning in solid space and linear time. They refer to this new view as holographic or holonomic. This view revolves around the idea that everything within the body-mind mirrors everything else. Again in the words of Grof: "Everything is a metaphor, and every metaphor is true."

RHONDA

Rhonda is in her mid-30s. She's a fiery little Latin woman who used to be a teacher but now tutors children who have learning disabilities and/or emotional problems. She came to me to do past-life therapy related to a man who was currently in her life. Fred is thirty years older than she is. Rhonda had been in a relationship with him for one year. She no longer wanted to be his lover and was having difficulty terminating the relationship because Fred insisted they had been brought together by some higher power.

During the course of the year, some unusual events had occurred which seemed to give validity to his use and/or abuse of this "power." On several different occasions, he called to warn her of problems with her car, i.e., a nail in the right front tire, a wire was loose on the distributor, etc.

After a heated discussion one night when she was attempting to terminate the relationship, he said he didn't want anything that would remind him of her and proceeded to give back certain objects that belonged to her. The next morning he called to report that the portable CD player had mysteriously reappeared (apparently teletransported itself) at his house.

Another incident occurred after she had written him a good-bye letter. He reported that he didn't want to read the letter because he already knew what was in the rough draft by "calling it up," which was an expression he used whenever he viewed something clairvoyantly. With precise accuracy he gave her an account of the contents of the letter.

By this time, Rhonda knew this was no ordinary breakup. He appeared to be using his "psychic" and prophetic abilities to manipulate her and control her life. Feelings of anger and frustration led her to discuss this with a few friends and therapists who gave her very little consolation, however, they each pointed out the apparent manipulation and control. She thought they must have had some past-life connection. Perhaps, by doing past-life regressions, she could gain some insight that would free her to get on with her life.

SESSION I

R: I see a stone structure and a group of men. It must be Mayan. I've been chosen to select a man from this group. I choose a man. I'm impressed with how large his penis is. He approaches me. I recognize this man as Fred. I'm having difficulty letting myself see what happens next. My mind is thinking about something I've read before and it's sort of infiltrating what I'm experiencing.

C: Just allow yourself to have the experience, whatever comes up. As you choose this man, what does it feel like? What kind of feeling do you have?

R: It's like being given a lot of power, and I don't understand why it's this way. I'm really aware of the people at my back. I don't want to look at the people, the audience. I don't want to do this, and I'm embarrassed to be in front of so many people.

C: What is the nature of the ritual?

R: Something to do with procreation and harvest. There's a lot of sexual energy. It's just charged with all these men and their erections. I don't like to have to be in a place to reject. To choose one means I have to reject everybody else. I'm in an awkward place.

C: How does Fred feel when you choose him?

R: Very proud. He likes the display of it.

C: How does he feel about you?

R: It feels like lust.

C: How do you feel about him?

R: I want to blame him. It's almost like he is taking me against my will, but it doesn't make sense. I thought he could have stopped this from happening. I'm embarrassed about this; enjoying it when I hadn't intended to and his knowing that. He's kind of gloating.

C: Like he's holding power over you?

R: Yes.

C: Is this ritual something that happens once a year?

R: It seems like this has happened before. As a matter of fact, it seems like I've chosen him before.

C: Can you describe what the ritual was like?

R: I'm dressed in white. People are standing in three sides of a square. I'm not sure what's going on. I don't want to be there. I just want it to be over with. I feel like I'm out of my body.

C: How does it feel now?

R: My first feeling is that it probably feels good. I'm enjoying the experience in spite of myself. In order for it not to hurt, I open up and in doing so it feels pleasurable. I can't deny that.

C: Do you have any relationship with Fred after the ritual?

R: I'm aware of him, sort of the same way I am now. It seems like he's always there, lurking around.

C: Let's go ahead in time. What's the next important thing that takes place?

R: I just have a sense that he's always lurking around and trying to pretend he's not there, like a peeping Tom. I don't feel safe because I always think he's there.

C: What are you not safe from, his lust?

R: I'm not sure if he will take me against my will. That's how I hold that image.

C: Do you have to go through this ritual again?

R: There's one way out of it. I can agree to be sacrificed down this well and I won't have to go through this again.

C: What do you choose?

R: I walk up to the well a lot and think about it. Seems like a real stupid choice to have to make in life. It's like a choice between physical death or emotional death. I don't know if I'm brave enough to go through it, but I'd rather die than go through the ritual again. I imagine what's down in the bottom of the well. I wonder if anybody ever survives it. What kind of satisfaction is this for these people?

Next I'm in the water and I'm yelling for Fred to save me. Now I know why I'm afraid of swimming in water when I don't know where the bottom is. It's a kind of a panic death.

C: What happens after you leave the body?

R: I'm looking at how pathetic all those people are still think-ing it's going to make their crops grow better by sacrificing women. Sex has taken over what used to be some kind of meaningful ceremony. An excuse for an orgy! I thought I was going to be able to teach and give them insight, but instead I got caught up in it. I feel like I've failed because I couldn't help them, and selfish for having killed myself.

Seeing this, it doesn't surprise me that I haven't made long-term commitments to men. I don't allow them to get close to me. I always end up rejecting them and hurting my-self. Half the time I feel like I'm punishing men and the other half I'm punishing myself.

SESSION II

R: I'm making love to a young man by a rock near a beautiful waterfall, somewhere in the southern equatorial region. It's a sunny day and the sound of the water is very peaceful. I be-come aware that a man, it's Fred, is watching us. I realize he has been there for quite some time and I also sense that he has the ability to know our thoughts and feel our emotions.

C: What is your relationship to Fred in this life?

R: He is the village shaman. I have been studying with him.

C: What are you feeling about him now?

R: I'm embarrassed, shamed, and angry that he would use his powers for such selfish pleasure.

C: Describe the village. Where do you live?

R: I live in this adobelike house with rectangular windows, open, without glass. It feels cool inside. I'm aware of the sun being extremely hot, and I am happy to have this house.

C: What is your relationship to Fred after this?

R: I always feel his presence. I think he's always looking in the window at me. I never feel safe or private again.

C: So what happens next?

R: I feel so shamed that I decide to leave the village. When Fred realizes this, he decides to leave instead. He just leaves without telling anyone and leaves the village without a healer. I think I have to take his place without being fully prepared. I'm very lonely and never take another lover. I'm extremely angry with Fred for having done this to me. I also begin to understand the inherent lonelinesses that comes with this position. I attempt to forgive him, but the anger and loneliness lead me to finally take poison.

C: What happens when you leave your body?

R: I see Fred wandering in the forests and living with the animals.

SESSION III

R: I want to fight the image because it's a past life that Fred has told me about.

C: Don't fight it. Just go with whatever comes to your mind.

R: Seems like a time when there were knights and castles. I am standing on a raised platform and I'm giving Fred my scarf. He is going to fight a jousting tournament. I give it to him to make somebody else jealous or hide my feelings about his opponent. I'm looking at another person as I give him the scarf.

C: How are you feeling?

R: Very confused and deceitful. Wishing I hadn't done it.

C: What was this about? Why did you have to give him the scarf?

R: They were quarreling over who would be my champion.

C: Do you have a relationship with Fred before this?

R: There seems to be jealousy because this other man has pledged to be my champion. Fred knows this. It's apparent that Fred is fighting for death, not honor. I realized it when they start fighting. I sense vengeance and know that he wants to kill him.

C: Can you describe who this other person is?

R: The other person is my lover. He's not my husband, so I have to hide my true feelings.

C: What happens?

R: It's a long, long jousting match. I think it's never going to end. I've complicated things and I can't take it back. Part of me doesn't want either one of them to be injured. I think it might be less complicated if my lover does get killed because then I won't have to worry about the mess I've gotten myself into. No! I can't let him kill my lover, so I stop those thoughts.

C: What's the outcome?

R: I don't know, I don't want to see.

C: Let's go ahead in time.

R: My lover has been injured. I think he may be dead. I see Fred put his foot on his chest and raise up the scarf. I feel really sick. How could I have let this happen? I can't look. He's not dead!

C: Let's go forward in time. What happens after you find out your lover is OK?

R: I make eye contact with him and start to walk away. It seems important not to show my true feelings. I think if Fred knows, then maybe other people do too. I wonder if my lady attendants suspect, and whether I should just give up this relationship. I still don't know the outcome of this tournament. It appears that Fred must have won. I never thought it could happen.

C: Who is your husband?

R: I know it seems weird, but he seems to be the king.

C: Can you describe the place where you live?

R: Rolling hills, woods all around. The buildings are made of reddish-white stones. It's a large building with a rectangular shaped courtyard.

C: It's a big building, sort of like a castle?

R: Yes, it's big enough for horses to be inside.

C: Let's go ahead in time. What is the next important event?

R: I think I must set up a meeting with my lover to terminate our relationship. I don't trust this man, Fred. He is my protector now and is always watching me. How am I going to do it? I'm in my room trying to decide whether I should send him a note. I don't have anybody I can trust to put this in writing.

C: Let's go ahead in time and see what happens.

R: We are all eating. It's difficult to look at my lover because I can't hide my feelings. I have to pretend everything is OK. I don't see Fred at the table. Nobody is talking about the results of the jousting or where Fred is. I sense that he's around somewhere, but I don't see him.

C: Let's go ahead in time again.

R: I'm having a conversation with my husband. He's shocked at the outcome of the tournament. He's very surprised that his friend, who he thought was very capable and worthy didn't win. I, too, am surprised. He wants to know why I gave my scarf to the other man. He's sort of blaming me for having done that. I don't have a very good explanation. I have no excuse, only the truth. I tell him the truth, that I have strong feelings for this other man.

C: What was his reaction?

R: Quiet, at first. I can't look at him. I don't blame him for being angry, although he doesn't seem to be. I tell him I'm willing to give up this relationship, but it will be difficult. I acknowledge how difficult it will be for him to be with me now. He needs some time to think, and he asks me to leave. I try to figure a way out of this. I could kill myself, but I need some help.

C: Let's go ahead.

R: I know it's very dangerous, but I want to see him again one more time. He seems to think there's a way we can escape. I say it would be disgraceful. We've both let the king down. This man Fred could kill me. Then I realize he still wants to kill my lover. He tries to get into a quarrel and fight again. He thinks he can win my heart.

C: How do you know this?

R: I just know it. I want to make sure he would never get me. I want him to kill me because I have caused all this. I should be the one to die. I have to confide in one of the women. I have to warn my lover to leave because he doesn't know he's in danger. I also ask her to help me get some herbs to kill myself. I tell her that my lover is innocent and that it's all my fault. I beg her to understand and help me. She puts a cloak over her head and I look into her eyes to see if she trusts me. Then I pray. I want Fred to die. He's so spiteful. I don't like him.

C: What happens next?

R: Fred tells the king that my lover has run away. He rouses others to go and look for him. Then I think for a moment whether my lover has acted as a coward. I search to find him and see if he's OK.

C: What do you mean?

R: It's like I'm able to psychically tap into him in the forest and I know he's all right. I think some men have gone out to search for him. I have extra guards at my room now and I'm worried this woman will not be safe if she tries to return. I try to send her a message. Then, I try to look around for other ways to kill myself because I don't think I have a chance.

Now it seems my lover has returned. I can see out a small window down into the court. My plan doesn't seem to be working very well. I'm tired of being stuck in my room. I'm tired of waiting.

"Kill me. I don't care. I just want out." The guard is jerking me by the arm. I decide I have to be public about what's going on. The guard takes me down to the courtyard where everyone is. My hands are tied. I think I'm going to be strangled. My lover and I are looking at each other.

I feel guilty and ashamed. I want it to be done! Nobody can win. Even our mutual deaths will not bring justice. The king also loses face. Before I die, I just want to expose Fred. He is always in the shadows. I realize now that he wants to usurp the king and take over the castle.

C: Do you say it?

R: I try to say it. (grabs spot on lower left abdomen near large intestine) This pain! I've been stabbed with a sword.

C: Who has done this?

R: It's Fred.

C: What's happening now?

R: A lot of confusion. I'm falling to the ground. There's a lot of fighting. I'm afraid for the king's life. Everything is crumbling.

C: What is the outcome?

R: The king is dead. There's a group of men who leave.

C: Where are you right now?

R: I feel really sick. I can't move. My legs are heavy and I can't move. My back. There's a pain near my shoulder. Someone comes and kills me. It's like a merciful killing. It seems like my lover had something to do with that to save me from more humiliation. I feel relieved.

C: Looking back on that life, is there anything important? Are there any guides who help you?

R: Someone is telling me that I'm OK and that I have a pure heart. No matter what happened, I still have a pure heart!

SESSION IV

R: I'm a gladiator. I'm putting on armor. The spectators are already out there and there is a lot of noise.

C: How are you feeling?

R: Sick. I don't want to be doing this. We're going to be punishing some people, killing them. People will be coming out these doors. I'm supposed to trample them. I have a horse and chariot. I'm starting to shoot across the field, people are starting to yell, cheering me on. A person has come out of the doors with his hands tied. He hasn't got a chance. I lose my life if I don't complete this. There is another gladiator waiting down at the other end. He will challenge me if I fail. I charge without looking at the person's face.

This seems to be a test of honor, but there is no honor except death for me. I decide to face my own death rather than charge the next victim. I want to charge the other gladiator because I have so much anger for being forced to do this. I charge him, but we both miss. We turn and charge again. He seems to realize my ploy and doesn't kill me easily or quickly as I wish. I have to keep charging him. I must die!

C: Why must you die?

R: (loud exhalation, body jerks)

C: What's happening?

R: I've been stabbed in the throat. I'm falling. As I fall I look up and see Fred. He is my trainer. The other gladiator is calling me a coward and tells me to get up and fight. I know he is a better fighter and should have overcome me by now. He wants to see me fight. I want to die. I stab him once and then he gets me. My energy is draining. I'm rising up from my body now.

C: What are you feeling now?

R: Retribution. I wanted to die and have the blood on Fred's hands. He thought I should get joy out of killing, but I wanted to defy him and take his satisfaction away from him. He could watch me die instead. As my trainer he had taught me to claim my victim and stand with my foot on his stomach and be proud.

C: So by dying yourself, that was your way of defying him?

R: Yes. I can see how in my present life he is still sitting on the sidelines and watching me, getting vicarious pleasure. It's a creepy feeling.

C: Take a few moments to relax now and get ready to have an experience in which you will live through what it is you need to do in order to let go and forgive Fred.

R: I feel lighter, my hands are tingling. There is an electriclike energy exchange between Fred and me. My guide tells me that it is all right and reminds me of the danger of allowing someone to take over my will, as I allowed Fred to do in all these lives.

I see Fred down below kneeling down. He thinks he has failed in my training, he blames himself. I feel myself going farther away, and getting lighter. My hands are still tingling, but it's getting less.

C: What's happening now?

R: I'm at peace. It feels good to no longer be controlled.

C: Does your guide have any more information regarding a closure with Fred?

R: It seems that the way he has gained control over me is that I have surrendered to him. My guide tells me to be alert for the code word of surrender. I must stay aware. My guide tells me to be at peace.

C: What normally keeps you from being at peace?

R: Anger, holding on.

C: What allowed you to let go of your anger today?

R: The anger was held in my jaw. When my guide told me to be at peace, I just released that feeling. Holding that anger has kept me coming back with Fred. Now I know I have a choice when Fred says things like, "You've got to surrender. How many times have you wanted to surrender to a man?" Or when he said, "You'll be back," after I said I no longer wanted to be his lover. I always believed him because I knew of his psychic powers. Now I know I have a choice. I have a great sense of peace after acknowledging this.

During the time period in which Rhonda was doing the past-life regressions, she had two dreams that demonstrate how her unconscious mind was processing the buried emotions related to her lover, who by the way was old enough to be her father.

DREAM #1

R: I'm carrying my abused sister in my arms while running away from our father who has sexually and physically wounded her. She appears helpless. I finally put her down and keep running away for my own life. He stalks me through a maze of junk, old buildings, etc.

At one point, I quit running and decide to retaliate, confront, and kill this man. He then drives away in a truck and I chase him, running on foot and carrying a large stick. I catch up with him and begin beating him to the ground. I can hardly believe I have overpowered him. He even seems to surrender at one point and submits to death. I continue to stab, but cannot seem to find his heart. I look for blood to spurt out, but it never does.

I awoke to find my fists clenched and my heart pounding. When I released the tension in my fists, I felt exhausted but quite relieved. I then started to worry that I might have actually killed Fred. My first regression session was just after he got out of the hospital for a heart attack.

Upon reflection, I realized I had to drop my abused self in order to confront this man.

DREAM #2

R: Two female friends and I have been captured by a power-hungry male. He has guards who keep us from running away. I keep wondering why we don't attempt to escape. It's like we're just waiting.

I begin to meditate. Each time I begin, a Buddhist type altar appears. I think it belongs to this man and don't want to use it.

I walk out from the meditation and feel the tension is released. This man has freed us. My two friends leave and I give some gift—a watermelon—in thanks. Then, this man writes on a piece of paper my name and the words, "Will you please sleep with me?" I respond after careful deliberation, "My heart isn't in it."

I was wondering whether I should sleep with him like a sacred prostitute who uses sex to calm the angry, hostile male. I decide no, because if he likes it, then I would have to continue because he was so into power that he would never let me go.

When I awoke I realized this is exactly what happened with Fred.

Rhonda's story has a happy ending. She is still on friendly terms with Fred, but has managed to free herself from the oppression of their romantic entanglement.

LISA

When I opened the door to meet Lisa for the first time, I was taken back. A middle-aged woman with a shaved head, dark complexion, and dark piercing Oriental-looking eyes greeted me. Except for her leather jacket, she brought to mind the image of a Tibetan nun.

Lisa had been battling breast cancer for two and a half months when she came to see me. She was divorced and the mother of several teenagers. She was a member of the Subud religion, and a mutual friend in her religious group had referred her to me. I began our session by asking her about her confrontation with cancer. She talked about her feelings of being exposed. Her hair had always been long and she had worn it down along her face. She was an attractive woman, but was dressed rather carelessly, as if to say, "What's the use of trying to look good anymore?" She went on to talk about her burning spiritual longing.

I've included Lisa's session in this section because her situation is a good example of how life will eventually put us in a corner and more or less force us to take a good hard look at ourselves. Her sessions with me followed a rather meandering course. I knew there were some things that she wanted to know, and some things that needed to come up from within her, so I acted as more of a sounding board for her, or a psychic mirror perhaps.

I began the first session by asking what she was learning from her present situation.

L: The biggest part is learning how to love myself and not be afraid of anything, that combined with letting go of all my attachments.

C: A crash course on your spiritual journey?

L: Yeah.

C: I can feel it.

L: Yeah, it's good. I'm not afraid of dying, but it's hard to let go of this life.

C: As you said that I had a feeling of how this is forcing you to acknowledge your vulnerabilities. When you said you weren't afraid of dying, it didn't feel true to me. Do you think you might still have some defenses buffering you from what a sensitive person you are inside?

L: That could be.

C: I get a sense that life has pushed you into a corner and made you admit that you really do want to live, that you really do have feelings, that you really are sensitive.

L: When you said that I saw an old woman right there at the corner of my breast. I know that it is me.

C: How would you describe this old woman?

L: She's a crone. She is bitter. She is longing for something, and demanding.

C: Bitter about what?

L: About being left, not being resolved. She is really stuck.

C: What is she longing for?

L: The Latihan. This is the term used in Subud for the mystical experience that is the central focus of our religion.

C: And what is she demanding?

L: She is demanding that I acknowledge her presence.

C: Is she demanding in other ways? Does she demand the Latihan for example?

L: Well, I don't know. I don't understand. It feels like she is in me, but that she isn't me. Could it be a past life?

C: Whether she is a past life or a metaphor isn't as important as the fact that she is really a part of you, an important part of you.

L: What do you mean?

C: Remember when you talked about your longing for spiritual union, and the pain and frustration you feel not achieving it? Well, you've tried, not only in this lifetime but in many others. You've tried so hard to attain that spiritual union and you feel confused and abandoned because you don't understand why you can't have it. That's where the demanding energy comes in. It's a third chakra approach to God. There is a part of you that is saying: "OK God, I've done everything I'm supposed to do and you better pay up now."

L: Yeah, I'm running out of time, so get on with it *now!* Yeah, I know that part of me.

C: Lisa, I want to back up a little here and look at who you are on a soul level. I feel this part of you, the crone, is representing something on a core level of your being.

As a soul you are a very vital and powerful being. You have come here from the inner planes where the spiritual laws are prevalent. Beings there exist in and act from divine love. It's very difficult for you to be in a world like this planet. You are like the prodigal son in that you have forgotten where you are from. But deep inside you are constantly judging yourself by the reflection of yourself in this world. You wonder what's wrong with the picture of yourself because you are seeking to have the inner knowing of who you are validated by your planet-side environment. But something is

out of sync, your inside knowing and your external surroundings don't fit together.

Before you came to the planet you were a young soul
who was very enthusiastic. Your soul is an emanation of the
will aspect of creation, and you were overzealous in your desire to whip the whole universe into shape. You lacked patience and understanding. You wanted to come along and
change everything into perfection with a broad sweep of your
magic wand without appreciation for time and the natural
unfoldment of things. You had very little compassion and acceptance for beings in their states of imperfection. This curtailed your ability to grow and learn in your native
dimension. You had fixed ideas and were not amiable to your
mentors when they attempted to impart their wisdom to you.
This is why you were eventually sent here. This plane is very
concrete and thus a great place to learn about how we are using our life energies. Whatever energy we put out becomes
relatively solid and we keep running into it until we understand how we have created it.

You've been here butting your head against the density
of this plane for a long time now. You are feeling anguished,
exhausted, and despondent about your ability to push things
into the shape that you would like them to be.

L: It seems like I've been that way forever, until recently. I've
had to confront not judging everyone. I'm learning how to
accept them instead of trying to change them, or the whole
world. I'm starting to see that I don't have to change it all, I
just have to be correct within myself.

C: Let's look at a couple of lives to see what it was like for you
when you first came here. Let's see how you've been pushing people around (laughter).

L: My family and ex-husband would love to hear that. Did I
have a choice about coming here?

C: Not really. There were things you needed to learn and this was the best place.

L: So that's the reason I came here, not to do anything for anybody else? OK, so much for my impact on the world.

C: Lisa, you can do things for others no matter where you are. You have an impact wherever you are. You are here to learn how to embody the transpersonal will of life without getting your personal will, your ideas and desires, in the way. This takes a lot of refinement, a lot of articulation. When you were sent here you were frustrated. You wanted to work on a bigger scale. You had grandiose ideas and were very idealistic. You thought this was much too limited a place, which is why you were sent here—to learn to appreciate the small and see that the small is just as important as the big. You felt curtailed by your mentors. You were angry when you came here. This is why I was sent here also.

You first came to the planet about ten thousand years ago, during the Amazonian time the Greek writers referred to. This was a matriarchal culture that had survived the large-scale destruction of Atlantis. Many angry and power-hungry souls who had been killed at that time were incarnating into the matriarchal tribes and taking over. It was in this context that you incarnated with your body of frustration and anger.

You were angry and you vented it. But you weren't really trying to go against the spiritual order of things, you really wanted to work for it. You felt thwarted and couldn't do as much as you wanted to. Part of your anger is a defense also. There is some confusion as to why you were sent here. You felt judged by your mentors, rejected. So part of your anger is pride, an attempt to puff yourself up and prove that you are worthy, that you are a good person. Your anger is a defense against the fear caused by the implications of the rejection you felt by your mentors. You have never really acknowledged that you fear not being a good person, and hence, you ultimately fear that God won't love you.

L: I know. That's one of the cruxes of my life that I couldn't understand. I know that I'm a good person, I know that. But there is a part of me that feels totally unworthy. I'm always playing right into that all the time.

C: What would it be like if you were really unworthy to God? For you, that's the worst thing you can imagine, the worst thing ever. What would happen then?

L: I don't know, I don't want to think about that.

C: And you've never allowed yourself to address this fear, to accept it and work with it. And now you're going to have to. You've been using all your power to defend yourself from this unspoken fear. You've been trying to prove that you are worthy, but in order to do that you would have to do incredible and grandiose things. That's where all of this started, your attachment to doing things your way, your idealistic vision of whipping the cosmos into shape.

You don't have to do grandiose things to be accepted by God, you are loved for being just who you are. Wouldn't a child who is vulnerable and in need of help galvanize compassion in your own heart more than a powerful confident child. God didn't tell you to go out and do great things, that was your own idea. And your desire to do these great things was coming from a very beautiful space in your heart. It was from a place of wanting to do good, to do what was right. This is the most beautiful and true thing within yourself, and you've lost touch with it.

L: With what?

C: The naive and idealistic desire to want to do all those great things, this innocence is the pearl of great price, the spiritual treasure of your soul. Because you projected it into your grandiose ideas, which you have felt powerless to accomplish, you have not been able to integrate this part of yourself and now feel unworthy. In addition, you felt you were rejected by your mentors for trying to do what you wanted to do. So to try to prove yourself, you've continued to try to accomplish things by forcing your will on the world. The more you fail to accomplish what you desire, the more powerless and unworthy you feel, and the more traumatic and charged this whole issue becomes. Hence, the harder you try to push things around in the world. The perfection you demand of the world and other people is the perfection that you're demanding of yourself.

So, how can you go inside and find the spiritual treasure. Going all the way down through the layers of defenses and insecurity, what do you find? It's like a fragile flower. You've been out in the world stomping around trying to do all these great things and there's this beautiful little flower and it's so delicate, so pure, and you've walked all over it and haven't even seen it. How can you go back to that part of yourself and just sit there with it, admire it, maybe even water it? And now your karma has reached a critical mass, you can't keep doing what you've done in the past.

L: Yeah, it made me stop. The cancer makes me just stop. I know that.

C: It's interesting, you know, facing death. It's like—all of a sudden—what really matters? So this is what it has taken for you to stop pushing things around.

L: Yeah, it's broken down any projection that I've ever had about what's OK and not OK. I can't get away, I'm right up against it and there's no pretending. All my ideas about what I need to do, where I need to go, it really doesn't matter any more.

If I ask you a question, like a feeling I've had, can you tell the validity of it? I feel I was a person in Crete. Is that something I can ask about?

C: Yes, definitely, I see you there. You were a man. What would you like to know?

L: I feel like I was part of a religion there that worshiped the bull.

C: Yes, yes. You were a priest in the cult of the Bull. You were a true believer and really pushed the religion onto people. This is a good example of some of that forcefulness we were talking about. You were really forcing others into this religion, but you were also trying to get something out of it for yourself, a sense of satisfaction, the spiritual connection you yourself longed for. You were projecting your desire for spiritual fulfillment onto other people, not integrating it for yourself. So the more you projected outwardly, the more dissatisfied you felt. The more dissatisfied you felt, the more you pushed other people. Your intensity became nearly maniacal. You were really evangelistic; you were going to save the world.

L: I really love this world. I really hate what's happening to it. If I felt how much it hurts me to see what's happening all the time I would be in pain constantly. But now I'm feeling it more, I'm also going into feelings I've never gone into before because I've always been so rigid.

C: I've been thinking about that, how minds tend to run in ruts.

L: Most of us don't realize that we're in ruts until something happens to us that breaks us open, and usually it's something painful. We won't break otherwise.

I've been feeling something else. It first happened when I was having sex. I saw this person looking at me. She was a young black woman and there was this feeling of great joy. It's really wonderful. Do you have any feelings about what this might be?

C: As you were talking I could really feel the energy around you, I could see it in your face. I see children all around you, your children, and later your grandchildren. This is in the South and you are a slave, but there is this beautiful spiritual energy. I see you looking up to God and having waves of ecstasy, real spiritual rapture, like St. Teresa of Avalon or something; you nearly levitate off the ground the rapture is so powerful.

L: So high, I mean it's the only time I've felt like that.

C: What's interesting about this life is that you were totally oppressed, you had no control, so much so that—

L: I couldn't do anything else.

C: You were so frustrated after you left the body in the lifetime just before this one that you were trying to break through. You've spent so many lifetimes trying to break through into a spiritual place and you were just at your wits' end. Your guides said to you, "Let us do something here." You were so frustrated that you finally gave in and let them set up this life for you. For you, there was real surrender in doing that because you've been trying so hard to do it your own way. When you surrendered there was a real opening there. You were willing to try something new. They put you in this situation where you were unable to act out any of your old patterns.

L: It almost seems as if it was a taste of what could be, but then I had to come back and see if I could do it again with all my old karma.

C: Exactly. It's like you've been all wrapped up in pushing energy around down here, tied up and very heady about it all. And this energy goes back a long way, like a train traveling with great momentum down the same old track. Your guides picked you up and set you in a totally different context, and you learned from it. This was your most recent lifetime, and why things are coming to such a head for you in this present life. Coming back into this life you ran back into that train of karma. You're meeting it with the awareness that you achieved in this life as the black woman, a life where you finally experienced the spiritual union that you have longed for. These two parts of yourself are meeting now.

L: It took until now.

C: You know it sounds pretty heavy to say "this big train of karma." I want to point out that it could change just like that! Get off that train! The only thing keeping it going is your belief in it. For example your guides took you off it and you had a new kind of experience. That place is still there and all you have to do is to get off that old track.

L: If I don't jump I'm going to get kicked off. I'm really glad I've been kicked, too.

C: It doesn't really matter if you die now or later. It doesn't really matter as long as you learn your lessons. You're making such incredible movement in your spiritual life right now. That's the important thing, that's what's going to carry on.

This makes me think of when you were talking about how much you love the planet. It doesn't really matter if the planet is destroyed, as long as somebody learns something. Life, you can't destroy life, it will go on, we will all go on. Do you have another question?

L: I keep coming across this native American.

C: It seems more like South American.

L: Could be, anyway I was a woman and there is something in that life that is in this lifetime—it has to do with healing something that happened then. It keeps coming up.

C: It was someone you were at odds with in your tribe. It was a moral or ethical issue. I see you weaving and thinking about this over and over. You're very upset about this and feel very strongly. You are at odds with the leader of your tribe. There is a major decision being made and you as a woman have no say in the matter. It is a council of men who are discussing this issue, and you feel they are wrong in what they are deciding, and it's eating you up inside. You're frustrated about not being able to voice your opinion or have any control in the situation. You were so convinced that your way was right.

This life was a karmic role reversal of your matriarchal lifetimes as well as a lesson in allowing others the freedom to choose their own course of action. In the past you've been so forceful about pushing people down the path you think they should go, but in this life you are in a situation where you have no power to do that. You didn't learn that lesson though because you were stuck on feeling they were wrong and you were right.

L: Yeah, and eating me up too! In my present life, the leader of the tribe was my husband. I had to go through it all again with him. In this life I had to get where I was so unattached that I could love him, even though I knew he was wrong and I was right. I feel like I'm finished with him.

C: I don't feel you're finished with him.

L: Does it have to happen again? Can't the forgiveness and acceptance be enough?

C: It's close. I just want to acknowledge that you did a lot in this lifetime. I'm saying you, not him.

L: Was I ever his mother?

C: Let me just finish what I was saying and then I'll answer that. In the future you will need to give him an opportunity to resolve with you. You've done your work, now you need to let him do his. You will need to maintain a place of compassion and acceptance as he deals with his feelings and lets go of his resentments toward you.

L: He's still around so maybe I can still do that. I feel myself go in and out of being able to do that. I know I'm not quite there because I still get reactive. Other times I touch into that place of grace.

C: There's one thing that's going on: you've used him as a scapegoat for your feelings against men, and the whole frustration issue you felt in that past life we were just talking about. In general you haven't healed those issues with the oppression you've experienced as a woman. You still have anger at men, and you've used him as a target for those feelings.

L: I really knew I was going through it. It's almost for all women I was going through it. I also knew it wasn't directly him this time.

C: You need to forgive yourself for using him as a whipping boy to vent the anger and frustration you feel in general and that you have projected onto men. Your original feelings stem from the time when you were sent here. You felt controlled and oppressed by your mentors, and you brought those feelings with you to the planet.

L: You mean he didn't bring them to me?

C: He is just one of the beings you have chosen to act out those feelings with. And in truth you were the one who oppressed him to begin with. He was one of the men who you controlled when you were back in the matriarchy. And yes, he was your mother once.

L: My mother?

C: He was very, very, strict with you. There is quite a history of a battle of wills between the two of you.

L: I hope it's over now. Can I ask you one more question? I went to Ireland and I felt like I was home. I also play the harp. So I want to know if I had a Celtic life, or maybe before the Celtic era. It feels real deep to me.

C: Yes, I see you there, but it's after the Celtic times. You're a woman and I see green rolling hills and the beauty of the countryside. I also see you playing the harp. Music is a mystical experience for you. When you played the harp you went into a trance, a state of rapture in the music and an almost religious attunement with nature.

L: I keep getting that I need to go into my music again. It's so healing for me, but it's real hard to give myself the space to do it. When I do I can be there for hours and hours.

C: Yes, it's a way that has worked for you in the past, and it's a wonderful path, a royal road for you.

L: I want to ask you about another thing that is happening. I want to know what it is all about. There's been a lack of male energy in my life for a long, long time. I feel this lack and need that male energy. Anyway I've known Mathew for three years. I've been doing camps for Subud kids and when I met Mathew he was going through his parents' divorce.

When he found out that I was ill, he moved into my house. There's this incredible sexual energy going on between us. He's 19. It feels really familiar to me; it doesn't feel incorrect. I find myself asking, "Who are you and where have you been with me before? What is this all about?" It feels very strange sometimes because of the age difference, but then I know that it doesn't really matter. Anyway, he's in my life now and I know he's like a moment. There's not a projection into the future. He's here now. I just want to know what's it all about?

C: My first sense is that the connection is on a soul level. He's like a spiritual brother. In this life he has not really awakened to who he is as a soul yet; he's searching for it. The spiritual bond you have with one another is a way for him to start connecting with that level of himself. It's his concern for you, the empathy and compassion for what you are going through, that is bringing his soul consciousness more into his body. That's where the main spark is coming from between you, but when you add that spark to all the hormones in his 19-year-old body you start a real sexual fire.

L: But there's so much integrity behind it. There's all this sexual energy going through him but it hasn't been fulfilled. He's really trying to understand what I'm going through. So it's real interesting.

C: You can't project any of your romantic fantasies, and he doesn't fit the negative qualities you project onto men. But here is a man bringing this spiritual love at a time when you're really vulnerable and searching for the truth and essence of your life, and on the brink of losing it all. It's a very poignant time, and here is this being who is resonating with the spiritual level you are searching for in yourself. In that sense he's like a teacher. Surrender to this love, trust in the integrity you feel.

. . .

At the close of this first session Lisa and I talked about how the cancer was attacking her feminine side and what that might mean for her. Several months later, Lisa came to see me again. In the meantime she and Mathew had become lovers. We picked up where we had left off with her relationship to Mathew.

L: It's been real good what's been happening between us, but I finally got to the place where I realized that the sexual thing had to stop because he was going to get hurt. So there's no problem with that. I'm still curious though. Is there something that we're supposed to be finishing up with this interlude, or is it something bizarre that was just real good? Where is this coming from? What kind of past connections did we have?

C: Let's start with your connection before coming to the planet. I think I said before that he was kind of like a big brother to you. There was a bit of a push/pull dynamic. You would open up to him and then pull away, wanting to be on your own. There's a sense of some rebellious energy there that turns into a power struggle at times, nothing major. Mathew has always cared for you and wanted to help you. From your side, you were fairly hungry for this kind of attention, because deep inside you have a lot of insecurities. When you were receptive, the energy flowed easily between you. At times you would begin to feel too vulnerable and too dependent, and you would pull away and act like you didn't need anybody. Can you relate to that now?

L: Well, barely; it comes every once in awhile, but it comes and then it's gone.

C: Let me take a look at some of your past lives together. The first one that pops out at me is in Egypt. Mathew is working for the Pharaoh; he is some kind of official. You are a woman who works in the palace as a servant. Your eyes are very penetrating, searching. I keep seeing your eyes. Your duties are pretty demeaning, like cleaning, etc. Mathew cares for you and takes pity on you. He wants to help you rise up from that position.

You become lovers, but you are always sort of walking on eggshells because of the lower caste you were raised in. Aside from that, it seems like a harmonious relationship. He dies before you do, and something about that really opens your heart. Ah, it's not until he dies that you allow yourself to feel the depth of your love for him. You are overwhelmed with appreciation for what he had done for you through that life. Your gratitude borders on feelings of obligation to him.

The next life I see is in Greece. I'm seeing that Mathew works in a building with colonnades. He's some kind of statesman again. He has a more prestigious role in this life. His character is more stern and anxious because of the responsibilities he has. He is an arbitrator, that's how you meet him. Your husband has been killed in a war and you have a child and no place to live and no means of support. So you're pleading your case to the government. Mathew ends up helping you again. He finds you a home and comes to visit you from time to time. He is married and has a family, but you and he develop a clandestine relationship because you really started pulling on him emotionally.

This puts Mathew in a bind, and he's not able to spend the time with you that both of you would like. He eventually terminates the relationship because it causes him too much stress. He gives you a large sum of money, and you leave that city with your little girl. You are really sad when you leave, but you know that it's right. You leave with respect and understanding, nonetheless, you long for him, as he does for you. This is the keynote to the karma you create in this life, the longing for one another and a feeling that it's not right to be together, or that you can't be together.

The next life I see is somewhere in Persia or western India; the culture is Islamic. He is in the employment of the king. He works in the palace. You are in the harem of the king, and you and Mathew are not allowed to talk to one another. But you do see him occasionally and there is intense eye contact. The women in the harem are pretty much cloistered, but his duties sometimes take him into those inner chambers of the harem. So both of you indulge in a steamy fantasy with each other, but it never gets consummated.

L: We would have lost our heads!

C: Yeah, so we're adding a little more forbidden fruit to the fruit salad. It's a frustrating and painful life for both of you, and you are both still stuck longing for one another in a situation where it is not possible to be together.

I was just starting to look for the next life when these words came into my mind: "It's because it really isn't appropriate for you to be in a romantic relationship." This has something to do with the work each of you must do individually.

The next life I see is in the same geographical area, a little more to the west. It's a desert existence. I'm seeing Mathew crossing the desert with camels. He's in charge of the caravans that bring supplies to the sultan. The two of you meet on one of these caravans. You are traveling with several other women to join the harem again. You are guarded, so once again you may not speak to one another, but the old psychic connection is still there, and the fantasies are just as strong. He is traveling a lot in this life, coming and going across the desert. He thinks about you a lot, while sitting around campfires and staring at the night sky while going to sleep.

L: Having romantic visions huh?

C: Yeah and hornier than hell. The forbidden fruit aspect really intensifies the longings you feel for one another.

Let's go on to the next life with him. I'm over in Italy now—don't know when yet. The land seems very arid and I see Mathew up in the hills being a shepherd. He has a very strong connection with the night sky. It's a real spiritual feeling but without a religion or philosophy attached to it. He also feels a beautiful communion with the natural world around him. He is a young man and lives with his family. This seems like some kind of feudal system. His family works on someone else's land. There is a large villa where you live. You are the wife of the feudal lord. You are aware of Mathew but there is that same taboo energy because you are not supposed to relate to someone of his position, and he can only dream of being able to speak with you. That same old energy is there between you, but you don't allow it to be conscious, it's just too socially unacceptable.

L: Why is it that we're always put in that situation?

C: Let's go back and look at that Egyptian life again. It started off with you having different social statuses. Because of that, and your upbringing in that life, you had a poor self-image. You always felt subservient and unworthy, so you didn't allow yourself to receive his love until after his death. Even though you were together as man and wife there was still this separation between you.

L: And it just kept getting broader and broader in later lifetimes?

C: For Mathew there was a lot of sadness because you were not able to receive his love. And for you it was painful too. Your love for him was great, but you were not allowing yourself to feel it. In those times you weren't aware of it, but this was painful for you. It had something to do with that push/pull energy you felt before coming to the planet. It was painful and frightening for you to feel your vulnerability because you have a need to feel strong and independent, which of course is a compensation for the insecurities you feel.

It seems to me the seeds for this pattern started then. The sense that neither of you could have the love you felt for one another.

L: So what are we trying to resolve then?

C: You're trying to fulfill the love.

L: It's the same pattern in this life, where it's just not OK. Yet the love is still there, and now it's been recognized and acted on. It's been strongly received, so strongly that I had to stop it, which I did. But still, I don't think there will be a discontinuation of the love. Ah, it's so complicated.

C: Maybe it has to do with just allowing yourself to feel the love, to have it. To feel worthy and vulnerable. When I said it wasn't appropriate—the kind of relationship you've been trying to have—it's because it's an exclusive romantic relationship. It has bound both of you in this narrow focus for many lifetimes. Both of you have been fixated on this romantic fantasy, when as souls you need to express and live in the love of the spirit. Your potential as spiritual beings is to live in that state of divine love, but you have tried to force that potential into the confines of an exclusiveness with one another.

L: Yeah, I was seeing how the romantic and sexual stuff gets in the way.

C: It doesn't have to once you get beyond it. Your relationship to romance and sex will change once you have gone to another level of spiritual love. It doesn't mean you can't have romance and sex after you unfold your potential for spiritual love. The completion and wholeness you will feel inside will eclipse the desperate and neurotic things that happen when you cling to romantic love.

L: Well, we never got to that part because of the situation, we just knew it was a limited thing.

C: It feels like it was set up in this life so you could move through and come to some resolution because you weren't really able to project the romantic stuff onto the situation.

L: I know, I kept saying, "Why couldn't he be born twenty years earlier?" (laughing) So that's the reason. Now can you help me go into my pain?

C: What does it mean to go into the pain?

L: It means understanding why it's there, and how I heal it. It means giving the pain its life so it won't stay on me any more. I didn't want to do that, and I still don't, but I am doing it. It hurts, and I can't recognize a lot of it.

C: How would you describe this pain?

L: It always comes unexpectedly. Anything can trigger it. It's just a wave of bleakness. Sometimes it's black, but most of the time it's grey or red and bloody. It's all held inside of me for a long, long time. For various reasons I wouldn't allow myself to feel it. Part of that is not wanting to burden other people with it. It takes me over when it comes. It takes me and I wail. I can't stop for a long time, and when I do I just buckle over; I'm buckling all over. Something is very lost in there.

C: Where?

L: Down in here. (she places her hands on her lower abdomen)

C: Can you imagine that you are inside that part of your body?

L: Part of me feels like I'm almost paralyzed by the fear that it holds, but I have to keep on walking anyway. This is a place I know real well. It's huge, it's so huge. It is in the shape of a monster. (whispering) I can smell it.

C: Are you almost there?

L: I'm real close. I'm outside, I'm just outside, but I feel the head. It's around me, it's reaching around me, pulling me in. Now it's touching me. (her body shivers)

C: What does it feel like?

L: It's grasping and clutching.

C: Is it still dark?

L: It's real dark.

C: What's the touch feel like? Is it smooth, slimy, cold, or warm?

L: It's clutching, spidery, and spindly. It's not warm or cold. It has no feel, but. . . . Oh, it's warm. It's all around me! (crying) I'm praying to go with it.

C: What is happening now?

L: I'm walking through a corridor. Pain is all above me with sharp angles, ready to fall on top of me and cut me to pieces. It's a building. I'm in a building now. That was just the corridor. Now I'm inside and there is this black water. It's all black water and if I open the door it's going to cover me up and engulf me. It's like a tidal wave, but it's all contained. I've managed to contain it all these years in this one room.

C: Can you go into that room now?

L: I can't. I don't want to open the door. I'm there. I'm standing in front of the door. My hands are on the door and I don't want to see in there.

C: You've already seen in there; there's just black water. Is there any strength or resource you could call on right now to help you open that door?

L: Yeah, God, ai, Allah. I'm with my pain now.

C: What's happening?

L: The pain's inside of me now and I'm at peace with it. It's all moving around, it's not locked in anymore. Just swirling around, swirling and trying to find a way to get out. But it can't come out until I say what it is. Oh God! Abuse, some kind of abuse somewhere, a long, long time ago.

C: It's all right Lisa. You can go back there right now. It's all right to see it, and feel it, and let this pain get out.

L: It's men! It's all these men. (crying) It's all these men and they are on me and through me. Oh God! They're ripping me apart. They're just destroying me with their lust, and I can't stop them. I can't stop them at all! It's a bunch of them. It's more than just a rape scene, it's a war, a violent rape. They're killing with their rape. Black helmets, fire. Ai, they've killed me. There's this huge gaping wound—ah, let that go!

C: What are you feeling right now?

L: It happened, it just happened, that's all.

C: Do you hate these men?

L: They couldn't help it. They couldn't help it. They were just doing what they were doing. They couldn't help it any more than I could help being who I was.

C: They were possessed with this war, violence, and lust? Just kind of insane?

L: Yeah. It's like they were insane. It's really an insane feeling. I can see their faces. Oh God it's so scary. (crying)

C: It's all right Lisa to let it go. Just allow your body to let these feelings and memories move through you so they can get out. You don't have to hold them in anymore.

L: (screaming) God! Their force came and stayed inside of me. (more wailing and crying)
    Oh God I hate them! They didn't just kill me, they killed my children. I want to kill them. It's so important. The impotency is so horrible. What can I do with it?

C: For now just feel it. Feel what it feels like to be utterly impotent.

L: Oh, God, it's horrible! (still crying) Oh God, there's a big hole, and I'm falling into it. It's a mouth, a huge mouth. It's eating me! (screaming and crying)

C: What's happening now Lisa?

L: It's dark, but I'm back in possession of myself. That's what happens when they take it away. Then they take you away, and you have to bring yourself back.

C: Who are they?

L: Whoever they are who says you can't be you.

C: And that's what happened to you when these men raped and killed you?

L: Yeah. They took away my power, they took away all the physical power of myself, and I couldn't go to the inner power.

C: Can you go inside right now and find that place where your inner power is?

L: It's that feeling of powerlessness, that's what it is. All
those times I felt powerless.

C: Lisa, go inside, close your eyes and go deep inside to the
place where your spiritual essence is. They could not touch
that part of you. What happened to you was a long, long time
ago, and it happened to your physical body, not your spirit,
not the real you. Those men could not rape or destroy your
spirit. They could not take that away from you. Feel that part
of yourself, and let it come down into this body, feel it completely moving down into you, all parts of you, into all those
places where the black waters were, every place where there
was pain.

L: The power of my spiritual self is holding the little child of
me, and rocking her, and consoling her, and holding her, and
protecting her.

C: *You've got it!* You've got yourself back!

L: So many times I've been in situations where I'm not allowed to be me, and I was powerless behind it. And that's
what it's all about.

C: Let's do something while the spirit is still with you and
your inner child. I want you to look back at what happened
to you, with your spirit and your child looking back at what
you've just experienced, at what those men did to your body.
Now let your spirit talk to your child. What does your spirit
say?

L: "Just let go, stay with you, stay, stay, stay with you, stay
with you, stay, stay. It's just your body, come back, come
back home, come back whole."

C: What does your spirit tell you about your cancer?

L: It's irrelevant, it's a reflection on the inside of what happened outside. It locked onto the inside. I have to take it off. What was outside has locked on.

C: Is it unlocked now?

L: It's coming unlocked.

. . .

Lisa left this last session feeling a tremendous relief. The psychic energy she left behind was so thick and sickening it took a considerable time to clean it out of my environment. I saw her just last week and didn't recognize her. She had a full head of kinky black hair, her cancer is in remission, and she has a new lover.

MARINA

Marina and I met at a week-long music camp here in my hometown. She is 30 years old. Though she studied biology in school, she now focuses on her avocation of being a musician and a healer. She presently works for a county agency called Planned Parenthood, and has a particular interest in abuse cases and women's rights. She has also been studying psychic work for about five years and does readings for clients and friends.

Marina has had two major relationships in her life: she was married for nine years, and, after her separation from her husband, she spent about two years in a relationship with another woman. She had recently separated from this woman when I met her. In the work we did together, she wanted to understand what karmic patterns were influencing her current life and what she might do to help work on them. After I led her into an altered state, I asked her to tune in to her soul consciousness.

C: OK, take a little more time to really experience the essence of your soul, its level of consciousness and purity. And now I want you to become aware of the karma your soul has chosen to work on in this life. You're not quite sure how you are going to see this. You will just have to wait and see how it appears in your conscious mind.

Can you begin to tell me any impressions that are occurring to you now?

M: I get a sense that I carry a lot of anger with me. There's also something about working on relating to people. And how to communicate what I know. I also need to work on my relationship to the feminine energy. This seems like a big issue. I have a fear of the feminine energy; it somehow seems evil to me. I haven't realized this before.

C: OK, can we look at how you chose your parents and the conditions of your present life?

M: I set up a situation in which I felt justified in having my anger, a situation in which I could explore that anger, feel it, and own it. I also set up a family situation in which I could experience my feelings of abandonment and isolation by entering into a dysfunctional alcoholic family. My mother left me when I was only 18 months old! My father raised my brother, sisters, and myself. He was a solid alcoholic. No one could ever talk about the fears caused by my father's depression and drinking, the fears or the loneliness that my brother, sisters, and I felt.

My mother abandoned me on all levels. My father was present physically but was absent in so many other ways that I also felt abandoned by him. He barely got me fed and clothed, and he really could not take care of my emotional needs.

The hurt from the family situation enabled me to get into my anger. So often for me hurt turns into anger, a defensive posture. I set up a situation with my older brother in which I was able to experience my theme of rejection. I adored him and he rejected me. He would ridicule me and refuse to even talk to me at times. There were rare occasions when he would notice me and play with me. It made me so happy, and those times made me like him even more. So the contrast of his rudeness made the rejection seem even more poignant.

C: Did you have any advice from guides before coming into this life?

M: That while I can be in a position of being a teacher, I must remember that I am the student always. That everything can teach me. And if one can assume the attitude of a student, one is open to learning much more. As one learns, one can teach others. The anger can be a motivator; learning about it can push me to new growth.

C: How would you describe the main focus of this life?

M: To find my joy in a body and to heal past wounds. It feels like a lifetime of great resolution on many different levels.

C: Is there one particular thing concerning this that would be really important for you to see at this time?

M: That there is no blame. It's not necessary to blame myself for the anger and the pain, nor is it necessary to lay blame on anyone else. The feelings just are and can teach me. That all the different parts of me are a great tapestry, which is beautiful to look at in its entirety. There are negative and positive tones but all are part of the whole. All are necessary to my learning as a being. And in this lifetime I have the opportunity to review the different negatives or transgressions of other lifetimes and to heal those events, to transmute them.

The tapestry can be mended where it's torn. The mending takes vigilance, perseverance, patience, consciousness, asking for help when necessary, and compassion.

C: Let's begin with the anger. I want to ask your soul if it's appropriate for you to reexperience the source of your anger today?

M: Yes.

C: Visualize yourself standing in a hallway. Down at the end of the hall there's a door. The door is closed. And as you walk toward that door you understand that when you open that door you will be ushered into the source—the original events, time, and place—where this deep-seated pattern of anger in your being is from. As you approach the door now, I want you to be precisely aware of the door handle as you reach out and open that door. Which way does the door open?

M: Toward me.

C: And what happens? What do you see when you open the door?

M: A bright, light nothingness. I see the essence of my being before it has become me.

C: How does anger come into the picture?

M: I am angry at being pushed out of the One. I can't go back.

C: Can you tell me what it was like when you were part of the Oneness?

M: Blissful, very high vibration, calm, even, lovely, homogenous. There is no pain, only a great expanse of love.

C: How would you express the love you felt at that time?

M: All-encompassing, glowing, and nurturing. I was love. There was no "I"!

C: What's the first thing you remember when things begin to change, as you move out of the One?

M: I feel squeezed and constricted. I don't want to go.

C: What's the next thing you remember?

M: I'm aware of a constriction, I'm being pushed out. I don't know what is happening. I feel like I'm being cast out, I feel an overwhelming sense of abandonment. It feels like I'm being forced. I don't want to go.

C: What's the next thing you're aware of?

M: I'm not alone. As lonely as it feels to be so constricted, there is another with me. We were pulled apart from one another. This other being feels angry toward me. This being feels that I am responsible in some way for the pain.

C: How did you respond to having anger directed at you?

M: I respond with anger. I feel that we should continue together. I feel there was a reason that we became individuals together. We should work together and support each other. I feel that we need to help each other, but he left me.

C: So you feel abandoned and rejected by this being?

M: Yes. It left me. It feels as though there is a contract and I can't believe I've been left. It is not right or fair for either of us. I feel like I have no support and have to search for myself, and that I would like assistance in this newness. And I feel anger at the process of individuation. Why should I be left out here completely alone? What's the point? I feel resentful.

C: Are you angry and resentful at having to take care of yourself?

M: Yes!

C: What would it take to release this anger toward this other being?

M: Understanding what the other being felt at the time could help me fathom the motivation he had to get away from me.

C: Going back to the experience, what would you say to that being who left you?

M: That I'm hurt. I feel very alone and I want your help. As I say that what I get is lots of fear, excruciating fear.

C: Can you go back and observe your birth again and be cognizant of what the other being goes through?

M: The other soul is in great pain and is fearful of being pushed out, incredibly fearful and confused. He wants to go back in but can't. He feels great grief. He feels some anger at me and feels that it is somehow my fault. I am guilty by association. My feelings of rejection caused by my individuation and my anger caused this other being to be even more fearful. Neither of us is there for the other.

C: So, seeing this, do you think you can have compassion for this being? Do you feel you can forgive this being?

M: Yes. I am sorry I caused him more fear.

C: Now can we go back and look at how, even before you had an awareness of your twin soul, you were angry at creation. You resented being pushed out without knowing what was happening, without having any control over it.

M: I didn't have any understanding of what was going on. I didn't think it was necessary. I didn't want to go. I felt so alone. I felt there should have been some sort of provisions made for me. How could I just get pushed out like that? I was frightened at the tasks in front of me.

C: Why did you think you were put out?

M: I felt rejected. I felt that there was something wrong with me. Something wrong with my energy.

C: Did you have any idea what was wrong with your energy?

M: I just felt unworthy. And that there was something wrong with me. So I think that I've spent a lot of energy trying to prove that I am worthy and protecting myself from the knowledge or the belief that I'm not worthy. There must be something awful about me.

C: Tell me something about the control that you wanted.

M: I wanted to get control. I felt so out of control as I was pushed out against my will. I wanted to be part of the decision. You know, if anyone had asked me, I might not have had so many problems.

C: If you had the control you wanted at the time, what would you have done?

M: If I'd had control I would have gone back to the One and never experienced the pain. I would not have accepted the task of being an individual.

C: Do you resist the task of being an individual now?

M: Yes. I can see now that I have expressed my anger by not bringing my energy fully into my body, by withholding energy from myself and from others, on all different levels and in all different lifetimes. In some lifetimes I have experienced my essence more fully. Those are few. They helped me know what it's like to have more of myself. There is always a part of myself missing. A great potential exists. So I have rejected and abandoned myself!

C: Have you felt guilt about that?

M: Yes.

C: What would it take for you to release your anger from the Point of Origin?

M: I just have to accept life. I'm surprised to see how much resistance I have to doing that. I don't want to. I can see that it would also be important to return to the Oneness in consciousness. I have some intuition that that's what I'm supposed to do, and I express my anger by resisting. And this makes me feel guilty, but the more guilt I feel, the more stubborn and angry I feel. It's a vicious circle. I can see that sooner or later I'm going to have to let go of my anger and play by the rules. I'm only hurting myself by resisting. That's really clear to me now.

C: OK, looking at your present life once again from your soul's perspective, let's focus on another issue that you want to work on in this life.

M: I can see that I have chosen to work on my relationship to the feminine energy. I have a fear of the feminine that I have carried through many lifetimes, in male and female bodies. As a male I have degraded the feminine. As a female I have indulged in self-destructive behavior because I felt the feminine was evil. I also was destructive toward other females. The persecution of the feminine in many different lifetimes has set up some incredible fear and protection in me as a female. My relationships with my father and my brother in this lifetime are examples of how I relate as a female to males.

C: Marina, we're going to have you go back in time again. Let's have you walk down a hallway again. At the end is a door that leads you to the source of your negative image of your feminine self. Open that door now and tell me what you experience.

M: I see a cave. It's a very primitive culture. Communication is very primitive and patchy. Not much verbal communication. I am an old woman with white hair. I have no teeth. I have dreams and can predict when to hunt and where the herd is to be found. I am old enough that I have seen the people change. At one time in my early days there was a place for both males and females. The energy is changing so that men have lost their place. The role of males is being reduced to impregnation and hard labor. When I was young the opinions of everyone were valued, and now there are only a few select that have input into any decision regarding the tribe.

I see unspeakable things happening. I saw my own son castrated for his willfulness and for being an uncooperative male. I carry guilt from this time for not speaking to the atrocities, particularly that I did not do anything when this happened to my son. The men and boys are subjugated and treated as servants. It causes me pain to see the women that would champion the men mistreated or ostracized, even mutilated sometimes, or killed. It is impossible to speak up even in the position I hold as visionary. I feel angry and powerless to stop this negative energy.

I have a dream of a battle, and I speak of it to the tribe and the tribal mothers. The dream is prophetic and comes true. It was a time of famine, and a neighboring tribe saw our wealth and our provisions. They attacked us. Many people are killed brutally. The dream I had was believed to have caused the disaster. I was ostracized and made to live on the outskirts of the village. I, too, feared that I had caused the disaster by my dreaming. I learn to fear my psychic sight and this ability that the mothers feel only belongs to women. I also fear the abusive women that are in power now. I see how they treat the males and cannot speak to it for fear of being killed or totally abandoned by the tribe.

These feelings are similar to the feelings I had at the Point of Origin. I have similar feelings of anger at being pushed out of my tribe. I also feel helpless at my lack of control. I'm afraid and feel rejected.

C: Can you explore another life in that period?

M: I'm still in those same primitive times. I'm a little girl. I learn that only women can think or make decisions. I'm reprimanded when I show a desire to relate to the boys or men.

I learn the tribal mothers' rule of what is right: that women are superior, if they play by the rules. It's not OK to have feelings. If we were allowed our feelings the subjugation of men and the cruelty could not have occurred. Women are abused if they show any signs of compassion or caring toward the cruelties that are happening. If a woman shows signs of pain or anger about the cruelty, she is mutilated.

As I grow I am trained to be a mother of the tribe. I forget all feelings of compassion. I learn to stuff huge portions of myself—the parts of myself that I would call feminine softness—and go for the power of being a decision maker in the tribe. In order to get the power, I have to cut off my sensitivities and feelings. My anger comes out in other ways. I act it out by becoming one of the women who persecutes the men and punishes the women who attempt to support men. The anger is indirect, manipulative, and vindictive. I feel my sense of guilt increasing, but it's also something that gets stuffed in order to maintain the status quo. I have to tell myself continually that I'm better than anyone else, that I have the supreme connection to the goddess energy, that I'm the chosen one. I have to keep reassuring myself that what I do and how I keep control is OK, is warranted. I make myself believe that this is the way it has to be.

C: Is there another life during the matriarchal times?

M: I'm surrounded by trees. I'm a primitive man covered with hair. I'm wearing a loincloth. I escaped from my tribe and live alone in the wilderness. I feel angry that I am alone and know that I will die in the harsh winter. In the tribe I was kept as a pet for the women. I was used as brood stock and had no other value. I was degraded by being tethered in the heat of the day and ridiculed and jeered at as the women passed on their work day. I feel like meat and that I have no worth or purpose. To be away from the tribe is to die. In this primitive time, the tribal unity is very important for survival. Alone I feel powerless and angry, hurt and rejected. I know I'm going to die.

C: Can you see another life as a man?

M: I see a jungle; it's lush and tropical. My skin is black. I am male. I wear a loincloth and I'm hunting. The tribe is male dominated, just the opposite of the skewed matriarchy that we've looked at. Women are not treated well. They are not treated with validity. They have nothing to say. I have a sense of arrogance in my energy, and sense that what I do is right. I feel better than anyone else, especially women. The arrogance protects me from knowing what I do is not very good. I put my anger into hunting and abusing my wife, an acceptable thing to do in this society. I hunt because I feel a need to kill. It's not a clean feeling of foraging for the nurturing of the tribe. It makes me feel good to kill.

C: In what way are you abusive with your wife?

M: I strike her physically and deny her needs. She does not always get food to eat, and when I feel particularly angry I make her sleep outside.

C: Is there anything else important for you to see in this lifetime.

M: No, I spend the rest of that life as an arrogant insensitive man. I'm killed by a wild animal; a tiger. The violence of my death is somehow satisfying, like a perverted indulgence in my anger.

C: What is the next life you see?

M: I think I'm in England. It has a Robin Hood flavor to it. I'm filled with anger about my lot in life as a serf. That's how I grew up. I never had enough to eat and there was so much poverty and illness around me. I'm filled with anger at my mother for not feeding me or taking care of my needs. I have to work so hard, even as a little boy, for so little in return. All that we harvest goes to the landowners.

When I grow up, I become a highway robber. I lie in wait for wealthy people, whom I despise. I rob from them and rape the women. That's my way of thumbing my nose at society and getting even. I rape women that seem the most snobby. Often I have seen them at the public markets and fairs. Their wealth is in such contrast to the poverty of my life.

C: What kind of feelings do you have as you rape the women?

M: Anger. Rage. A sense of getting control and making them hurt as much as I hurt inside. A sense of getting power where I feel I have none.

C: So it makes you feel powerful?

M: Yes. It also increases my feeling of guilt and circularly my anger increases. I feel powerful and in control when I rape. And I feel like I'm making the wealthy pay. It makes me feel more angry on another level, because their pain mirrors my own. So ultimately I feel worse. The rage continues to grow. I'm a very unhappy individual.

C: What happens later in that life?

M: I am killed during one of the robberies. I'm shot with an arrow.

C: What do you feel like as you're dying?

M: I feel relief at being able to let go of that life and the misery I experienced since the moment of my birth.

C: Can you move to another life now?

M: It seems like I'm in the Alps. I don't know where. I'm a peasant girl. I work really hard. I'm toiling in the fields. I carry heavy loads to fields high up in the mountains. I'm barefoot and my feet bleed. The work I do makes my body hurt, so I have resistance to my lot in life and anger about the hard work. My parents have their own farm and it's a collective community. I spend a lot of time out by myself in the fields, which are so far from home it takes a day to travel there by foot. So I sleep alone in the fields. I was once raped by a passing group of bandits, so I have a lot of fear. I feel helpless. I'll never know anything different. I'll always be in the fields alone and unprotected.

C: How did you feel after you were raped?

M: I felt helpless and alone. I was not able to deal with it in any way. I told no one. I had made a choice as a little girl not to speak. I'm mute. There was no one in my family that would help me. I was not accepted as a family member other than for what work I offered. I made a choice to isolate myself from them because of physical and sexual abuse. I wouldn't talk. I didn't want to communicate. I wanted to shut everyone out because I felt angry at my lot.

   I don't bear any children when I do have a lover. He leaves after being with me for a year. I die a young woman; I just don't want to live anymore.

C: Is there another life that would be important for you to see today?

M: I see a fire in the fireplace in the Victorian era. I am a woman and I'm wearing a high-collared dress that is restrictive, hot, and uncomfortable. I'm wearing a corset that is killing me. I can't breathe a full breath. My ribs ache.

As I was growing up I was not allowed to do the things that I saw my brothers doing. I'm allowed to ride as they are, but they don't let me go alone or wear comfortable clothes. I was taught to sew in even stitches and run the stuffy house and rule the servants. I'm taught I have to look pretty. I feel angry at having to stuff my feelings, of being uncomfortable physically, and having to do women's chores in the house. I'm frustrated and upset. I also feel powerless to change my lot. I hate women's clothes. I hate women's chores. I hate being female.

As I grow up I'm not allowed to do what I really want to do. I'm forced to marry, but he dies and leaves me with my family house and enough money to live quite well. My woman friend moves in with me and becomes my companion until I die. We sleep together but don't have a sexual relationship because the society is very repressive. I begin to wear men's clothes and to do more of the things I wanted to do. Simply go riding by myself, for example. As a girl I was resentful and angry about being a girl. I wanted to be a boy and have boys' adventures, but instead I had to learn how to sew in even and tiny stitches, and keep the servants in line. I had a lot of anger about being female.

C: What was your marriage to your husband like?

M: It was very removed. I didn't see him much. I was for the most part left to my own devices during the day. We didn't talk much when he was home. I didn't like him. He was dull and calloused.

C: Why did you marry him?

M: So I could survive and remain in my family home after my parents died. As a woman in that time I had no way to make money. It was necessary to marry for survival. There were no options for me as a woman as far as making money.

C: So you were glad when he died?

M: Yes. He died in an accident. He fell off a horse and broke his neck.

C: Marina, is there another life for you to recall today?

M: I see a massacre occurring in the plains of the North American continent. I'm an Indian man. There's a lot of fear and helplessness. Masses and masses of my peoples are getting killed by white men and by renegade Indian tribes. I have great pain in my heart that this is happening. And I knew that it would happen. I have anger and a sense of helplessness. I need to be able to protect my people and I cannot. I feel that the killing is inevitable with the white man moving across our lands in such numbers.

C: What's your position in the tribe?

M: Medicine man. Shaman. So I see and I know what will occur and what does occur, white faces murdering my people.

C: Is there anything more in that life to look at?

M: There's a lot of sadness in that lifetime. I feel very sad.

C: Why was it important to see this life today?

M: Because of the helplessness and the anger. Because I hadn't connected to this energy in this way before. And because it needs to heal. Also because of what's happening to Mother Earth. I know and see that she is raped as the women in my tribe are raped. It's a sin against our natures.

C: Are the feelings similar to the feelings you had at the Point of Origin?

M: Yes, a sense of helplessness and confusion. I don't understand what's happening. In this life as the Indian I feel very isolated and alone. Me and my people are being exterminated—my response is to get very angry.

C: You mentioned communication as one issue you are focusing on in this life. Why is this an issue with you? What have your patterns been in the past?

M: I have been quite closed with what I know in other lifetimes. I have been withholding this knowledge and have not shared it with those who really deserved it. I have not been able to share it with people who might just have need of it.

C: What was your criteria for that?

M: In the lifetime that I'm seeing right now, people had to prove that they were pious. They had to prove a grand religious intent and purity. That was a very difficult criteria for one to match. There were few, very few that measured up to my standards. Few people had the benefit of my knowing.

C: What time period are you in, and what is your capacity? Why were you the person, making these decisions?

M: It was in medieval times, and I was a part of the Catholic church. It's a time I have looked at before and become conscious of in this current lifetime. I felt much better than others. I was at a place where I was a decision maker in the church. I had a lot of power to make decisions about the fate of my subjects. I was a part of the Inquisition. I could decide who lived and who died in the name of the church.

C: Looking at that now from this perspective would you say you were completely fair in how you carried out your role?

M: I can see that it was very unfair.

C: How were you unfair?

M: How I see that now? I see that no person has a right to make decisions about someone else's path or to judge others on their spirituality. All of the people that were murdered were wrongfully killed. They had wonderful attributes that need to be exalted in the world. I, because of my fears and my power in the church, was able to persecute and operate to stamp out the healing energy, at least to do what I could toward that end. The abilities of the persecuted to rely on their own healing energy challenged my reality and the reality of the church, and what I felt was right and good.

C: In other words, they challenged the Christian dogma?

M: Yes. In my eyes they were witches. I know now that they were healers and had grand things to offer. They had a sense of nurturing and ways of healing that in that lifetime I could not express as a man or as a priest. I can see now that it was threatening to me.

C: Is there anything else that played a part in some of your decisions? Is there a level of anger that you were acting on?

M: Mmm, but I couldn't have seen that at the time.

C: So looking at that from this perspective, what were you angry about and how were you acting that out in that lifetime?

M: I was angry at feeling that the same thing had been done to me. In another lifetime I was a healer and had been tortured and killed and deemed a witch. In this priest lifetime I carried that anger with me and I continued to do the same thing. It was a blind anger.

C: Are there any other lifetimes that relate to this need to learn how to communicate what you know?

M: I see stars. I'm gazing at the stars from a balcony. It's a stone building. I'm in the desert, a dry, arid place. I'm a man and a teacher. It's part of the ancient Egyptian culture. I feel full of myself. I feel I'm at least one notch above the rest of the world. I feel superior because of my knowledge and my abilities as a clairvoyant. Being a teacher I use that to make myself feel better than others.

C: What else do you see about this life?

M: I'm strongly competitive with my teacher, who I now work with in partnership. I always felt like I wanted to be like him and have the abilities that he has. I do have similar abilities, but I always want to be better than I am. And I resent him for always being better than me. I compete with him and challenge him in an arrogant manner. You probably know this already, but I just realized that you are my teacher in this life.

C: Yes I was starting to get that sense. What's important for you to see about this life?

M: This is about power issues. And wanting to be one-up and have the control and power. It's important to look at that because of the resistant quality. Not letting a more forgiving energy in where I could learn something. I am defensive about my abilities, arrogant. So I don't even know that I'm not that great. Not that I'm not OK, I'm just not as great as I want to be.

C: Let's go forward in that life and see if there's anything important that happens.

M: As I move forward in the lifetime I feel a growing sense of frustration and helplessness, because I set my sights on something that I want to be rather than who I am. I become more hopeless that I would ever attain my desires. I grow into a bitter old man. My teaching abilities deteriorate. I'm no longer teaching for the right reasons anymore. I'm teaching to get control and to get power and prestige. I forget my students' needs; they are secondary to me and my needs.

C: In other words you're using your position to bolster your sense of self-esteem.

M: Yes. I have a sense that it's not right to do that, and I'm called on it by my teacher. The guilt I feel, and try to deny, makes me feel even more hopeless. And I never find a way out of that before I die.

C: Marina, is there anything else you need to look at today to help clear the issues we've been focusing on?

M: The first thing I experience is a tunnel inside of my physical body, dark and moist. As I move into it, it becomes the One. Nothingness. Absolute serenity and calm.

C: OK, why are you shown this now?

M: To remember the One. To remember how it feels to leave behind the anger and the resentment and the feelings of isolation and rejection and to feel how it feels to be absolutely complete, a part of everything.

C: Are you able to open yourself to that experience?

M: Not completely. There's some tightness in my third chakra.

C: And why does it have trouble opening to the serenity of the Oneness?

M: It has trouble receiving. I don't feel that I deserve to receive because of the things that I've done in past lives. The cruelties and the way my power has been misused.

C: Maybe there is something else you need to look at to help you forgive yourself. Is there anything else that's important for you to look at today about these issues? It may be another past life you need to look at, or it may be anything else your higher self or guides want to show you at this time.

M: It feels like a study or an office. There's somebody sitting at the desk checking off the things that we've looked at today. There's more to look at but it doesn't need to be done today.

The importance of being able to forgive the past is under-lined in order to move forward. It's important to release the guilt about the anger I've carried with me through all my life-times and move forward. I can see that I need to become more conscious about how these themes work into my life at the present time.

C: What would help you integrate these experiences that you have had today?

M: I see my guide. He's a guide that I've done a lot of work with in the past few years in a conscious manner. He appears as a huge black Jamaican man with really dark skin and he offers me a sense of protection and a positive male-father en-ergy in my life. He offers me a sense of strength. He's an in-credibly joyful being. He often appears to me with a huge smile on his face. He talks to me a lot about movement in the body and finding my joy here. So we look at what's stopped me from having my joy. I feel guilty for what I've done in my past lives and the way I've misused power and directed my anger by getting control over other people. This guilt makes me feel like I don't deserve to have joy. So the process of for-giving myself is very important.

C: How does he help you forgive yourself?

M: I see myself in a field with many other beings. My Jamai-can guide and others. They put me in the center of this circle of support and love. I remove things from my third chakra that represent my need to get control. I see and remove pad-locks, chains, the scepter from the Egyptian life, a spear and a bow and arrow, the priest's hat and cross, and a big ball of darkness that represents how I used power against other be-ings and myself in an effort to get control and thwart the life process because of the anger I held toward the cosmos.

We put these things in a pit and destroy them with a cleansing fire. This allows the energy of the anger and the guilt to be released, dissipate, and transform so that there is room for forgiveness, understanding, and compassion in my soul. They put me in the middle of the circle with my clothes removed. On all sides, the beings here to assist me are massaging me. At first I have difficulty receiving the energy. Gradually the resistance I feel to receiving such love and assistance lessens.

The ritual melts away the tightness in my third chakra. And then I melt into the feeling of oneness, of being able to receive and allow more of my energy to flow out in a helpful way in the universe, a complete clear circuit. All these beings here to help me in this ritual remind me that I'm not alone, and that if I'm open to it, there are people here to help me. The ritual makes me aware that the isolation I have felt has a lot more to do with how I view it than what is actually occurring. So I'm learning more about myself and my process and acceptance of the life process. The importance of the lessons I've learned in all my lifetimes and in between lifetimes, the destiny of my soul is to become more and more infused with light so that I will give guidance to other beings still in bodies. I still have a lot of work to do on this planet.

C: Could you talk about how you will be different in a body after this ritual?

M: I feel softer. There isn't a need for protection because of the forgiveness I feel for myself. I don't have to protect myself from knowing about my past actions and the fear of thinking that I'm unworthy. So I'll have less of a need to reject other people or a feeling of having to protect them and myself from how awful I've felt that I am. I have a greater allowance and acceptance of my friends' energy and love and can respond in a new clearer way. I see myself less withholding than I have been. I see more energy in my body and more of a desire to move and be in it—in my body and in the moment.

C: OK, I'd like you to relax a moment and feel yourself drawn up to a soul-level perspective to a place above all these lifetimes, and look back down on your present life. Is there any last thing that is important for you to see and understand right now at this time to integrate into this lifetime and go forward?

M: The importance of the process of being in the moment. Trust in the process of life and of my life as a being. Faith.

C: Is there any part of you that feels unresolved or uncomfortable in any way about this session today?

M: There's an energy in my third chakra that is still resistant. It's the skeptical part of myself. It's saying: "You haven't really let go of the anger and control issues. There is still a lot of work on forgiveness that needs to occur before you're on your way."

C: It seems like the skeptic inside you could be an ally as far as keeping you honest in the future. Would you be willing to let it serve that function for you?

M: Yes.

C: Is it willing to help you in this way?

M: Yes.

C: Ask it how it would be willing to serve that function for you.

M: It will communicate itself to me by a tightness in my third chakra. When I feel that I'll know that there is something a little off so that I can look at whatever it is and examine it. And at that point see how I need to change my energy to feel better.

C: Do you or your skeptic need to communicate anything else at this time?

M: No. We're shaking hands. It's a deal.

· · ·

In Marina's sessions we see how complex and convoluted our karmic patterns can become. Her initial feeling of helplessness, abandonment, lack of control, and belief there must be something wrong with her from her Point of Origin, were compensated for by anger, will to power, and a false sense of superiority. Throughout the lives she reexperienced, we see the polarization of these core feelings being acted out. In some of the lives, she embodied her sense of abandonment and powerlessness, whereas on the other hand she had lives where she sought positions of power in which she acted out her defensive anger and resentment for feeling victimized. The theme of rape was a major vehicle, and metaphor, for these polar feelings; in some lives she was the victim of rape, while in others she was the rapist.

Her fear of the feminine is also a complex issue. Beginning with her experiences in the matriarch, what she originally despised in the power structure of the matriarch, she became in order to survive and gain the power she desired. As a man in a following life, she then experienced the results of her negative identity as a matriarchal leader. The abuse she received in this life turns into abusive actions toward women in subsequent lifetimes, which in turn generates lifetimes as a woman where she suffers the same sort of abuse from men in her life.

In Marina's sessions we also learn how important it is to address the sense of guilt we carry; it is often one of the biggest hurdles we must overcome in order to take an honest look at ourselves. So much of our present identities are constructed of rigid defense materials to protect our conscious self from the ugly or unacceptable things hidden beneath our socially acceptable facades. The healing metaphor at the end of her sessions is a good example of the self-forgiveness that is so critical in our endeavors to heal ourselves from the hardships of the dramas that we have lived.

Implications of Karma

Where are all our karmic lessons leading us? Are we learning to have more power, wealth, sensual pleasures, complete freedom, and bigger more charismatic egos, or is there a more sublime purpose?

Let's begin with some conclusions about this process of transformation we as souls participate in. In *Other Lives, Other Selves,* Jungian analyst Woolger delineates three stages of psychological integration worth summarizing here: the realistic-cathartic stage, the symbolic-archetypal stage, and the integral-mystical stage.

In the realistic-cathartic stage we relate to experiences in a literal way, and in a linear cause-and-effect sequence. In this stage we treat a complex or karmic pattern as if it were real, as if it were based on traumas from previous experiences. Often this includes some form of catharsis, an awareness of, and release of related emotions.

These complexes normally involve events in which the ego-self has been profoundly hurt. Hence, Jung's maxim: "A complex arises where we experience defeat in life." In *any* life, I might add. Based on these "defeats" we construct formidable defenses, rationalizations, and entire life styles to avoid further painful events. Unfortunately our defensive maneuvers only result in fixating us in our traumatic egoic realities from one life to the next.

Woolger points out that cathartic release is not always successful in helping a person release trauma. Further regressions to prior or more dramatic episodes may only entrench people more in their emotional hells. In therapy, as in life itself, we often have experiences but miss their meaning.

Hence, there is a need to move on to the next level of integration, the symbolic-archetypal.

In this second stage we begin to search for the meaning, "for metaphor rather than realism," as Woolger puts it. At this level, growth occurs through an understanding of the symbolic implications of our life-dramas. For example, in Lisa's struggle with her cancer she finally arrived at the symbolic meaning of the life-threatening aspect of her illness, the sense of powerlessness because some external force had taken away her ability to live her own life.

In this symbolic stage of unraveling our personal histories we look at the recurring themes in our life, and lives, and begin to detach ourselves from identifying with them. If we fail to do this, we will continue to repeat life after life in which we act out the symbolism of our personal myths. The astral or emotional body does not age as does the physical body. It exists beyond three-dimensional time and continually revisits the past. Here traumas and belief systems are imprinted in the dreamlike mythical stratum of the psyche, the metaphoric symbolic level of psychic reality. We therefore are confronted with the task of reading and changing the myths of our lives. In order to do this we need to develop an objective perspective, what Jung referred to as "the transcendent function," or what some meditation groups refer to as the "witness point."

It is also from this transcendent perspective that we begin to reconcile the many conflicting polarities within ourselves. We have seen in the readings how a soul will often flip back and forth in consecutive lifetimes experiencing dramas that mirror one another. One of Jung's dictums puts it this way: "You always become the thing you fight the most." In Marina's regressions we saw her soul alternate between being the victim of rape and oppression and being the perpetrator of rape and oppression. Until a soul is able to achieve a transcendent perspective, and hence begins to disidentify with its complexes, it will continue to spiral through lifetimes of action and reaction, lifetimes of contrasting opposites.

Reconciling the opposites through integration of the shadow side of the psyche is laborious and humiliating, often bringing us to the verge of despair, disillusionment, and ego-death. In terms of karma and past-life therapy, it often means reliving and accepting those lifetimes in which we lived out the grotesque and macabre human aspects that symbolize the ugliness, anger, resentment, and self-loathing our souls can succumb to. Through acceptance, forgiveness, and dis-identification or ego-death, we move from this transcendent position onto the integral-mystical stage.

At the first level, the realistic-cathartic, events appear to be literal: real power struggles, real rape, real cancer. In the second stage, the symbolic-archetypal, the mythic level of re-ality reveals itself: needing a leg to stand on, being cut off from feelings, losing our head, life is a burden, etc. Finally life is simply what it is, in its "suchness," as Tibetan Bud-dhists might say. Or, to restate Stanislav Grof, "Everything is a metaphor, and every metaphor is true."

At this stage, the integral-mystical, the enlightened soul transcends the dualism within itself. Indifferent to the play of opposites in external reality now, it comes down from its meditation cave on the mountain and reenters the market-place. In Zen Buddhism there is a series of pictures of a monk and an ox that depicts the various stages of spiritual unfold-ment. The last picture shows a potbellied monk riding the ox and entering into a city with "bliss bestowing hands," where he then lives among winebibbers and butchers.

In *Other Lives, Other Selves*, Woolger recounts one of Jung's dreams to demonstrate the implications of this final stage. In his dream, Jung was on a hiking trip and stopped at a small wayside chapel. He expected to find a customary im-age of the Virgin Mary or a crucifix on the altar inside the chapel. He found a yogi seated in meditation instead. Upon a second look Jung realized that the yogi had his, Jung's, own face. Jung woke with the realization that the yogi was meditating him, that Jung himself was being dreamed by the yogi. Jung knew when the yogi awoke, i.e., reached enlightenment, that Jung would no longer exist.

Working with karma then is not just a matter of erasing old patterns from the psyche, as if the unconscious mind is a mere collection of video tapes. We need to transform the basis for how we relate to the world, and indeed to our own sense of self. Until we do, we continue to create karma in the same old ways.

This brings us to the more sublime dynamics of karma. There is an evolutionary force pushing us beyond our basic physical and psychological needs. There's an old axiom that says: "Straight is the way and narrow is the gate." As we near the end of our journey on the spiritual path, the cosmic karmic computer sets up situations in which we have less and less choice to do anything other than "walk the straight and narrow." In other words the critical mass of karma can get so dense that we find ourselves in the proverbial corner in which the only way out is to grow in consciousness.

There are two important aspects of this higher work we are confronted with: developing a conceptual framework for the way in which we as individuals relate to a greater reality, and participating in a method whereby we consciously integrate into this greater reality.

As past-life work progresses, our sense of self expands. Gradually we house a whole family of other selves in our present consciousness. The small abode of our egos exists in the kingdom of the soul. Meditation techniques, life style, and attitudes to align our ego's will with that of the soul, are now appropriate extensions of our endeavor.

Whereas the ego is active in organizing and directing the conscious self, it must eventually learn how to be passive and subservient in relation to the soul. For the ego this is a paramount task. Jung's vision of the individuation process evolved around the ability of the ego identity to reorient itself to the guidance and whole-making impulses of the Self. Jung envisioned this as an ever-increasing opening of the ego to embrace into consciousness the transpersonal dimensions of the Self.

Once this longing for reunion is satisfied, the soul experiences a profound sense of relief and acceptance back into the heart of creation from which it has felt cast forth. Our sense of identity then assumes transpersonal connotations and we gain a calm assurance that we are Life. The omnipotence, omnipresence, and omniscience of Life are the vital, sustaining, and guiding factors shining through the translucence of the holographic microcosms of our souls.

To encourage this transformation we need to establish life styles based on this essential reality. Most popular religious systems, especially here in the Western world, are not adequate. They are from an earlier stage of development of the psyche. At best they are like nursery rhymes and fairy tales from our previous periods of spiritual childhood. At worst, they wreak rationalizations and the manipulative or addictive tendencies of our neurotic egos, which have twisted and perverted the teachings of inspirational beings. Religion has been referred to as the "opiate of the masses." It often promises salvation while providing insidious systems for denial of the responsibilities involved in the transformation of the ego-self.

There is a need for a method whereby we can learn to trust the greater reality through actual participation, hence allowing the transpersonal forces to move through us. In meditation, for example, we learn how to relax the various tensions in our being and allow Life to circulate through our being. When we can transpose this experience of meditation into our everyday life, we begin to fulfill our destiny as a soul. We will then cease to function from a self-centered, closed-system mentality that generates karmic patterns.

Everyone knows that if we want a good harvest we must plant good seeds. Moreover, we will not even get a harvest if we don't plant anything. All our psychological experiences—especially those thoughts and feelings we hold at the time of death—are part of our soul's harvest, for better or worse. The best way to advance is to refrain whenever possible from dwelling on negative thoughts; accept, indeed *appreciate*, karmic lessons; plant good seeds; and remember, we grow and learn best through love.

Freedom and free will have always been sacred concepts here on planet Earth, especially in the Western world. So often what in reality is championed as freedom, is merely a defense of the freedom to choose to be dominated by our personal desires, aversions, and will to power, hence karma; hardly freedom at all. In truth, our only freedom is the choice of when we are going to master these tendencies of our personal sense of identity so that we can in turn surrender to the greater will of Life.

In Asia, the nontheistic religion of Taoism addresses the ultimate reality with a term that simply means "The Way." When we become masters of our own fate, we are not free to do whatever we so please. A Master is a being who has freed himself or herself from the laws of karma by relinquishing attachments and personal identity, and learned how to *follow* "The Way." The Zen Master Sengstan once said that the Great Way is not difficult for those who have no preferences. When love and hate are both absent, everything becomes clear and undistinguished. If we make the slightest distinction, however, heaven and earth are set infinitely apart. If we wish to see the truth, then we can hold no opinions for or against anything. To set up what we like against what we dislike is just a disease of the mind.

The Western world of late has been exploring the ancient wisdom of the East. A synthesis, a marriage is taking place in the fields of physics and psychology, and to a lesser extent in religion. The offspring, a new generation of symbols and paradigms, is forthcoming. You are the explorers and the pioneers. The work you do now within your own psyches to eradicate the karmic residues will affect the bio-morphic fields of the human race. Your quest for the Way will lay the foundation for the next step on the path of the evolution of consciousness for humanity. A step we are getting ready to make.

But let's not be too optimistic about this great New Age. There are extremely powerful groups who comprise the "powers that be" on the material plane. These include such organizations as the Trilateral Commission and other international covert alliances of the world's wealthy/power elite working diligently to establish a global economic totalitarianism under the guise of the "New World Order." Theirs is not a new world order, but a worst-case scenario of the old way of doing things here on the planet. In the name of profit they are ruthlessly raping the Earth of its natural resources and destroying our ecosystem at an increasingly alarming rate. The human race is being used as beasts of burden and consumers by these gods of the almighty dollar.

In Giaff's message on the soul, which I included in the introduction to Part One, he makes reference to the mythical battle of Armageddon. I edited out some of his original message and decided to place it here at the end of the book because it speaks to the worldwide crises we face today.

. . .

Once again the body of Earth is heavy with pain and disease of the collective energies of the race. Even now she labors in the throes of a healing crisis that will like a fever burn away the negativity and life-threatening elements weighing upon her. In those times of Atlantis, a new tone of cosmic energy was brought to the planet. At this present time, twelve thousand years after Atlantis's final destruction, the body of the planet is beginning to entrain or resonate with that new tone. The cycle of karma generated at that time is now coming to fruition. Once again the planet is faced with worldwide destruction as the forces of the Universal Law confront the insurrection of power-hungry souls, those wayward Lemurian and Atlantean souls still karmically bound to the planet and bent on enslaving humanity for their own gain and indulgence.

The frequency of your planet is being changed. Not only the vibrational rate of consciousness, but the atomic structure of your world is being altered. I beseech you to relinquish your old ways and adjust yourselves to the new frequency of consciousness manifesting in your world, whether it be in the wake of worldwide destruction or through the radical transformation of existing structures. Regardless of your origin as a soul, whether you are here from some inner dimension, another physical evolutionary system, or part of the human kingdom proper, all of your individual fates are invariably woven into the collective drama being acted out on the body of this planet. The battle of Armageddon, the legacy of Lucifer and his lot, these mythogems haunt you as a race.

We are here now, watching over your planet. Throughout the critical period we will be here lending our support, reaching out to you from the Spirit, urging you to walk toward the light and allow those old ways to fade into the darkness behind you. We can not do it for you. We can only encourage you to go forward on the path of your evolution.

Let me just emphasize that for you who have become ensnared in the karma of planet Earth, there is no individual salvation. It is only through rectifying your actions and thoughts in accordance with the Universal Laws, and then working toward the healing of the evolutionary system you are now involved in, that you will be able to untangle yourself from the collective karma of the planet and continue along the path of your perfection as a soul.

Postscript

Our earth-bound brains are not accustomed to probing the dimensions of life that have been presented in this book. I have often had profound experiences in past-life regressions fade like dreams from my normal awareness. Reading over this manuscript over the year or so that I worked on it, I found a deeper understanding each time. I therefore encourage you to reread this book one or more times over the years ahead.

APPENDIX A

Many New Age people and writers have glorified the Golden Age of Lemuria. For example, in *The Lost Continent of Mu*, James Churchward maintains that many thousands of years before the Pleistocene Age, more than 50,000 years ago, the continent Mu flourished on a landmass in the Pacific Ocean. He shows that written records of Mu are many and widespread around the globe.[1] Often called the Motherland of Man in these ancient sources, the advent of language and all the arts and sciences of human civilization are attributed to the Motherland, as is the advent of the human species itself. Churchward has nothing but good things to say about the inhabitants of the Motherland of Mu.

In *The Twelfth Planet*, on the other hand, Zecharia Sitchin traces all language and culture to the Sumerians in the Mesopotamian Valley. His translations and interpretations of ancient symbols and texts indicate there was a race of "gods" who the human species was created to serve. These gods were often depicted with wings and in association with im-

---

[1] Accounts of Mu appear in the Naacal tablets discovered in India and in another closely related set of stone tablets found in Mexico (the actual writing on both sets is in the alphabet of Mu and both are over 15,000 years old), the Troana Manuscript and the Codex Cortesianus, from the Mayan Indians in the Yucatán, in the Hindu classic, *Ramayana*, in the *Life of Solon*, by Plutarch as well as other Greek philosophers. Legends, artifacts, symbols, and monuments abound through the islands of the South Pacific, Central America, the cliff dwellers of the Southwestern United States, and the Zuni Indians. And finally, the Lhasa Record was a manuscript found in the Buddhist temple at Lhasa.

ages that evoked the impression of rockets and space flight. Hence Sitchin attempts to make a case for a race of extraterrestrials from an undiscovered planet that exists in an extreme elliptical orbit in our own solar system, who brought civilization to Earth and created the human race as beasts of burden. Sitchin refers to biblical and Mesopotamian texts for his thesis. For example he quotes this passage from Genesis: . . . the sons of the gods saw that the daughters of men were beautiful; so they took for themselves such women as they chose. . . . In those days, when the sons of the gods had intercourse with the daughters of men and got children by them, the Nephilim were on earth. They were the heroes of old, men of renown (Genesis 6:2, 4).

Though modern theologians have shied away from these enigmatic verses in Genesis, Jewish writings from the Second Temple associated them with the ancient traditions of "fallen angels." Sitchin, on the other hand, surmises that the Nephilim were those who came here in space ships.

The term *Nephilim* usually translated as *giants* in translations of the Old Testament, stems from the Semitic root NFL (to be cast down). Sitchin goes on to show that the term *shem* is a Semitic derivative of the Sumerian word *mu*, which he interprets as a "Boat of Heaven," a vehicle in which the gods roamed the skies. From ancient glyphs that evoke the image of a rocketlike object—and other indications in texts—Sitchin claims that a shem was a spaceship. Hence, he maintains that the People of the Shem were the people of the spaceships. Is it not also a possible interpretation to assume that the Semitic derivative of *mu* refers to the Motherland of Mu? Could the Nephilim be the fallen angels (Lucifer and his host) who were cast down to Earth because of their cosmic insurrections? Is it not possible that these fallen angels could have been the "gods" who founded Lemuria, and later colonized Earth?

In my experience with regressing students and clients, I have been urged to consider that the legend of Lucifer refers to a group of inner-dimensional beings who were sent here to initiate and guide the evolution of life on our planet. This group of power-inflated souls was working at odds with the Divine Plan and was sent here as an opportunity to rectify their self-aggrandizing attitudes.

My first experience of regression work involving Lemuria occurred with a young man in one of my classes. I personally worked with him as he returned to his native dimension prior to coming to Earth. He relived being a member of a group of scientifically-minded souls who were carrying out experiments and controlling life forms in another dimension. Eventually the group was curtailed in their endeavors because the work they were doing was out of harmony with the greater good. Many of the group were angry about being sent here and they projected that anger into the life forms they had been assigned to help develop. Having further complicated their karma, these resentful souls were then required to incarnate into these life forms to straighten them out and create a suitable vehicle for human evolution. I subsequently worked with several other people who recalled a similar story.

Both Edgar Cayce and the guides who write through Ruth Montgomery speak of the "Things." These were half-animal half-human creatures. In *The Stories of the Origin and Destiny of Man,* Cayce is quoted to say that there were soul-entities who existed for hundreds of thousands of years before the first inhabitants of Atlantis who had cohabitated with animals in order to experience material existence. These creatures were freakish, with tails and hoofs, etc. Ruth's guides in *The World Before* also imply that these souls somehow mated with animals when they say that "God" later made it impossible for them to mate and have offspring with animals.

Cayce also talks about the Sons of Belial, though not drawing a parallel between them and the legend of Lucifer, who were at odds with the Sons of God. I must say, however, that in general I find both Cayce's and Ruth's guides' rendition of the origins of life on this planet to be metaphysically dressed-up biblical accounts of creation. Ruth's guides have the Lemurians going around the planet "spreading the gospel of the One God." Both Ruth's guides and Cayce tell of not one, but five Adams, who start the five races of man simultaneously around the globe. My feeling about this is that Cayce, Arthur Ford, and the other guides working through Ruth, are all members of a soul group of evangelistic Christians who are networking to preach a New Age gospel. Though their information is probably the most substantial in this field of metaphysical anthropology, the overlay of Christian dogma is suspect.

This may all seem a bit obscure and irrelevant to the theme of this book, but it's important because the legacy of Lucifer possibly explains how the evolution of human life on this planet has been plagued with an unusual number of negative qualities. I'm suggesting that the inordinate amount of will to power, avarice, and obsession with scientific manipulation evident in our history can be traced to the karmic themes implanted on Earth by the fallen angels. Their influences are still diligently working to control the planet. All of our individual karmas are woven into the fabric of this cloak of original sin that shrouds our evolutionary system.

APPENDIX B

The second controversial period of history that plays a significant part in our present collective experience was an Amazon social system that existed in Old Europe. I believe this occurred after the earth changes that caused the final destruction of Atlantis around 10,000 B.C. After the rebellion and the civil war that caused the earlier destruction of Atlantis—28,000 B.C.—my psychic impressions suggest most of the power-hungry souls took control of the remaining landmass of Atlantis and lived out their predilection for power and dominance there. When their remaining domain sank beneath the sea, many of these souls chose to incarnate into the matriarchal tribes that either survived the Flood or sprang up in the Dark Ages that ensued after the cultural center of Atlantis was totally destroyed.

Historical records and archaeological evidence of this period are scarce. The only archaeological evidence I am aware of indicating the Amazon motif are the Greek vases from 700 B.C. Scenes such as a hero slaying an Amazon queen are portrayed. On the other hand, a few early Greek writers, such as Herodotus, described a society ruled by fierce women in Lybia. Later, 50 B.C., Diodorus Siculus, a citizen of Roman Sicily, traveled and wrote. During his lifetime accounts of Amazon women still lingered in Lybia. Siculus wrote about a nation of Amazons in which women wielded all the authority. Men were not allowed to be warriors, hold government or public office, and were confined to domestic affairs and labor.

Contemporary objective authors writing on the goddess religions trace the myths of the Amazons to matriarchal tribes. In *The Goddess Within*, Jennifer Woolger surmises that the goddess Artemis is a remnant of the tribes of female hunters from Anatolia (present day Turkey). Merlin Stone, in *When God Was a Woman*, maintains that the mythical Amazons were inspired by an earlier race of women who worshipped a warrior goddess and hunted and fought in Lybia, Anatolia, Bulgaria, Greece, Armenia, and Russia. Though Riane Eisler quotes Stone extensively in her otherwise brilliant book, *The Chalice and the Blade*, she, like many feminist writers, completely ignores references to the Amazons while glorifying matriarchal times. On the other hand, radical feminists evoke the Amazon image as a model.

My own introduction to this period of history occurred through past-life work with a woman I had a relationship with for four years. As we traced the karmic history of this relationship, we came to a series of lives in this Amazonian period. These lifetimes were responsible for some of the most traumatic aspects of our relationship. So profound were our personal realizations that she began teaching a workshop called "Healing the Feminine." I would attend the workshop when both men and women attended. She would guide people in past-life regressions back to these times and then concentrate on healing the traumas each person experienced.

We traveled and she taught this workshop in many states. We were continually amazed at the similarity of the accounts from this period. We also noted that women who were the most verbal and adamant with militant feminist attitudes in the workshops normally regressed to lives in which they were in positions of power in this era. In fact it was not uncommon for these women to be so horrified by the atrocities they had taken part in that they would refuse to talk about what they experienced in their regressions. Marina's descriptions, in Part Two of this book, of what this period was like is very general and toned down compared to what I myself, and most of the workshop participants experienced.

Marina's past-life sessions do demonstrate, however, that what's wrong with the world today cannot be simply blamed on the souls who are in men's bodies now. I'm not denying that the patriarchal values dominating our present lives are inane—indeed life-threatening—but let me point out that souls incarnate as women today have have also incarnated as men. In fact, most of the aggressive and angry feminists I have worked with have relived past lives in which they had been male chauvinists.

It's difficult to interpret what the balance of power between men and women was like in prehistorical times, including both the more primitive matrifocal social structures and the Golden Ages of Atlantis and Lemuria. My sense is that in general it was much more equal than in either the Amazon era or subsequent development of modern patriarchal society. Similarly, in matrilinear tribes worshipping the creative powers of nature in the form of a goddess, I don't believe the personal freedom and integrity of the male was curtailed or devalued.

Fear of the feminine gender, and its subsequent oppression on a collective level, in my opinion, was caused by a racial memory from this Amazon period of the matriarchy. The patriarchy, to a significant degree, was a paranoid reaction and defense against the abuse visited upon both sexes during this era. I don't believe the Amazon experience was the only cause for the development of patriarchal values, but this period of history was undoubtedly pivotal and pertinent.

The dominator model for society can be traced back to the Lucifer aspect of the Lemurian culture. This authoritarian and misapplication of the hierarchical structure of power was seeded in Atlantis after the destruction of Lemuria by those souls who were attached to power. This element clashed with the theocracy of Atlantis and eventually led to a cataclysmic civil war. Those powerful souls reveled in their power to destroy the existing theocracy and indulged themselves in scientific accomplishments and imperialistic exploits on Atlantis until 10,000 B.C. When their powerful nation sank beneath the sea, along with all their wealth and scientific accomplishments, these souls were not eager to incarnate into the spiritual communities of Egypt, Peru, and China/India/Tibet. These outposts of civilization had been colonized over a long period by the souls who had been involved in the theocracy of Atlantis. Frustrated and curtailed in their efforts, most of this group of souls incarnated into matriarchal tribes. The peace-loving, egalitarian nature of the social fabric was hence altered. In the Amazon culture we see the dominator model imposed on matriarchal society. Both men and women suffered oppression and damage to their psyches in the Amazon era.

BIBLIOGRAPHY

Arroyo, Stephen. *Astrology, Karma, and Transformation.* Sebastopol, CA: CRCS Publications, 1978.

Bache, C. *Life Cycles: Reincarnation and the Web of Life.* New York: Paragon House, 1990.

Cayce, Edgar, *Story of the Origin and Destiny of Man.* New York: Berkley Medallion Books, 1973.

Churchward, James. *The Lost Continent of Mu.* Albuquerque, NM: Brotherhood of Life, 1991.

Clow, Barbara Hand. *Eye of the Centaur.* St. Paul, MN: Llewellyn Publications, 1986.

Goldberg, Bruce. M.D. *Past Lives, Future Lives.* New York: Ballantine Books, 1982.

Grof, Stanislav. M.D. *The Adventure of Self-Discovery.* Albany, NY: State University of New York Press, 1988.

———. *Beyond the Brain.* Albany, NY: State University of New York Press, 1985.

———. *The Holotropic Mind.* New York: HarperCollins, 1990.

Langley, Noel. *Edgar Cayce on Reincarnation.* New York: Warner Books, 1967.

Lundsted, Betty. *Transits: The Time of Your Life.* York Beach, ME: Samuel Weiser, 1980.

McGregor, Geddes. *Reincarnation in Christianity.* Wheaton, IL: Quest Books, 1978.

Montgomery, Ruth. *A World Beyond.* New York: Ballantine Books, 1971.

———. *Here and the Here After.* Greenwich, CT: Fawcett Publications, 1968.

———. *The World Before.* Greenwich, CT: Fawcett Publications, 1985.

Neufeldt, Ronald W., ed. *Karma and Rebirth: Post Classical Developments.* Albany, NY: State University of New York Press, 1986.

New English Bible. New York: Cambridge University Press, 1971.

O'Flahery, Wendy Doniger, ed. *Karma and Rebirth in Classical Indian Traditions.* Berkeley, CA: University of California Press, 1980.

Schlotterbeck, Karl. *Living Your Past Lives.* New York: Ballantine Books, 1987.

Sitchin, Zecharia. *The Twelfth Planet.* Santa Fe, NM: Bear & Co., 1976.

Steiger, Brad and Frances. *Discover Your Past Lives.* West Chester, PA: Whitford Press, 1987.

Stevenson, Ian. *Twenty Cases Suggestive of Reincarnation.* Charlottesville, VA: University of Virginia Press, 1966.

Woolger, Roger J. Ph.D. *Other Lives, Other Selves.* New York: Bantam Books, 1988.

Woolger, Jennifer, and Woolger, Roger J., Ph.D. *The Goddess Within: A Guide to the Eternal Myths that Shape Women's Lives.* New York: Fawcett Columbine, 1987, 1989.

For twenty years Charles Breaux has been contributing to the field of modern psychotherapy and holistic health, as a counselor, teacher, and writer. Formerly the director of the Berkeley Holistic Health Center and a member of the board of directors of the Health Enhancement Institute in Santa Cruz, CA, he holds a master's degree in humanistic psychology from the University of California at Berkeley. After many years of lecturing, teaching seminars, and maintaining a private practice of clairvoyant counseling and past life therapy, he now lives and writes on the Olympic Peninsula. He is also the author of *Journey into Consciousness*, which explores the relationship between Tantric teachings and Jungian psychology, and ways of working with the chakras in self-transformation.